I Thought The Sun Was God

The Spiritual Journey

of a Descendant of the

Last Satsuma Samurai Clan

by Masako Kimura Streling

"Moving among these many worlds makes her story
an intriguing, engrossing, and eye-opening tale,
one that deserves a special place in any women's
studies course or any class on modern Japan."

— Clarion Book

Produced by:

FriesenPress
Suite 300 – 852 Fort Street
Victoria, BC, Canada V8W 1H8

www.friesenpress.com

Distributed to the trade by The Ingram Book Company

Table of Contents

Dedication

I am indebted to my husband, Carl O. Streling,
for his love, kindness, and perseverance.

Foreword

I have always been fascinated by spirituality, and have found much comfort and inspiration in God. My work as a composer over the last ten years has been focused on multi-culturalism and spirituality. I have studied, experienced and witnessed almost every religious system around the world, often working with leaders of the five faiths. From Islam to Buddhism, Hinduism, Judaism, Sikhism to all forms of Christianity, I have participated in almost every possible religious ritual known to man, in an effort to process my own place in the Universe, and gain a deeper understanding of spirituality. When I was approached by Masako to help her with her memoir, I asked myself, why would Masako choose me? I soon discovered the answer in our parallel experiences.

In this book, Masako processes her life and her journey with spirituality. In a quasi stream of consciousness style, she details the challenges she faced as a young girl raised in a poor family steeped in the traditions of the samurai and Eastern religion. As a child, she "thought the Sun was God". She recalls the different images imbedded in her memories of life in Okinawa before, during and after the fall of Japan.

Like many of us, Masako thirsts for an understanding of what is beyond herself. The theologian Karl Rahner, calls this the "real". All human beings, at some point in their lives, have this desire to reach for something outside of them to help understand their own existence. Throughout her adult life, Masako develops a thirst for knowledge of Jesus Christ. On this journey she continually tries to balance the Eastern traditions of spirituality with her new found love of Christ. Through her life experience, she learns that leaders, more times than not, fail their followers. And followers, often times, fail themselves.

Eventually, Masako and Carl accept an invitation to become lay missionaries for a priestless church. They soon begin one of the most challenging chapters in their lives when they're posted to the Kainan church in the Wakayama Prefecture, Japan.

Wide eyed and naïve, basing their decision on trust, without any title or contract, Masako and Carl put forth every effort to build the community of the Kainan church. They served the local population without any real financial or spiritual acknowledgement from the Society of St. Columban Missionary. Led astray by the Columbans, Masako and Carl find love and understanding in the Kainan community they were sent to serve. In the most fascinating way, Masako reveals the true landscape of the life of a missionary and the realities of working for the Church.

After three years of service as lay missionaries in Japan, with broken spirits Carl and Masako return to America with no place or church to call their own — much like my own situation working for the Vatican. For the next fifteen years Masako struggles with her experience working with the Columban priests. For a time she loses her faith completely, as I did. However, her spiritual journey continues in the most profound way. It is a struggle we can all relate to as she searches for life's meaning through her own experience, academic study and deep contemplation of some of the world's great contemporary philosophers and theologians.

In her attempts to forgive the Columban priests and herself, Masako enters into a rich, meaningful relationship with God. She discovers a forgiving God, a God of understanding and wisdom, a God who accepts all forms of religion and spirituality.

Once again, her spirit returns to her childlike innocence and sees "the Sun is God".

Masako's journey is an eye opening and inspirational story of how one maintains one's own spiritual center through personal hardship and religious hypocrisy. After helping Masako edit her memoir, I processed and learned more about my own spiritual journey, my own place in the universe, my own self and my relationship with organized religion. I now understand why God brought us together to share in our common experience. Masako's journey and perspective bring clarity to the paradox of organized religion, the realities of working for the Church, God, the Universe and our own personal spiritual journey in life.

In the most beautiful way, by witnessing Masako's life struggle, I learned that the Church is not in the Columban priests, not in Rome, not in the hearts of the corrupt, jaded or disengaged. The Church and the meaning of spirituality live within individuals who inhabit communities around the world. It lives in the individuals who give even when institutions continue to take. Individuals like Masako and Carl and the local community they served in Wakayama. Masako, like so many of us, had a dream to make the world a better place. In this memoir, you will witness how much she endured throughout her life for her dream. At the same time, you will be inspired by her samurai spirit, and her discovery and understanding of a loving, forgiving, personal God. A God who is always with us; waiting for each one of us to let Him fill our hearts with compassion, personal peace and love.

-Matthew Ferraro
Composer & Arranger
of Music, Film, Media & Performance

Prologue

It is June 16, 1931, on the Yaeyama Islands in the Okinawa Prefecture. Roosters crow in the distance, greeting the dawn. A farmer's horse and cart clatter in concert with the echoes of the bells of Buddha's temple. I enter the world, breathe deeply of the salt air, and am given the name Masako (正子) by my father. I grew like a weed.

I remember vividly when my father told me why he named me Masako. I must have been about six or seven years old. It means righteous, or one who walks straight toward her goal.

I wrote what he told me in my diary, with the understanding of a child. I must have been in the sixth grade. But my diary was lost or destroyed during our voluntary evacuation to Taiwan in 1943–1944. My father led the evacuation. He predicted a big bombing of Okinawa Honto, the main island of the Okinawa Islands. The Yaeyama Islands were spared from a land battle during World War II, but massive casualties due to starvation and Malaria killed off over half (about 54%) of the islands' population.

Many years later, with an adult understanding of what my name meant to me, I decided to write a piece of prose about it in English. At the time, I was recovering from the first of eight surgeries in 2003. Subsequent surgeries followed every seven to eight months for five years thereafter.

MY NAME SAKE

I love my name.
The writing of my name in Japanese consists of five straight
*   strokes: (正)*
It means: To walk straight toward her goal.
Straight, right,
not wrong, not bias,
fair, square, with all four sides equal.
I help my siblings see right from wrong.
I love my name Masako
because it means I was given the name as a path to follow
*   my life.*
I am a possessor of the sense of right from wrong.
So, I am a righteous child to translate my name literally.
Suffix Ko (子) at the end of my personal name means
I am a female child.
I seemed to know dimly from my birth, my mission in life:
to serve others, and to sacrifice my self-interest.
Is it any wonder why
I did not want to come out of my mother's womb?
I was comfortable and secure in there.
On June 16, 1931, I was forced out, to be born
later than my time to be born had been predicted.
I was angry and cried loudly.
I looked so furious and homely with thick reddish hair cover-
*   ing my face.*
My nails were long, punching with two fists tightly clenched.
My father said to me,
"God sent you into this world with enough to eat
and enough talents to accomplish His mission".
That, I held tight in my fists, I dared not lose it.
How did my father know that?
What exactly were in my hands so tightly clenched?

My father practiced no religion.
He was a very sickly, unknown artist.
I love my name
because I love to serve justice
even at an early age.
I protected and fought for the weak and oppressed.
I fought with clenched fists — all I had with neighbor-
*   hood bullies,*
when they called me a "half-breed"—not pure. Her blood
*   is tainted.*
Even to this date, the many scars on my body witness
*   those events.*

I love my name
because my name believes in God,
and my name said openly that God helps me seek knowledge
*   of Him.*
I love my name
because my mind thinks always,
in a feminine body, too.
I love my name
because my name is vulnerable,
and full of naiveté
I love my name
because my name is a twin — very intelligent,
and yet so very dumb.
I love my name
because I am loyal to my husband, my friends,
and my family, and
most of all to my faith community, the church.
I love my name
because I serve wonderful meals.
That is my mission in life:

to serve.
I love my name just the way my God made me.
I love my name, Masako: (正子)
I continue to seek my gifts;
what exactly was in my hands,
I tightly held when God sent me into the world?
I will see them when I open my hands
when I freely submit my life to Him.

Little did I know — what I tightly held in both of my hands when I was born was the gift of God's love. The "stubbornness and directness of my nature" prods me to seek the truth. This trait ultimately led me to carry my own heavy cross.

Chapter One:
Signs of the Times

"Today will be stormy, for the sky is red and threatening.
You know how to judge the appearance of the sky, but you
cannot judge the signs of the times" (Matthew 16:3).

Every time I read this scripture passage, it brings me back to the
years 1945-50, shortly after World War II ended in Okinawa.
I saw American soldiers asking the farmers whether or not a
typhoon was coming. The answer they received from the farmer,
in broken English: "No sweat, GI., typhoon no come."

What prompted me to dare begin writing a book at the age of
seventy-eight? I have never written a book, nor have I ever had
any desire to write a book, but now I am driven to do so with
the same energy that drove me throughout my life.

It is a different kind of energy from the physical. It was the
Spirit who took me away from Okinawa to America. It was the
Spirit who drove me to the baptismal font at the Mary Seat of
Wisdom Church. It was the Spirit, who drove me to study the-
ology at Loyola University of Chicago. This is the place where
I began my search for Jesus. It was the Spirit, who sent my
husband Carl and me to a mission field in Japan for three chal-
lenging years.

I can't do many things at the same time anymore. Nor can
I do things as fast as I once did. My mind thinks that I am
functioning as well as I did when I was younger. I can do but

one thing at a time now. And now, at this time in my life, I am driven by a burning urge to complete the last things before I die.

Augustine said, *"Our hearts were made for God, and they are restless until they rest in Him"* (Confessions I:1). Why else do we need to know the meaning of life itself? In the heart of every human being there is a quest for truth, a quest for justice, a quest for peace, a quest for love, a quest for mercy. In the heart of each one of us, we have this longing for something over and above our immediate reality.

Qoheleth, in the book of Ecclesiastes said, *"There is an appointed time for everything, and a time for every affair under the heaven" (3:1).* However, he warns that man does not choose the right time to act (3:11). Perhaps the appointed time can only be understood with the light of faith. As my spirituality has matured from the ups and downs of life's journey, I am able to look at my life as a precious gift from God. I feel the need to share with others the joy of living life, and the wisdom that one should find in living life. I also feel the need to share in the satisfaction of appreciating the simplest of life's pleasures through our human activities.

Both the bitterness of failures and the joy of my accomplishments are crying out from inside of me like a child, compelling me not to waste their memory, but to celebrate and to live each day with gratitude. Putting my experiences down on what seems to be endless blank sheets of paper might enable them to live. I thus wish to open God's gift to me—my life—to see what is in it.

What I celebrate most of all at this stage of my life is freedom of time—my appointed time. This miraculous freedom allows me to sit here on my back patio, looking over the golf course and savoring the simple pleasure of past memories. A beautiful yellow dandelion over there on a hill brings the memory of my mother.

My parents visited from Okinawa Japan in 1971 to meet my husband Carl for the first time. One day when I came home from work, mother had cooked a supper of rice, boiled spinach, grilled fish, and miso soup. On the dinner table was a beautiful bouquet of yellow dandelions.

In my mind's eye I can still see how my parents looked when we began our first trip across America. From our home in Park Ridge, Illinois, we drove an old pickup camper, borrowed from my sister-in-law, Beverly, and her husband Bob. Carl put it on his pickup truck for our camping trip to Indiana, Kentucky, Georgia, Florida, North Carolina, South Carolina, Tennessee, Kentucky, and Ohio.

My father, an intellectual and an artist, kept a journal detailing every bit of America's people, landscape, and food. His journal was published in the Yaeyama island of Ishigaki newspaper over eight consecutive weeks, from February to April 1972. I treasure those clipped articles that have discolored with age as they rest in my files.

When my mother saw wave after wave of wheat and corn in the vast farmlands, she said, "America is God's country."

She pondered, why is God so unfair? She thought that Japan had so little land for farming and wondered how the leaders of Japan thought they could go to war against America and win? She imagined what they must have thought about the size of the United States of America in comparison to Okinawa. The entire size of Japan is equal to the size of California. Why would people risk their lives to get to America, except to take part in America's abundance?

It is the appointed time to savor the simplest pleasures of life that nature brings. The changing colors of the oranges on the trees, signal that the harvest is near. The streets are like autumn flowers adorned with crimson colors of red and deep orange. It is time.

It is time to go to the fruit market to buy *kaki*, a pear shaped Japanese persimmon. As a Japanese artist dedicates a kaki to the beauty of a woman in the season of autumn, a Japanese poet uses the word *shibui* (渋い). *Shibui* means simple with subtle complexity. This word is used to express the subtle beauty that radiates from the wisdom that one has accumulated. A beauty that is like the beauty of the kaki persimmon, which radiates with deep yellow and red from within.

Chapter Two:
Memories of the Past

*"Memory is more than looking back to a time that is no longer;
it is a looking out into another kind of time altogether where
everything that ever was, continues not just to be, but to grow
and change with the life that is in it still."*
—Frederick Buechner, *The Sacred Journey*

COURAGE

I have many happy and sad memories of my childhood before I discovered there is good and evil in the adult world. Good and evil occupied by my parents, grandparents, my aunts and uncles, my brothers and my sisters, my teachers, adults whom I trusted.

I was in heaven when I was a little girl, unaware of how little I had. I remember when I was told that I had to borrow a dress from my cousin for a picture of me with my brother Hiroshi. We did not have proper shoes. Both of us wore *getas* (Japanese wooden clogs) in this precious picture that I am now looking at. When I think about that day, I weep. How can I love you, God, for bringing me into the world in this condition? This knowledge of Jesus in the manger cannot ease the pain and humiliation I felt as a child when richer kids taunted me because I didn't have even one good dress to call my own. I never cried, like my brother Hiroshi, even though I was so humiliated, ashamed, and angry for being poor and unaccepted. I fought the bullies that taunted us with everything I had. My clenched fists, my body, my soul.

I remember learning to become a neighborhood terror, grabbing the food of other children so I could eat, a steamed sweet potato, or a rice cake. I got away with this because I was the best student in the class. I would threaten the other school children by telling them if they ever told, I would not tutor them. I also learned to beat them physically whenever I needed to defend my little sisters or myself. Later I learned that reward should not be expected from anybody, even from my own siblings. Was it my destiny, God, to sacrifice myself for them? I did not want any of my younger siblings to experience what I experienced.

POKKURI

Pokkuri are Japanese lacquered high clogs or wooden shoes made for young girls. Ordinary Japanese shoes are called *geta*, which are wooden clogs or sandals. The geta has two supports that look like stilts to keep one's feet off the ground; and, to keep Japanese socks, called *tabi*, from getting dirty. The color of tabi is always white. The dusty coral roads of those days are not like today's blacktop and concrete. Pokkuri are made a little differently than geta. They are built high, about two inches from the ground, made in the shape of a ship, then lacquered in various colors. A hollow hole is dug in the wooden sole and bells are placed inside the hole. As a girl walked, the bells rang, giving a sound like 'pokkuri', a hollow but beautiful sound. You may still see them today worn by a *maiko* (dancing girl) trained to be a *geisha* (an artist, professional dancer of ancient Japanese dance) in one of the ancient cities of Kyoto, Japan.

It was a New Year's morning when I received a pair of pokkuri; I was about four or five. I was so happy, and I wanted to show them to my maternal grandmother who lived next door. I went to Unme's house to show her the beautiful pokkuri before my mother dressed us in a *kimono* (robe) and *obi* (sash) according to the instructions from my father. My father, who sat in the correct Japanese manner on the *tatami* (mat), with both of his hands rested on his thighs, instructed my mother as to how we should look. My father was an artist and brought up among the elite. He knew how we should look. This "dressing up" was a New Year's ritual.

With the beautiful kimono and pokkuri, we would pay a visit to our grandparents of both sides, followed by visits to uncles and aunts. At each visit, we would receive an *otoshidama*, a New Year's gift of money. We could hardly wait to come home to count the coins we received that day. Some children visited temple with their parents to pray for blessings of health and prosperity for the New Year; but my parents did not take us to temple that morning. They never did. That was the ritual of New Year's Day for other people, not us.

That day, I visited Unme to show her my beautiful new pokkuri. I was so excited I had to stop at the toilet. The outside toilet was a four foot deep pit dug into the earth, with lumber laid across it so you could squat and do your business. I did not want my pokkuri to get wet as I peed, so I moved forward, trying to hold my pokkuri with both of my hands. I lost my balance and fell in the pit.

Thank goodness my grandmother came to save me before I sank deep into the filth. Back then, there were many cases of children drowning in toilet pits. As I screamed, she and my aunts fished me out of the toilet pit and scrubbed me at their family well with a brush. I lost my beautiful pokkuri in the toilet pit and did not have them to wear for New Year's Day that year. The elders told me that, because my life was saved, it was a good omen to start the New Year.

TAIWAN

My father moved with his family from my birthplace, Ishigaki Island of Okinawa, Japan, to Taiwan and back three times, looking for a job so he could feed us until World War II ended. We moved from house to house and place to place. Taiwan and Korea were some of the few territories Japan occupied. The Japanese were allowed to live here without having to get a passport and visa until 1945, when Japan agreed to an unconditional surrender to the United States of America. Japan ceded all territory rights, and whoever lived in those territories had to return to Japan.

I don't know exactly when my father decided to seek out his brother in Taiwan for help, but it must have been around 1936. I understood that my uncle had an important position as an ambassador. With the help of my uncle, he found a job as an accountant in a government office. But eventually he quit and returned to Ishigaki Island because he could not bear to see the pain and humiliation my mother endured from my uncle's circle of friends. My mother was judged a peasant woman, even though her father was a high-ranking official in Okinawa, according to *Shizoku* (their social class) standard. She knew how to speak and act properly only within her own culture of Yaeyama. She did not know how to bow, when to bow, or how low to bow in the Japanese way. She became the laughing stock of my uncle's circle of friends and their wives. Eventually even my uncle shied away from us too.

While my parents were enduring their lives as best they could, every summer my elder brother Hiroshi and I were sent to Ishigaki Island to pay homage to our paternal grandparents. Hiroshi was the first son and I the first daughter of my parents. This birthright had its privileges, but it was also laden with a heavy duty. We were both respected and feared by our siblings because of our place in the family. We were respected because we were the eldest, but we had the responsibility to be role models and to take care of the younger siblings. Filial duties were expected. As we learned to be obedient to our parents, grandparents, uncles and aunts, so we expected our younger siblings to be the same to us.

Prior to the summer trips, my father would make nametags for both of us in case of an emergency. We wore them on our left chest. He took us to the train station and helped us board. I held Hiroshi's hand tightly every time we traveled together.

One time when I boarded the train, I did not feel good. I remember that day, because before we were to leave by a train I had been swimming in a school pool with a couple of friends into the late afternoon. Something happened there that day, though I have no recollection, other than going to the pool.

At sunset I was not home. My parents knew where to look for me. They found me floating on the water. I was motionless and unconscious. The next day I had to board a train to get to Taihoku where my aunts lived. They were to take us to Kyurin seaport where we were to board a ship for Ishigaki Island to see our grandparents. I do not know why my father did not cancel the trip, but he didn't. I am not quite sure how long the train ride was from Tainan to Taihoku, but by the time we reached Taihoku, where our two aunts came to meet us, I was burning up with a high fever and sent to a hospital. The doctors explained to my parents that they were not sure if I would survive. If I survived the next three days, I would be able to go home.

When he received the telegraph late that night, it read: *Masako kitoku* (Masako is in critical condition). He took the first train to see me in the hospital. I remember lying in a bed breathing with the help of an oxygen tent. To me, it looked like a mosquito net. I heard my father whispering into my ear, "Masako, when you get better, I will buy you a beautiful *boshi* (hat) with many beautiful flowers on it, like the one you have always wanted, and an apple, the biggest one I can find."

So, I got well. My father bought a hat so large it almost covered my eyes. I suppose he bought it large enough so I could wear it for a couple of years. With my favorite boshi on my head, and a large apple in one hand—I dared not drop it and clutched it close to my heart—holding my father's hand, we walked out of the hospital to the home of one of my aunts. While my aunt took care of me, my father boarded a train to Kyurin with my brother Hiroshi to see him off. Hiroshi left aboard a ship bound to Ishigaki to visit our grandparents by himself. My father and I returned to Tainan via train a few days later.

I never swam with my friends again. I am the only one of my siblings who cannot swim. Something serious happened at the pool that day, but I cannot recollect what it was. I only remember that I have always been afraid to swim after that incident.

Shortly after we came home to Tainan, we returned to Ishigaki, My parents heard rumors that Hiroshi was not being properly cared for by his grandparents. Fortunately it was no more than a rumor; we found Hiroshi healthy and happy there.

Being assured that we would be well cared for by our grandparents, my father left Hiroshi and me with them. He took the rest of his family and returned to Taiwan, where for a second time, he looked for a job. This time he did not look in the city where my uncle lived. We went to Taihoku where my two aunts lived. I was only in second grade, and I cried every night because I missed my parents and siblings. I was neglected, although Hiroshi was well cared for. My parents heard another rumor that proved to be true—namely that I was sickly and undernourished.

My teacher must have noticed something very wrong with the way I looked and dressed, and with the contents of my lunch box. Every lunch hour, she gave her lunch to me and ate mine. I must have been one of the shorter students in her classroom. I sat in the front row. At our noontime ritual we opened up our lunch boxes, said a prayer, and ate. She saw me open my lunch box every day and it was always the same—a bed of rice with shaved dried tuna fish seasoned with soy sauce.

My parents returned to Ishigaki and found me with hair unwashed and matted so badly a comb could not get through it. I was wearing dirty clothes, with bare feet. When I saw them coming toward us, I ran to them crying. My sister Chiyoko thought I had lost my mind, because of the way I looked and acted. I don't know why my grandparents neglected me, although I can guess. As far as my grandparents were concerned, I was only my mother's daughter, not their granddaughter.

We returned to Taiwan during the last part of World War II for the last time. My father led one of many refugee groups from Okinawa to Taiwan, after a governmental order was issued to evacuate the populace from Okinawa. He was one of many refugee group leaders chosen because he was knowledgeable and experienced in living and traveling the land. The refugees were to live in temples, schools, or any public facility where people could be housed. We lived in one of the temples with other refugees. The sanitary conditions were horrible. When any sickness attacked, it seemed like I was the first one of the seven siblings to get sick.

I remember my father going from one house to another, selling his and my mother's belongings to raise enough money to get medicine for me, but there were no medicines to be had. Every morning he and the rest of our family went to the seas and rivers to gather *asari* (clams) to make soup. The belief was that clam soup cured hepatitis. True or not, I survived my time in the temple. Today, more than 65 years after that illness, my blood test shows that I did suffer from hepatitis A and B.

FIRST DAY IN SCHOOL

It was my first day in school. We were instructed by our first grade teacher of the Ishigaki *Shougakko* (elementary school) to sit down beneath a big tree. I believe it was a coral tree or perhaps a banyan tree. We sat until our names were called. The shade of the tree helped protect us from the hot sun while we all waited. Behind us were our parents. We were instructed to stand up when our name was called so everyone could see with whom he or she were starting the first day of school.

It was hot that day, even though it was only the first Monday of April 1938. All students started school the same day no matter what grade they were in. It felt like I was waiting end-lessly before the teacher called my name. I had waited excitedly every day for that moment to come. Finally, it had arrived and I heard those magic words: Kimura Masako!

I jumped up and pointed to my chest. "Banu!" I said.

I was so proud to let my teacher know of my presence. I felt everyone's eyes were on me, but they laughed. *Banu* is a word in the Yaeyama dialect, meaning 'It is I' or simply 'I am'. Nobody wanted to admit to speaking in the Yaeyama dialect, which was my mother's tongue. The Yaeyama dialect was our first language taught to us by our mother. My siblings were ashamed to admit it because speaking the Yaeyama dialect was a sign that one was uneducated.

Although the Okinawa dialects resemble ancient Japanese; and have been recorded in *Kojiki* (the Ancient Chronicle of Japan) and *Manyooshu* (the oldest book of poems), their use was discouraged by the Japanese Ministry of Education. During the period from 1903 until 1955, students were punished if they ever used the Okinawa dialect in school. The authorities wanted us to learn Japanese, the national language. At that time (around 1903), if a student violated this rule he or she was forced to wear a *hogen fuda* (dialect placard) around the neck. The child was never allowed to take it off without permission. The hogen fuda was meant to instill great shame on the one who had failed to speak proper Japanese.

When we were in elementary school, students who spoke the Yaeyama dialect instead of speaking *Hyojungo* (standard Japanese) were punished by the teacher and forced to stand in the teacher's office for a couple of hours. Although that form of punishment might have been better than wearing a hogen fuda around the neck all day and night, it was another punishment with shame.

SIGNS OF SPRING & SUMMER

As a child I looked forward to two signs. One was when the bright red blossoms of the *deigo-no-hana* (Coral Tree) began to open its brilliant red flowers. It was the sign that spring was around the corner and a new school year would soon begin.

I was excited. It signaled the time when I could learn many new things. As an adult and a Christian, I am still excited when I see the blossoms of the Coral Tree begin to open because it signals that another Easter Season is around the corner. It also signals a profound truth: A new beginning. It represents a new chance to start over.

According to Wikipedia, the web-based encyclopedia, the Coral Tree is a common name for Erythrina. These are trees growing up to 98 feet in height and found in tropical and subtropical regions worldwide such as Okinawa, Japan, Los Angeles, California, India, and Argentina. Every spring the Coral Tree displays beautiful bright flaming red flowers everywhere in the regions of the world where it grows.

Indeed, it is God's gift for the regions where the summer visits early. It is planted on the streets or in parks. When it is in full blossom, it attracts people like cherry blossoms attract people in springtime in Japan. When the coral tree is adorned with leaves, it becomes a lovely shady tree.

In Okinawa, the Coral Tree is grown in schools or parks and is used as a shade tree. It grows not only in height but also in width, making a canopy. It is where we played, rested and dreamed as children. The blossoms of the Coral Tree bring many wonderful memories of my childhood.

For me, the Coral Tree is also profoundly proverbial. It tells me that life is one continuous cycle of learning. It tells the time to learn and the time to rest as it knows when to blossom and when to grow leaves as, "….the sun knows the time for setting" (Ps 104:19).

I liked school because it was where I could be free from domestic chores to learn many new things. I was forever asking why, searching for the reasons for things, trying to make sense of things, which was not a good virtue, according to my grandfather. He said I was to always listen, learn, obey, and not to ask any questions.

"But," I would say, "I want to know why."

I suppose I was a good student because at least some of the whys were answered. However, I often sensed some sort of disapproval in my grandfather's voice at these times. I still do not understand why a child's quest for knowledge evoked anger in him.

My father said I was a gifted child, and learning was not difficult for me. I was a good student. I am, in fact, still a student. I will always be a student. Although the academic degree I earned qualifies me to be a teacher, I have never been quite comfortable as one. I am most comfortable simply being a student.

The next sign I looked forward to seeing was the vibrant yellow *nanohana* (rapeseed) and mustard flowers covering the fields as far as my eyes could see. It was the sign that summer was approaching.

As much as I loved school, I also looked forward to summer. We were off from school for the whole month of August. However, we still had to do homework every day. In addition, we were expected to write an essay on how we spent the summer.

I found myself as delighted as a child in 1996 when, after moving from Chicago to California, I discovered these two tree blossoms again. Every year, when the naked coral trees begin to dress themselves with brilliant red blossoms, I know spring is near. And when I see the once-empty fields covered with the deep yellow rapeseed blossoms in spring, I know summer is approaching.

Tradition has it that when the Spanish Catholics of the Franciscan Order came to the Pacific Coast region of California to spread the Christian Faith (1769–1823), the padres sprinkled mustard seeds along the way during a Spanish expedition to mark their path. These seeds took hold in the California soil, delighting the eyes of many. I recently learned that the Coral Tree is the official tree of the city of Los Angeles. It is also the prefectural flower of Okinawa.

Although we lived within walking distance of the ocean, we were not allowed to go there without a teacher's instruction. We were taught to fear and respect the seas and the deep mountain areas. We were not allowed to play in these areas. We were told only gods live there. Occasionally, our teacher took us to the ocean during the semester year to learn to swim, but I did not care for it because there were too many jellyfish in the sea. Once, I was attacked by one of these jellyfish. It stung. I screamed! When the teacher heard me screaming, she took me and rubbed limejuice all over the wounded area to relieve the pain. No wonder I don't swim!

Chapter Three:
Beginning

I want to share my story, the story of my life, as candidly, logically, and truthfully as I can, in the hope that glimmers of truth shine through. Some may call my story a journey of faith, but I prefer to think of it as the story of my spirituality and what it means to be a woman created in the image of God. Know that my story may not move chronologically nor is it comprehensive as an autobiography. I only mention the people and incidents that impacted my life and helped form who I am today.

ISHIGAKI

Ishigaki Island is part of the Yaeyama archipelago in the Okinawa prefecture of Japan. It lies about one hundred and twenty-five kilometers east of Yonaguni, the most western of all the Japanese Islands, and about 400 kilometers west southwest of Okinawa Honto. At 24.4° N and 124.2° E it lies between the East China Sea to the north and the Philippine Sea to the south and west. It shares the approximate latitude with Miami, Florida, or Nassau in the Bahamas. Although it is a small island—approximately 200 square kilometers—it has its riches: the lush greenery of the mountains, the colorful fish of the emerald seas, traditional local festivals peculiar to Okinawa, and spectacular sunsets over the East China Sea, which are simply unforgettable.

Visualize the blueness and clarity of the ocean water and beautiful beaches with white sands. The coral is still living even today. The island has a subtropical climate with mild winters and hot summers. The average temperature during the year is 72°, with winter temperatures around 61° and summer temperatures in the high 80's. You can easily understand why the island is known as a place of everlasting summer, or 'Japan's Hawaii' to the world. Precipitation is very high and is affected by the rainy season and typhoons. As a child, I loved the torrential rains that followed typhoons. How I enjoyed going outside with bare feet and letting the raindrops fall on my face! The dusty coral roads were once again washed clean, and I imagined the leaves of the trees dancing with me. Oh, the joy of the wind's cool breath before the heat came — followed by yet another typhoon.

The typhoon is a way of life for the islanders. The season begins around June and continues through November, peaking in August and September. Typhoons regularly visit four or five times a year. I remember living in a thatch-roofed house when the typhoons struck the island. Sometimes they lasted three or four days. They began with the rumbling of thunder in the distance, followed by heavy rain and strong winds. It would grow pitch dark outside. In that darkness, the sea and rain roared like demons. The islanders patiently waited through the night until morning would arrive, still as stones in their houses that shook like wheat in a basket. I liked that time because everyone was home, including my mother, taking care of us. For once, I was free from my big-sisterly duties. My father would tell us a story or two.

Ishigaki Island lies in what is known as typhoon-alley because almost every typhoon originating in the South Seas passes through it. Generally by the time typhoons reach Ishigaki, they are at the height of their strength. They rage, destroying thatched-roofed houses, uprooting trees, and flattening and flooding rice and vegetable fields before moving on. Thatched-roofs, in particular, are torn by strong winds. The winds send the thatch flying around like a flock of birds in the sky. When a typhoon has moved on, the Islanders start to gather themselves and help one another rebuild before the next storm arrives.

The word *"Tsunami"* is Japanese. Its literal meaning is "harbor wave". Tsunamis are caused by earthquakes, volcanic eruptions and other underwater explosions. I don't remember a tsunami ever visiting Ishigaki Island while I lived there. My grandmother Unme often mentioned tsunami when we passed a street that took us down to the beach from her house. What she referred to was the Tsunami of 1771 that attacked Ishigaki Island. 10,000 people died. It devastated the coastal regions, sucking the houses, people and everything else into the seas. The only remnant today is the road that leads to the beach from Unme's house. The road drops steeply at about a ten-degree angle. The coastal region was rebuilt since, and one can now find houses, fish markets, restaurants, and business corporations there.

On this beautiful island I was born the second child. I was born the first daughter of my parents as an illegitimate child of my father in a back parlor room of my maternal grandmother Unme's house. It was a time when Imperial Japan was moving toward an invasion of Southeast Asia, all the way down to Australia. The invasion was justified to the people as the quest for a unified Asia.

At the end of World War II, Japan fell under the control of the United States of America. The US Constitution became governing law. As a free man, no longer under the control of his father, (according to the Treaty), my father's first act was to petition to marry my mother. She was a peasant farmer's daughter as my grandfather called her. At that point we were no longer considered illegitimate children of my father.

My father married my mother. Their interests and background were vastly different. Moreover, my father was a Japanese citizen, for his father was born on one of the four main islands of Japan, Kyushu, in the Satsuma district of the Kagoshima Prefecture. While my mother, an Okinawan, was also legally a Japanese citizen, she was considered an Okinawan. To understand my mother, one must understand the many layers of historical prejudices Okinawans suffered. I have decided to cite a brief history of Okinawa to explain why they suffered to such a degree, and to illustrate my mother's feeling of humiliation from the treatment she endured.

BRIEF HISTORY OF OKINAWA

Occasionally people will ask me where I'm from, or how I met my husband. I am not sure why they want to know how I met my husband. Obviously I am an Oriental, and Carl is a Caucasian. I always answer that I am from Japan, which is where I met Carl.

"Oh," they will then sometimes ask, "what part of Japan?"

"Okinawa," I will say.

Often, I notice a look of puzzlement on the face of the person I am talking to, who is perhaps unaware that Okinawa is in fact part of Japan.

Japan is an archipelago of 6,852 islands, not all of which are inhabited. The four largest islands are Honshu, Hokkaido, Kyushu and Shikoku. Okinawa is a chain of approximately 160 islands. It was once called Lewchew—the Mandarin pronunciation. It is a prefecture of the Nation of Japan.

Geographically Okinawa is a long way away from what most people consider to be Japan.

Okinawa's history and culture are in many ways quite distinct from Japan. Throughout Okinawa there exists a strong influence of Chinese culture, both aesthetically and linguistically. It is very hard, therefore, to discuss the history of Okinawa strictly in terms of Japanese history.

In my research, I came upon a wonderful book written by George H. Kerr, entitled *OKINAWA: The History of an Island People*. It is touted as the first comprehensive history of the Ryukyuan people by a westerner. Many of my references will be from this book.

According to Kerr: "The name *Okinawa* means literally 'a rope in the offing'. This is an apt description of the long, narrow island chain. On a map the island chain itself suggests a knotted rope tossed carelessly upon the sea."[1] Of the approximately 160 islands only 48 are inhabited.

There was once a small, independent nation known as Ryukyu. It was peace loving, unarmed, and governed by the Three Kingdoms. They were known as the brave men of the South Sea, and called themselves *Umin-chu* (fishermen). They maneuvered their crescent-shaped canoes, called *Sabani,* with skillful hands, crossing the rough, wild East China Sea on fishing expeditions. Some of them were sent to travel the same high seas to look for trade in far away foreign lands. These were indeed brave men, for these were dangerous waters. Brave or not, the destiny of this people was always oppression from the larger neighboring nations, albeit Japan, Mongolia, China, Korea, and even the United States of America. In the eyes of these larger nations, the welfare of Okinawa and the Okinawans has never been considered important.

The basic structure of society and language indicates that in ages past they were closely akin to the early Japanese, although the ancestry of the Ryukyuans is disputed. I, however, offer my own interpretation of Ryukyuan ancestry as mixed with Japanese, Micronesians, and Europeans. When you visit the ancient fishing village of Itoman, which is located about 10 kilometers south of Naha, the capital of Okinawa prefecture, you will meet individuals who look Portuguese. These people are

---

1   George H. Kerr, "Okinawa –The History of an Island People," p.22

a remnant, perhaps, of past intermarriages between the different cultures.

Looking at a map, Ryukyu—now the Okinawa Islands—is located right on the pathway to all the provinces of the empire as the empire's "Sea Frontiers". Some of the early settlers were wanderers from Northern Asia moving southward through the Japanese islands. Some from "Mongolia or Manchuria moved southward along the Korean Peninsula"[2] to invade the islands. Some were shipwrecked by violent storms and rescued by Ryukuans. Their purposes for passing through the Ryukyu Islands were many. Traders, who were carrying luxury goods and spices from markets of Southwest Asia and the Indies to the ports of China, Korea, and Japan, stopped over there for a brief rest before completing their trip. Ryukyu became an important relay point for trade. This led to an increased level of prosperity for the Kingdom.

"Thus, we may assume that Malay, Mongol, and Caucasoid Ainu stock mingled in the Ryukyu Islands."[3] In addition, Sea Frontier people from Spain, Portugal, Holland and England had an eye on these islands, but to colonize these small and poor islands was not a profitable endeavor.

This mingling of cultures that were not of Japanese blood, however, was the biggest reason why the Japanese considered them inferior. To be considered a Japanese (Yamato race), one must be purebred. Any mixed blood would not be admitted to full membership of Japanese society.

Another reason why Japanese think Okinawans are inferior "...was the Okinawan use of pork as a main article of diet. This was part of the Chinese cultural heritage. Many Okinawans established themselves in the metropolitan centers of Japan

---

2   George H. Kerr, "Okinawa- The History of an Island People," p.21

3   Ibid, p.22

(and in Hawaii) as proprietors of piggeries. In Japanese eyes, this placed them almost on a level with the despised Eta, the butchers and tanners and shoemakers of the old days."[4] Because they ate animal flesh, my grandfather referred to Okinawans as (毛唐) hairy foreigners!

Yet, another embarrassment to the Japanese was the way Okinawans dressed, and the peculiarities of how they talked in their own dialect. In short there were, and remain, many reasons why the Japanese had disdain for the Okinawans.

Despite the prejudices leveled against them, the Okinawans have a kind, simple nature that does them credit. They are not so ritualistic in their manner of speech, or in their actions, as the Japanese. In the early 1800's Napoleon discussed Okinawan history with Captain Basil Hall and learned much about the peace-loving nation. Hall's grandson later wrote that "the most prominent race-characteristic of the Luchuans is not a physical characteristic, but a moral one… their gentleness of spirit and manner, their yielding and submissive disposition, their hospitality and kindness, their aversion to violence and crime."[5]

Their gentleness of spirit is best expressed in the Okinawa word *mensorey*, a greeting of welcome to whoever enters the island, be they friend or foe.

Kerr points out that this: "… submissive mildness brought about the kingdom's downfall. England, France, Russia and the United States each thought to use Okinawa. In June 1853, Perry landed a token force from the USS Mississippi, marched into the royal castle at Shuri, and asked for Okinawan cooperation in exchange for American friendship. He also demanded permission to establish a military base at Naha."[6] It did not happen

....

4   George H. Kerr, "Okinawa-The History of an Island People," p.449

5   Ibid, p.4

6   Ibid, p.4

then. But, the Islands, "too small and too poor to attract attention in time of peace," were eventually doomed to rise to international prominence during crises among the world powers.

Its destiny since the 1600's was that of a vassal state of Satsuma, my paternal grandfather's legal domicile. In 1951 the San Francisco Treaty put Okinawa under the American Administration, but political equality with other prefectures of Japan was never achieved.

Since this is not a complete book of the history of Okinawa, I shall be very brief from the time the Kingdom was governed by three kingdoms to the present time:

Okinawa History is broken down into six parts: (1) Buraku or communal village period, (2) Aji or Warlord's Period, (3) Kingdom's period, (4) The First Ken or Prefectural period, (5) The U. S. Occupation Period, & (6) The Second Ken Period.

Like other humans in the prehistoric age, the Okinawa people lived on hunting, food gathering, fishing, etc. From about 300 BC, the island people gradually formed villages and engaged in agriculture due to the possible decrease in wild game. They had to produce food and learned to store it for future use. The wealthy began to rule over the poor. Local chiefs, or *Aji*, emerged to rule their territorial communities.

Around 900 AD, greater chiefs, called Aji, started building castles on the island chain. This was known as the Aji Period and lasted until 1314. During this time, powerful Aji overcame the less powerful Aji. They engaged in international trade with the neighboring countries in Asia and struggled consistently to maintain their power.

An Urasoe Aji named Shunten, who built Shuri Castle, became the first King at the age of twenty-one in 1187. However, the Shunten Dynasty ended in 1259. A man named Eiso established a new kingdom at Urasoe Castle in 1260. In 1296 Mongolian troops made an unsuccessful attempt to take over the kingdom. The Eiso Dynasty wasn't strong enough to rule the entire kingdom and gradually weakened. Two additional kingdoms emerged in 1314. The three kingdoms were called *Nanzan* (Southern Kingdom), *Chuu-zan* (Central Kingdom), and *Hokuzan* (Northern Kingdom).

The Three Kingdoms that governed Ryukyu, known as Sanzan Jidai, lasted from 1322–1429. In 1429, these three kingdoms consolidated their powers. This led to the unification of the Ryukyu Kingdom by Hashi the Great. Shuri Castle became the political, economical, religious, and cultural center of Ryukyu and established relations with Ming China.

Emperor Ming of China helped establish the Sho Dynasty by naming Hashi the Great as the first Sho Dynasty, which helped establish foreign trade. Under the Sho Dynasty, Okinawa enjoyed its most stable period politically, economically, and socially. This period is known as the Golden Age. The emperor of China called Okinawa the Ryukyuan Kingdom, or *Syureino Kuni*, the Kingdom of Courtesy. Thirty-six families of Chinese immigrants settled down in Naha, the capital city of Okinawa and introduced continental civilization and culture to the Ryukyu Kingdom.

Chinese emissaries periodically came to Okinawa to hold coronation ceremonies for the new king. A remnant of this period is a relic of the relationship between China and Ryukyu. It is Shuri Castle, one of the biggest attractions of Okinawa's tourism today.

The reason why each Ryukyu Kingdom started to send emissaries to China in the years 1372–1439 was because Japan had never looked upon Okinawa as one of its own. An isolated island far out on the sea, Okinawa needed to find a way to take care of its citizens, and it looked to China. For five hundred years they looked to China for cultural guidance and faithfully carried themselves as tributaries of Chinese Courts.

"Undoubtedly in part the Okinawans were deeply moved by a sense of moral obligation, for they took Confucian discipline and precepts seriously. China was the 'teacher' upon whom they looked with veneration."[7]

But for three hundred of these years they were under heavy obligation to Japan. Heavy taxes were imposed on the island people. Okinawa became one of the poorest prefectures in Japan. The Satsuma Coveted the Ryukyuans profitable trade. The Japanese from Satsuma, a southern clan of Japan and my paternal grandfather's ancestry and my root, invaded this peaceful Ryukyu kingdom with 3,000-armed troops, claiming they had the right to take back Okinawa in 1609. King Sho chose non-violence as a tool to negotiate. When the Satsuma invaded they found a warehouse full of armors, which the Ryukyuan kings had not used for a hundred years.

During the Satsuma invasion, under the leadership of King Shō Nei, the people of Okinawa developed a martial art, called Karate, in order to protect themselves in some way using only the hands and feet. It has been said that Chinese Kung Fu and Okinawan Tii were combined to create Karate. *Karate* means literally 'empty hand'. The reason that Karate developed on Ryukyu was because of the prohibition against carrying any weapons by King Sho Shin.

Subsequent to the invasion, Satsuma made substantial profits through the imposition of *Nintoozei* (taxes) on every inhabitant of the Miyako and Yaeyama Islands. Through Chinese trade, Satsuma was able to buy European warships and modern weapons and became powerful enough to overthrow the Edo Shogunate.

The medium of exchange for paying the tax imposed for men, women, and children was in millet, a type of grain or rice. However, women generally paid their obligatory tax with cloth.

7   George H. Kerr, "Okinawa-The History of an Island People," p.130

There are many songs and dances expressing how they prayed for a good harvest and rain to pay the tax. But the gods were not kind to the islanders. There was not enough textile material or rice left after paying the heavy tax to feed and clothe their families. They had only Sago palm to survive during this period of dire poverty in Okinawa, and they began raising Japanese Sago palm for food. This period is known as *Sotetsu Jigoku* (Sago Palm Hell). Is it any wonder why Okinawans dressed peculiarly?

Eventually the Shogunate was abolished, and a Meiji government was established in Japan in 1868.

In 1879, the Ryukyuan kingdom ended. This event is known as *Ryukyu Shobun* (disposition of Ryukyu). Okinawa was no longer under Satsuma. Thereby, "Ryukyu Han is abolished and Okinawa Ken is established in its place. The last king, Sho Tai, and his family were exiled to Tokyo. This was the symbolic break with the past. For the first time in five hundred years the palace ceased to be the seat of authority and the symbol of nationhood. It was immediately occupied by Japanese troops from the Kumamoto Garrison."[8] Governors were appointed and sent to Okinawa from Tokyo. None of them were natives of Okinawa. Governing officials were largely from Kagoshima (Satsuma). However, the "colonial relationship" did have roots in the Satsuma's invasion of the Ryukyus in 1609 and subsequent taxation. My grandfather was one of those officials.

With Ryukyu Shobun, the first Prefectural Period of Okinawa and cultural programs were introduced. However, in 1872, when the abolition of clans and the establishment of prefectures under the New Meiji era occurred, Okinawa should had been freed as a vassal state from the Kagoshima Prefecture to become the Okinawa Prefecture, but it did not happen until the year 1879. Even after Okinawa became one of the prefectures of Japan under Emperor Meiji's edict, the Ryukyu Sovereignty

8   George H. Kerr, "Okinawa-The History of an Island People," p.382

issue had never been solved. Many scholars refer to "the colonial relationship of Japan and Okinawa" during this period.

Under a national program entitled *Fukoku Kyohei* (enrich the nation and strengthen the military), Japan's aggression in Asia and the Pacific eventually led to wars against neighboring nations, as well as against the United States.

The Battle of Okinawa was fiercely fought from April 1 to June 22 in 1945. With the defeat of Japan on August 15, 1945, Okinawa came under U.S. control, and the Occupational Period began. After 1945, Okinawa became known as the "Keystone of the Pacific" or "An Unsinkable Aircraft Carrier." Still, the Okinawa Sovereignty issue had not been resolved. Under Japan's policy toward America, America placed military policy as the priority, and took away the democratic rights and freedom of Okinawans accordingly to the San Francisco Treaty of 1951.

Due to a strong reversion movement by the Okinawans, the U.S. Government returned Okinawa to Japan on May 15, 1972, ending 27 years of US Occupation. Thus, the Second Prefectural Period of Okinawa was born.

Although Okinawa's sovereignty was never solved, Okinawans have never given up their anti-war stance and peace-loving spirit. Even now, Okinawa is trying to get the disproportionate amount of U.S. military-based land returned to Okinawa for industrial development. Shedding Okinawa's economic dependency on U.S. military bases is a prerequisite for obtaining a normal, healthy economic development. Another movement in Okinawa is the restoration of the use of the native dialect and cultural pride of Islanders, known as Umin-chu.

Lastly, I suppose the Japanese who came from prefectures other than the Okinawa prefecture looked at Okinawans as a different level of citizenship. The Okinawans were a lower class of citizen because they were different from typical Japanese. "The ugly problem of this social discrimination had not been overcome. The Japanese government was winning the campaign to have Okinawans think of themselves as Japanese subjects."[9]

In general, there was little done by the Japanese government to help the Okinawans overcome the widespread Japanese sense of superiority toward the Okinawans as second-class citizens. That was the world of Okinawa in which I was born and lived.

I sensed this irregularity when I was growing up. I will never forget when I was waiting my turn to see an authority interviewing each applicant for passage to enter the seventh grade. I noticed a photocopy of a family registration that accompanied the application to the Yaeyama Girl's School that read "illegitimate daughter of Kiyotaka Kimura."

Instinctively, I knew the answer to the question I must ask, and so I went to see my grandfather, Kimura Naotaro. I had no fear then of going to my grandfather's house to question him. "Grandfather," I asked, "why am I an illegitimate daughter of my father?"

Instead of answering my question, he asked, "Where did you get that information?"

I held up the application. "In this paper," I said.

"Your unpolished behavior should be proof enough that you are an illegitimate child of your father."

I knew this was meant as a reflection on my mother. I left my grandfather's house, telling him that I didn't need any further education since I was a daughter of a peasant woman. Ultimately, my father convinced me that education was needed if I was to prove to my grandfather that I was a gutsy Kimura woman. Sometime after that incident, my father arranged a meeting with school officials so that I could enter the Yaeyama Girl's School. This school was the equivalent of middle school today.

Thus, I was raised in two different worlds; one held my paternal grandfather as a remnant of the Satsuma Samurai

---

9   George H. Kerr, "Okinawa –The History of an Island People," p.448

and his son, while the other held my father and my mother, an Okinawan living in Ishigaki island with a peculiar culture all its own.

Although my mother never expressed her feelings to me regarding the discrimination by her parents-in-law, I had seen it, and I suffered for her.

Even today, Japanese who live in America seek to make sure they are not mistaken for Okinawans because the very word *Okinawan* often carries a negative connotation. My siblings tell me that the Japanese now have a better understanding of Okinawa as one of Japan's prefectures.

MY PATERNAL GRANDFATHER

Is it our right to become our own gods?

In the brief history of Okinawa I wrote, prior to 1945, Japanese civil law permitted parents to control their children's lives. Accordingly, my paternal grandfather, Kimura Naotaro, a Japanese business tycoon and remnant of the Satsuma samurai clan, exercised his right not to permit his sixth son, my father, to marry my mother, an Okinawan.

Although my grandfather was known and praised as a philanthropist for his heroic deed of a saving action toward his own, a family of temporary residents of Yaeyama (Ryukyu Shimpo, April 13, 1904), his treatment of my mother and my father, his son, was completely different.

According to a newspaper article, he organized a group of charitable people to help save a family whose wage earning husband was recruited by the Japanese Imperial Army, which left the family without anybody to care for them.

As I said, my grandfather had two sides to him. He considered Okinawans second-class citizens because they were not his kind and primitive. He believed their blood was tainted.

To accept my mother as a daughter-in-law was unthinkable. Besides, she did not speak perfect Japanese.

Not speaking perfect Japanese was highly indicative of your social station. In those days, prior to the end of World War II, many Okinawans falsified their names in order to get employment in Japan. Is it any wonder why I was ashamed of my mother? She was considered an uneducated, unfinished woman who had been conscripted into the role of my father's wife. Ironically, the shame I felt for her, I am now wearing as my own because I don't speak perfect English.

I witnessed horrible injustices in my immediate family circle for as long as I can remember. My mother was never considered a family member. She ate at a separate table with my grandparent's servants and their seventh son, Shichiro-san, who had severe physical and mental disabilities. Encephalitis, caused by a high fever, left him with the mental acuity of a seven-year-old. But even with his diminished brain capacity, and his inability to speak, he knew how to love us with his smiles and actions. He would show us that he was waiting for our visit by his loud scream when he saw us coming. He was our most lovable and welcoming uncle. He died of malaria during World War II.

My questioning heart began to rise with fury during this early stage of my life. Did I inherit the strength and spirit of the samurai? I must have to some extent; although, I failed in having the valuable traits of women of the samurai class, those being humility, obedience, and self-control. I inherited the Kimura strength and loyalty, which were based on Confucian law. This defined the personal relationships and the code of ethics of the warrior class. A woman was required to show subservience to her husband and filial piety to her parents. I was, in truth, very faithful to my duty as the first daughter of my parents, and I tried not to dishonor Kimura. I was a descendant of the Satsuma samurai. I lived that tradition of frugality, loyalty, and honor.

As I mentioned, my paternal grandfather was once a very powerful man who held an appointment from the Japanese government when he was only eighteen years old. Grandfather was one of the government officials responsible for developing the fishing industry, coal mining, ocean liners, and establishing underwater telegraph and cable stations between the main island of Japan and Okinawa.

Eventually, he left his governmental position and decided to purchase land with the intention of opening a commercial business with Osaka, Japan. To do that, he moved from Naha, Okinawa to Yaeyama. There he tried sugar manufacturing using Taiwanese laborers in the Inoda farming district. He opened the first drugstore and became one of the pioneer developers of business between Okinawa and Osaka, Japan. He discovered producing dye from the Hirugi trees, a kind of Mangrove tree found in the muddy, salty and brackish coastal land of Yaeyama Island. The workers first separated pulp from its bark and the core of the tree. Then they cooked it to a starchy state. This natural dye strengthened the cotton rope of fishing nets because its durability kept them from rotting.

But as the world changed from a Feudal society to an industrialized society to a technological society, by 1950 my grandfather's factory, too, was replaced by the manufacturers of chemical dye and nylon synthetic fiber. Consequently, Yaeyama seas once filled with one, two or even three-masted fishing boats faded away as the sails were replaced with gasoline/diesel engines, because they ran faster and more efficiently. The fishing boats no longer needed cotton net or natural dye.

A review of the life of Kimura Naotaro confirmed that even though he was a brilliant young man, and a descendant of the Satsuma samurai, he could not escape from the effect of the changing world, particularly from political and economic revolutions.

All of the business attempts he made failed due to either his poor business acumen, the changing world, or by annual visits of typhoons. The most difficult thing he must have dealt with was that his subordinates stole his ideas and ran with them. He was more of a scholar than a businessman. I grew up during the years of 1931-1950 when my grandfather's business was on its last leg. I tasted the life of dire poverty, and poverty made me ponder life's absurdities. I ask myself, how did I find meaning in the absurdity of life during those days?

Unfortunately, termites destroyed the family manuscripts during World War II. However, my brother, Hiroshi, kept records as my grandfather told him of his ancestral history. My Grandfather was the eighth generation of the house of Kimura, a descendant of the Last Samurai clans whose leader was Saigo Takamori. Culturally, the first son had the responsibility of carrying the family name so that it would live perpetually. In that sense, Carl's and my name will cease to live when we die, since we did not produce any children. Because of this, my mother lamented as though God forgot us.

Samurai, (侍 — Kanji, or Chinese Character used in Japanese writing) were military nobility of the pre-industrial Japan, Meiji era. According to the Kenkyusha's English-Japanese Dictionary, the word, Samurai means "those who serve in close attendance to the nobility." They were the ancient Japanese soldiers from traditional warrior families, such as the house of Kimura — my grandfather's house.

By the end of the 12th century, the Samurai became almost entirely synonymous with Bushi (武士).[10] The teaching of Samurai/Bushi is rooted in Confucianism and influenced by Shinto and Buddhism, 'allowing the violent existence of the samurai to be tempered by wisdom and serenity.' Their moral

---

10   Wikipedia — Bushido

code stressed 'frugality, loyalty, martial arts mastery, and honor unto death'.

What makes the Japanese unique, even in today's world, is that the samurai code of ethics still lives in our blood and flesh, (Yamato-Damashii or Yamato spirit).

In the Bible stories of Israel's tribal wars, the winning tribe would wipe out the entire losing tribe, not only all the people but also the animals, so that nothing remained except memories of that lost tribe.

Japan exercised this practice during the Shogunae era (1192-1868). In 1877 my grandfather's grandfather, Kimura Kijiro, and his son Kimura Yoshitaro, were on the losing side of a civil war known as Seinan-no-Eki (Southwestern Satsuma Rebellion) led by Saigo Takamori (January 23, 1828-September 24, 1877).[11] Saigo was known as the last true samurai and one of the most influential samuri in Japanese history during the late Shogunae era and the beginning of the Meiji Restoration era (1868-1889). The Meiji Restoration led to enormous change in Japan's political and social structure.

Saigo Takamori (the leader of the Satuma domain) and Kido Takayoshi (the leader of the Chushu domain) built the foundation of the Meiji Restoration. These two leaders supported the restoration of the Emperor to power, which was to abolish the samurai right to be the only armed force, thus returning the power to the Emperor.

However, Saigo was one of the most vocal and vehement opponents to the negotiated solution, which demanded that the last shogunate, Tokugawa, be stripped of their land and special status, returning everything to the Emperor. Saigo also disagreed with the modernization of Japan and the opening of commerce with the West.

---

11   Wikipedia — Saigo Takamori & Satsuma Rebellion/Seinan-no-Eki

During this time, Saigo resigned from all of his governmental positions in protest, and returned to his hometown, Kagoshima, where he established a private military academy for the faithful samurai who had also resigned their posts in order to follow him from Tokyo.

Saigo was eventually and reluctantly persuaded by his own samurai students to militarize them to become a rebel army, and he led close to 30,000 ex-samurai in Satsuma against the central government to Seinan-no-Eki or the Satsuma Rebellion. According to my grandfather's account, Saigo's men actually numbered 15,000. The Imperial troops were modern in all aspects of warfare, using warships and firepower to systematically reduce the rebel position. The rebels fought with swords and bows and arrows.

Saigo fought for nine months. At the final stand at the Battle at Shiroyama, his rebel army was dwindling to about 400 (my grand father's account 372). Saigo was badly injured in the hip. He committed Harakiri, and the last 372 of his loyal men were expected to do the same. However, my grandfather's grandfather, one of his loyal men, left Satsuma, exiling his children, grandchildren, and wife to Ryukyu. Ending the Satsuma Rebellion by the non-samurai was the first victory won by the government. Thus ended the era of the Shogunate dictatorial leadership and class distinction in Japan, marking the beginning of the Meiji era.

Saigo's objections became reality. Imperial Japan stripped the Samurai of their property, limited their role, and eliminated the rice stipend, reducing them to mere peasants.

Time passed, and when Ryukyu became the Japanese prefecture of Okinawa Ken, my grandfather's grandfather decided to gather his family up — they were all scattered by then. He took them to Okinawa. My grandfather Kimura Naotaro was nine years old when he went to Okinawa as a child. When he reached middle-school age, he was sent to Kagoshima for higher education.

I remember watching the film *The Last Samurai* (2003),[12] an epic American film drama starring Tom Cruise and Ken Watanabe. While watching the movie I remembered my grand-father and my roots, the Satsuma Samurai. The reason I decided to watch the film was that 'its plot was inspired by the 1877 Satsuma Rebellion led by Saigo Takamori.' The last scene was very touching — even the Imperial soldiers kneeled and bowed around the fallen Satsuma Samurai, who had taken their lives by Seppuku, according to Bushido, The Way of the Warrior. This is my heritage, my roots, my soul.

Later in my life, I learned that this code of ethics was no dif-ferent than that of the Old and New Testaments. Both teach that life does not belong to oneself. Serving others makes life mean-ingful and fulfills the purpose of the Maker, who created our being. The big difference I discovered was the focus on personal relationships. The Scripture focuses on the personal relationship of the Self, Life, God, and the World, while Bushido focuses on the complexity of relationships, affiliations and obligations between the master and subordinate relationships — which demand loyalty and obedience with one's life.

My grandfather lived out the rest of his life on Ishigaki. He became a permanent resident; and by doing so, he claimed that he was a citizen of the Okinawa Prefecture. He was reduced to a mere peasant as Saigo predicted. My mother took care of both of my paternal grandparents until the end of their lives.

The history reminds us why Saigo objected that the last sho-gunate be stripped of their land and special status, returning everything to the Emperor. Indeed, Imperial power always led Japan into various wars. On August 15, 1945, Emperor Showa (Hirohito) announced the defeat of Japan and renounced his

12   Wikipedia — The film, "The Last Samurai"

divinity. Thus ended World War II. The Japanese surrender ended the reign of the Japanese Emperor.

UNME, MY MATERNAL GRANDMOTHER

Unme was my maternal grandmother. She had *hajichi* (tattoos) on the knuckles of both hands. She lived in an Okinawa-style thatched-roof house on a plot of land. She had a stone fence dividing the boundary line between her neighbors. In her back-yard there was a vegetable garden, papaya trees, banana trees, a pig house, and her outside toilet. She grew sweet potatoes, daikon, spinach, and green vegetables in her garden to provide her food. She also raised a couple of pigs in the pig house for profit.

I asked her why she had tattoos on the knuckles of both hands. She explained that the tattoos meant that she was taken or married.

I also asked her, why we called her Unme. She explained, that it was her identity. She was a high-ranking official's local wife, no longer a peasant woman.

When I met her she was old, wrinkled, and bent. She dragged her right leg as she walked. She was well respected by the villagers. Whenever someone needed someone to lead a cel-ebration of birth or prayers of petitions, she was called. She said that, when she was younger, she went down to the ocean with a bamboo fishing pole to catch her dinner, or go clamming, or to gather seaweed. Whatever she did not eat, she salted, cured or dried. She cooked food with firewood that she gathered.

With a portion of the money she earned selling her pigs, she bought butchered pork meat so that she could salt and cure it for future need. Another source of her income was raising silk worms.

I often went to visit her, and we talked about anything and everything. I loved listening to her stories, as she peeled the sweet potatoes she had just cooked, which were too hot for my child's hands to handle. She treated me in the most special way and as her equal.

Her house had a dirt floor and *kamado* (a stove/furnace) made of mud on one side of the room, and on the other side was a floor woven of bamboo and rope to sit on. What looked like an altar rested on the stove. It held a mound of salt and a dish of ash to hold an incense stick. She used a large V-shaped iron-cooking pan with a cover made of the same material as her thatched roof, to cook sweet potatoes. That way the potatoes steamed evenly. Every day she cooked the same amount of sweet potatoes to feed herself and her pigs.

One day I asked her, "Why are you so bent and crippled?" This is what she told me as she peeled the sweet potatoes for us to munch on.

"I was taken by one of the emissaries sent by the Governor to govern the Yaeyama Islands. Those emissaries were so powerful they took any woman they wanted. I was a beautiful woman then, otherwise they would not have taken me. I had three daughters and one son by this particular emissary, and I was his local wife."

She continued, "When the village strong men found out I was taken by one of the emissaries and was pregnant, they gathered together and attacked me, breaking my back. This way, no one would want me. Eventually I recovered and was able to raise my four children. It took some ingenuity and my strong will."

My Unme was also a very spiritual person. God must have also guided her. Her life was not easy. Her only son, who she had hoped would take care of her in her old age, was killed in a wrestling match.

Without her help, my mother and my father could not make ends meet. When my father was thrown out of his father's house without any job skills and being sickly, Unme took them in and gave them her back parlor room to live in. As was the custom, when the first son of my parents was born, Unme wrapped her grandson in a blanket and took him to my paternal grandfather's house to pay a visit in the hope he would be given a name. When she attempted to show him his grandson, my grandfather refused to even see him, much less name the child. So my father named him Hiroshi and registered him as an illegitimate son. When I came into this world two years later, again my Unme wrapped me in a blanket and took me to my paternal grandfather's house.

As predicted, my grandfather refused to see me or name me. So my father named me Masako and registered me also as an illegitimate child. My grandmother used to tell me that I was born very sickly. I caught every childhood disease there was in the world, including polio, but miraculously, I healed without any paralysis or physical detriment.

"There were two boys who were severely crippled," she told me. "One summer afternoon your father found you sick. You were limp when he picked you up to take you to a doctor. When he came to the medical office, there was a herd of children with their parents waiting for a doctor to treat them. In the end, you were the only one who survived without any paralysis of your limbs. Most of the children died. Two boys survived with severe paralysis. One of those two survivors is the son of the owner of the largest pharmacy, Yamashiro. You were spared," she repeated.

I often wonder what was she trying to tell me with that story. Was my grandmother Unme trying to tell me that I was different from the other grandchildren?

When I was growing up, society taught us that being different from the others was not a good thing. We had to look like everyone else, one and the same. Why? Japan is a racially homogeneous nation. We all had the same haircut and wore a uniform, which identified us by what grade we were in, and from what school we belonged. If we didn't look like every other child, we were treated as odd, different. Using an analogy of the table, my grandfather taught us that a table can only be a table and can function as a table when all of the parts – the four legs, the tabletop – are nailed down by a hammer. When one of the nails decides to come up, it shall be hammered down. You are one of those nails holding the table. Independent thinking or action was discouraged.

One day Unme told me about Hiroshi's encounter with our grandfather. Obviously, Hiroshi told her because my grandmother was taking care of us. When Hiroshi turned seven years old, he entered the first grade in Ishigaki Elementary School. At the front entrance to the school was an old man with a bow. He was using it as a cane. The old man stood there every day watching Hiroshi pass by. After several days, the old man approached Hiroshi and asked him his name. The old man took Hiroshi's hand and put some coins in it. He then left Hiroshi without saying anything. This continued for several months. Finally, he announced to Hiroshi, that he was his grandfather, Kimura Naotaro, and invited Hiroshi to come visit him at his home. He promised to show Hiroshi his factory where many workers were employed. It was Kimura Senryo Kojo (the Kimura Fishing Net Dye Making Factory). Eventually, I was also invited to his house. He educated Hiroshi and me in the disciplines of *Shodo* (Japanese calligraphy) and *Bushido* — the samurai code. A few more words about the samurai code of ethics: It teaches us to honor our family name, always act justly, obediently, and be faithful to your duty with self-sacrifice.

My grandfather gave my father a job as a factory worker supervisor so we could finally live in our own home. Unme taught me that I was to never forget my grandfather and never to shame him because we were his grandchildren. Those were her words as we moved away from her home to our own. I must have been about four or five years old.

UNME'S MULBERRY ORCHARD

In the front of Unme's house was a mulberry orchard. I took my younger sisters, Chiyoko and Takako, to the orchard to pick ripened purplish-black berry fruits. I climbed up in the tree like a monkey, and I ate more than I put in the basket. When the basket was full, I came down from the tree and divided the fruits equally into two baskets, giving each of my sisters their fair share. I was allowed to climb into the tree only when the trees were laden with ripening berries. The real purpose of the trees was not for the fruits, but for the leaves, which would feed the silk worms. Every season, Unme's house turned into a silk-worm farm.

I watched the silk worms as they went through different stages of their development, from a tiny worm until they grew up to three inches in length. Next, the worms began to spin their cocoons. After spinning a cocoon about the size of a small bird's egg, the cocoons would be boiled to harvest the silk. Although the farms had to be kept clean, or the silkworms would die, the smell of the workrooms was unbearably rank. This was another way that my grandmother earned her own living.

MY MOTHER, MYSELF, SELFHOOD

"But who do you say that I am?" (Matthew 16:15).

" Who do you say that I am?"

Jesus' question to his disciples disturbs me to no end these days because I am forced to deal with the ultimate question of selfhood, myself, my mother.

My mother was known to be a village beauty. She was chosen to be a rich farmer's bride. Apparently she was told that with her beauty, she could have had anything she wanted in this world. But she had a plan of her own, a plan that demanded a high price of severe humiliation and suffering, and I was there as her witness. When I got to know her, she was no longer a village beauty, but a worn out old woman with nine children.

But why? What possessed her to choose such a path? She knew it would be hard. Yet she chose that path so deliberately and steadfastly. What she wanted more than anything in life, were the children of a particular man, my father, who was a sickly, unknown artist without job skills or the means to support her and their children. How did she get to know my father? They were not in the same social class. She used a woman's ingenuity, and decided to use her natural beauty to get a job at *Kimura Senryou Kojo,* my grandfather's Fishing Net Dye Making Factory.

During one summer vacation, my father came home from the University in Kagoshima Prefecture, Japan, where he was studying toward his major in Fine Arts with a minor in Business. He saw my mother in the yard working. He approached her and drew her image on a canvas. Bingo! Eventually, when my grandfather found out that their relationship was more than a boyfriend-girlfriend relationship, he threw my father out on the street, and my mother lost her job. Shortly after that, my brother Hiroshi was born, and I was born two years later. My father and mother were in dire need of money.

Although my father was the sixth son of a Japanese tycoon, who almost governed the small village of Arakawa on Ishigaki Island, my grandfather could not find it in his heart to help him.

Despite this, my mother kept telling us we were never to question our paternal grandfather. However, I became defiant of his absolute authority. Why? I will tell you something that

I have never shared with anyone else before today because it breaks my heart even to this day. I helplessly witnessed my grandfather beating my father with the Kimura family sword. All the while my father was just sitting there on the tatami, a Japanese straw matted floor, without flinching. I can still hear the sound of the harsh brutal whack of my grandfather's sword as it lashed my father's back.

There was one thing no one could stop me from doing— thinking. My quest for the deeper question of life and its meaning had begun at this very early stage. I kept it in a chamber deep within myself, like a dark thought, and pondered over such philosophical issues as absolute power, justice, and truth. These unanswered and repressed thoughts raged in me. Most of the time my anger was targeted at my mother, for she was an easy prey.

I tortured her with harsh words. Those words came out of my mouth smoothly without any effort on my part. The words were unforgivable. I knew that. I also knew that my act of lashing out at her was not proper conduct for such a young person. I grew more and more withdrawn and became a silent adolescent. It was the most difficult time of my life. I found the world was nothing like what I learned from school, books, my grandfather or my parents. With the fervor of a revolutionary, I became an activist in the town. I joined the youth group and made speeches criticizing the government and its agenda. I was about seventeen years old when I heard that my father was con- templating taking me out of the last year of high school to help him support the family. I begged him to reconsider.

"*Tochan* (daddy), how could I help you without a high school diploma? I don't know how to work in the farmland!"

Eventually, he agreed to let me finish my twelfth year of high school. About that time I noticed my mother was pregnant again. I became furious, and my anger was uncontrollable. One day she asked me why I was acting like a mad bull.

"I just gave up my dream," I said, "that someday I might become a lawyer. Instead I am to help you raise the children you already have, and now you are carrying another child. You have no business carrying another baby. You can hardly feed the ones you already have: Hiroshi, the first son and the oldest, me, the first daughter, Chiyoko, the second daughter, Takako, the third daughter, Isoko, the fourth daughter, Iwao, the second son, Masayoshi, the third son, Kimiko, the fifth daughter. You should abort this child."

That child was her last. My father heard our conversations in another room, and he called me over to him.

"Masako," he asked me, "do you know why a baby's hands are made into fists when he or she comes out of a mother's womb."

"I don't know, Tochan." I said.

"Each child," he explained, "is given two gifts from God, one in each hand, to help him survive in this world. Do not worry about how we will feed this ninth child."

In the end, I submitted to him, for it was my filial duty to assume the responsibility of helping them care for that child until she became twenty-one years of age. When she graduated from university, my duties as the first daughter would then end. For years, I sent money so my siblings could go to the universities, which I could not. By the time the last graduated, I was already around forty years old. Paradoxically, my mother struggled to have all the children she wanted to have and keep them happy. Japan was calling on all women to "produce and procreate" for the nation, but I wanted no part of it for myself or for Japan—not then or later.

I wanted to retrieve what I had lost—my childhood, and the opportunity to become someone who could exercise her own talents. What good is it to have an above-average intelligence as God's gift, as my father often told me, if I was not given any chance to develop it? This feeling of injustice grew like a flame in the depth of my heart. It was my deep desire to search for self-worth.

I had a strong conviction that someday I would be free. That conviction kept me alive—that conviction, coupled with my mother's word that I'd be rewarded because I was so faithful to my filial duty. The reward I wanted was freedom from child-bearing. I desired deeply to be childless. To be childless meant I would be free to do whatever I wanted to do. This desire to be free and childless was so desperate that it became my daily prayer. In essence, I killed the most important capacity of womanhood by my desire. Too late have I realized that the most precious gift is motherhood.

What I received from my peasant mother was her strength and will to persevere.

MY FATHER

". . . if there were no suffering, man would not know his limitations, would not know himself" (Viktor E. Frankl).

My father lay in an Intensive Care Unit in Yaeyama Hospital in Okinawa, Japan awaiting his summons. His outstretched arms were attached to an IV tube inserted in his trachea so that a ventilator could help him breathe.

"What does *life-support* mean?" I asked a friend of mine who is a nurse.

"When you cannot breathe on your own, a tube will be connected through your nostril or mouth to a ventilator which will help you breathe," she said.

The more I thought about that, the angrier I got. Only God gives the breath of life, not a machine! If he could, my father would unplug all these awful things connected around him and free himself from the fetters of modern medicine. He had lain in that condition since his surgery on February 4, 1993. Then he went into an eight-month coma. Yet a team of doctors claimed that the surgery was successful, even though it only meant prolonging his ruined body. He died on March 15, 1996.

I often wonder if he knew whether he was alive or dead. Most of his bodily functions had deteriorated. He could no longer read, and it was very difficult to communicate with him any longer because his hearing was completely gone. I was very happy to see him once again, of course, although he was no longer my father as I remembered him. He was now a person who belonged to God. It is amazing that he remembered me. He told me that I was one of his nine children, his first daughter, who caused him so much grief that he took up smoking to ease the pain. He said that he had never regretted having me. I wished I could tell him how much pain he had caused me too, but now I was grateful for all that pain.

Do his memories of life wander around on this earth, in his wife, in his children? Perhaps, the reason he was alive was so that he could retain the memories of his wife and nine children. Maybe it was the sandy and dusty roads of the coral island where he walked in his life—mostly in drudgery and hardship. He could not just yet give up.

He was laughed at because he was not man enough, so they said. His children were ashamed of him because he did not exhibit the image of a father, whatever *that* meant. He was no provider. He was no carpenter. He was no fixer-upper. He was no fisherman. He was no farmer. Instead, he was an intellectual, an unknown artist, and a learned man. But why did we, all his children, love him so? He was such a source of our suffering.

I miss him deeply.

I don't miss him because he no longer buys me apples or straw hats with all kinds of colorful flowers around the rim. I cherish all the colors of the flowers on the straw hat on the wall of my memory: the bright red, soft pink, and dazzling white of the hibiscus flowers. I miss him because I will no longer find his weekly letter in my mailbox to add to the six boxes that I have accumulated over the past forty years. To think that I will no longer find his face at the dusty airport saddens me still. To think that I won't have him threshing around when things get tough. I would like to have died with him. Even the hibiscus on the rim of that hat withers with sorrows in the absence of him. They say that hibiscus was in full blossom when Buddha reached his last state of ineffable bliss of Nirvana.

Father was a different man; a misfit, like me. He broke all the social taboos and stood firmly on the ground. Yet his greatest weakness was his ill-health. He suffered from chronic asthma attacks. My little hands of prayer were often directed to the Sun whenever I approached the little unbeaten path I had to pass through to come home from the school. I prayed that I might, just might, find my father's smile instead of his relentless wheezing.

His greatest strength, however, was his love of his children. One day I was feeling sorry for myself and lashed out at my father for using me as his instrument to help him raise his nine children. I told him that he was irresponsible having nine children he could not support. It hurt me to say that, and it was said out of pain. I was hurting because my natural ability and intellectual quickness had waned by this time too. At age forty-two, I was struggling to recapture the lost dreams.

But my father said that I would learn someday in my life that the most important thing in one's life is the gift of children and loving them. I didn't know what he meant when he said, *loving them,* for I had never heard him say that he loved me. I had never seen him touching my mother or demonstrating any physical manifestation of love. Yet I knew he loved me; someone told me he loved me. Strange that he told someone else that he loved me. Why couldn't he say that to me?

And why was it that I couldn't directly say that I loved him? Whenever the nine children got together, we talked about our lives and our parents. There were times when we would break into cascades of laughter, and we felt the warmth of our parents. But why was it so hard for me to say "I love you, Tochan"?

I can still hear his voice whispering in my ear when I was roaming about between life and death under an oxygen tent, suffering from pneumonia. He was my guardian. He knew, that if I got through that night, I would be all right.

He whispered, "Masako, when you get better, I will buy you a beautiful boshi with many beautiful flowers on it, like the one you have always wanted and an apple, the biggest one I can find."

I can still see him clearly in my mind's eye. A fragile man whose hand tightly held the left hand of his daughter and led her out of the hospital a week later—my seven-year-old self trying to hang on to my father, the apple, and the hat ever so tightly so that I wouldn't lose any one of those treasured possessions.

That apple was, indeed, the biggest and the most beautiful one in the world. All my little right hand could do was hold onto it with all my concentration. That straw hat, too, was the biggest and the most beautiful one in the world. All you could see was the hat hanging low, caught by the bridge of my nose, as if a wreath of flowers were dancing up and down. Yes, Tochan, it was a long, long time ago. Even though I could not see where I was going because my new hat was too big for my head and hung so low it covered my eyes, I was content. I was content with the feel of my apple in my hand, and my hat on my head. I was content to be led by you, my father because we were going home together.

Since that day, many things have happened.

Whenever I departed for the USA to be with my husband Carl, you, father, stayed alone at the airport. Even after all had boarded the plane, you remained to catch the last glimpse of me, as if you could stop the wheels of time. The departures did not get any easier.

I made my last visit to my father in January of 1993 before his surgery, which was scheduled for February 4, 1993. His eyes told me that he loved me.

He said, "I am sorry. They have taken all of my clothes including my teeth. I am very tired today. In a few days I will feel much better—please pray for me". I saw him broken, humiliated, and emptied. We both knew this was the last departure we would share in our journey of life together on earth.

I am glad I made that trip. It was the last time he was able to communicate. After his surgery, as I mentioned, he went into a coma for eight months. When he woke up from the coma, he was not able to speak, see or hear.

With whom do I share this last journey of my own life when the time comes? Is this what my father meant when he said that he wanted to give all his life for his children, so that they would share their love thru the loneliness of his death? As far as my father was concerned, money, fame, and power were not important achievements in life. He longed for the unrequited love of his mother. Because of this longing, my father decided to give the love he never received — to his children.

My father came from a prestigious family and was reared by a wet nurse. At that time in Japan, the rich often employed wet nurses. He also had three other nursemaids pamper him. His food was custom cooked to suit his palette. The rich only ate the white meat of the fish. They did not eat pork or chicken. Their tastes were catered to.

As I write this today I remember why I heard so many complaints from my father at the dinner table. Because of his upbringing, he could not stomach the many "peasant" meals my mother served him. She was raised the daughter of a farmer and considered a part of the lower echelon of society.

Brother Patrick, a character from *Blue Highways — A Journey into America,* by William Least Heat-Moon, brings a poignant point to my father's last words. In the book, Brother Patrick says, "I don't endure life without a woman, I choose it. Not for a woman so much as for a child—I would like to have had a son. That's the emptiness."[13] That quote speaks to the pain of absence I feel as I hear the voice of Brother Patrick. Heat-Moon summarizes: "It seems like a gift of giving up a gift. For he so loved God he gave up his only unbegotten son."[14]

Was my father sorry that he could not give me what I wanted during of my life? Because what he wanted, I did not want any part of. Childlessness was not a curse. It was a blessing for me. All my young life I prayed to not have a child because children were obstacles in my personal pursuit of truth. I thought, how could I bring a child into this life where I, myself, am still unfulfilled? How can I bring a child into this world while hunger and poverty persist in my heart? A deep hunger persisted inside my soul like nothingness. The hunger was like an abyss seeking its being. I was very selfish, even a husband was not in my plan.

I did not believe then, nor do I believe now, that men and women get married simply to procreate. Children are the fruits of their love. Therefore, love was, and love is, and love will be the reason for marriage. Love is meant to heal the inevitable loneliness of human life that we are all destined to face.

I remember, Tochan, you were the son of a business tycoon whose bloodlines trace back to the Satsuma Samurai. I heard your father call you half a man. I was there. He was beating you

13   William Least Heat-Moon, "Blue Highways — A Journey into America," p.87

14   Ibid, p.87

with the Kimurai family sword. I was frightened for you. I was only seven or eight. I hated you for making me believe you were half a man. All because you became an artist and married a peasant woman out of your class. You were laughed at and made fun of by the local strong men because you could not harness a horse or plow the field for planting. You were a storyteller and drew beautiful pictures. You taught me how to write the alphabet. You said it was called *Eigo* (the English language), and said that people who spoke it looked different from us. Their hair was blond and their eyes were blue. That day, as you told me that story, I dreamed about that land as I stroked the foreign kewpie doll you gave me. I loved you too, Tochan. I had the talent to become a lawyer, if I'd had a chance.

During the U.S. occupation period, Japan adopted the U.S. Constitution as its governing law. I was fascinated to learn that the "United States Bill of Rights" legally protected the "natural right of liberty and property"; and, it guaranteed "a number of personal freedoms." I wanted to learn more about the Rights and the Responsibility of the U.S. Constitution and how it related to the individual. I knew that knowledge was power. I wanted so much to help build a just society.

My mind was quick then. But I had to give it up for you, Tochan, when you asked me to. Maybe I could have made a difference in the Japan that proclaimed man superior and woman inferior. I wanted to change the concept of absolute power a father has to rule over his children's lives, like your father did to you. It was really tough, Tochan, I thrashed around like wheat in the thrashing machine, and I rebelled, but in the end, I submitted because I loved you then, and I will love you forever.

I can still see you there on your hospital bed. As you waited for your summons, you were not like Buddha, whose face is serene with lips slightly parted in the smile of one who has passed beyond every power in the earth or heaven to touch.

Your eyes were not closed—as though in meditation—as you sat beneath the tree in a lotus position. Instead, your face was contorted. Your toothless mouth was opened wide and cried out in silence, and your eyes were tightly shut as if to bear the agony of death.

As I search in the depths of my memories, I am confronted by another face—the contorted face of Jesus on the Tree. I cannot say for sure whether his mouth is open or closed; his eyes shut or open. I only see a face that says to love other people is to suffer when they suffer. As Buddha well knew, that is the price that love exacts from us all.

I remember, Tochan, the teaching embedded in my memories from you. You have shown me how to suffer, how to die, and how to rise above adversity in spite of it all. No matter what your father told you that day when he was beating you with the family sword, you were a descendant of the Satsuma samurai.

You told me once, "Masako, I was there when every one of my children were born. You were different from the very beginning."

My father finally confirmed what my Unme was trying to tell me. I was different. I was uniquely me.

Why have you given me the added burden of the name *Masako* (righteous) as if to be different from the others was not burden enough? To correct what, Tochan? To correct your wounds? Or to correct the Teaching of the Old, which suggests that the ultimate aspiration of womanhood is to be a good and faithful wife, and a wise mother, a selfless, voiceless being? Is it any wonder why I looked as mad as hell at my birth, Tochan?

I remember my resistance when you tried to dress me up in a Kimono so that I would at least learn to walk daintily, like a Japanese doll.

"I am not your goods to display," I said to you.

I resisted, still, when my mother served me a fish head while you and Hiroshi ate the best part of the fish.

I always asked, "Why do I have to eat the head of the fish? When do I get a piece of fish like my brother?"

You would be a very smart girl," my mother would say, "to eat the brains of the fish."

But being a smart girl paid very little, I thought. One day, when I saw my mother's portion of fish was the tail, I stopped complaining. It was that day when my eyes opened to see the reality of my life.

There are many untold stories about my life in the United States that I have not yet shared with you, Tochan. But I want you to know that I was just as fearless and courageous as an adult as I was as a child. Indeed, I am different even today. I still want to push my boundaries. I still want to challenge myself. I am a misfit and an activist at heart.

I remember our last conversation when we were reminiscing the hard old days—your cascades of laughter, and your cries, and much, much more.

I remember when we were all together in our first garden, and I yearn for the return to that lost garden once again. Thank you for your gift of this bitter fruit, a taste of life, this *difference*, this gift that prods me to seek the truth.

Tochan, I want to tell you what my professor at Loyola University, Sister Camilla Burns, told me when I was sharing part of this story with her. She reminded me that fish signifies life. You had married the right woman, my mother, who raised your nine children. My mother fed me the head of the fish; to you and Hiroshi, she always served the body part of the fish, and she ate the tail.

"You, Masako, and your mother are the life of Kimura," sister Burns said, "and your mother helped your father help create a new generation of Kimura." The mixing of the blood of the Satsuma Samurai with the peace loving Okinawan will carry the new generation of Kimura.

FILIAL DUTY

My hunger and thirst for freedom became increasingly difficult those adolescent years. What was so wrong with being a girl, with being my father's daughter? Back then, I did not know what I was hungering and thirsting for.

In place of God, I was given the filial duty to earn my way to life's happiness. Why was I chosen to be the family sacrifice?

I remember that whenever living got tougher, my mother used to say to me, "Masako, you are made perfect. There is not a thing in this world you cannot do because you are Kimura. I sacrificed my happiness to bear the children of Kimura."

Little did I know just how prophetic those words were. In my child's mind, I perceived those words of my mother as a piece of music. Words that formed a military march I used to hear at home, school, and all over the village. As such, I marched to her tune.

She used to say to me, "You are a good girl and a good example for your siblings to follow. Someday," she added, "you will be rewarded because you were so devoted to your filial duty."

I was chosen to be my mother's right hand helper when I was only eight or nine years old; and, until her last child, Kayoko, graduated from university. My filial duty as the first daughter of my parents ended in 1971, at age forty. It took thirty-one years before I became free from my duty. I paid the price for a long time, in my own mind, for the unthinkable thing I said to my mother. I struggled to overcome the hurt and disappointment I was enduring.

My youngest sibling Kayoko, the last child of my parents, came to visit us in 1983, one month before her wedding.

I asked her, "Why come see me now, Kayoko? Don't you need the money you spent to come see me for your wedding?"

She replied, "I needed to come to see you now, *Nene* (elder sister). After I get married I will not be free to do everything I want to do." Then she looked up at me for a moment and lowered her voice. "Why did you want me aborted?"

Obviously she too was carrying self-inflected guilt. Holding my tears back, I sat down.

"Kayoko," I said, "I was too young and stupid. Please forgive me."

With that, we both cried.

"Kayoko, I am so glad our mother decided to bear you. You are the best child of our parent. You are the prettiest and most fun to be with. You are not like me."

Since she had only one week before her marriage, Carl and I asked her where or what she would want to see. We took her to Niagara Falls via Canada and showed her parts of our beautiful country. Then we brought her back to Chicago on time for her to return home for her wedding.

As she was walking away from us toward the boarding area to board the airplane, I reflected that Kayoko was, more than any of my siblings, the child my father envisioned.

Now, I would like to share the details of my filial duties. My mother took my sisters and me to work every day during the month of August, when school recessed for summer. While my mother worked, I would be under a nearby tree tending to my younger sisters and doing my assigned homework. I don't remember who took over my job when I was going to school. It might have been my father.

I began serving my duty at an early age, when my eyes had fully opened and recognized that my parents needed my help. As a young adult, I was expected to send money to help my parents raise and educate my younger siblings. I remember vividly having my sister Chiyoko, who is two years younger, to one side of me, my other sister, Takako, who is four years younger, on the other side, and my baby sister, Isoko, strapped to my back, as I did my homework while my mother toiled as a *kezuri*, a skilled worker at a *katsuobushi* (dried Bonito) factory. *Bonito* is a kind of fish.

What do I mean when I say that Isoko was strapped on my back? A baby tender carries a baby on her back. It is a form of babysitting that we call *komorisuru*. This was the accepted form of babysitting.

My mother would take a six-foot long, one-foot wide sash, long enough to go around the baby and me and wide enough to hold the baby's bottom. I would lean forward as my mother put my baby sister on my back, her stomach against me. I placed my hands behind me to hold my sister so she would not fall. Mother would lay the sash on the baby's back, going under the baby's arms, over my shoulders and across my chest, then back around under the baby's bottom. This required opening the width of the sash enough to hold the baby's bottom, thus placing the baby up and onto my back. The left and right ends of the sash came back around to the front and tied around my waist.

The baby came off my back as often as she cried, either when she was hungry or wet. My mother would then nurse the baby or change the diaper.

No one in our culture had any idea that carrying a baby on a young child's back, while the child's bones were developing, would have consequences in later years. The consequences for me were five spinal fusion surgeries to mend the damage caused by carrying my sisters on my back.

My mother's job at the katsuobushi factory entailed shaping each piece of the quartered, steamed, and dried Bonito meat into a smooth, oblong piece using various knives. To look at the finished product, you would think it was a piece of dried wood. Because these knives were her tools and source of her income to support her sickly husband and her children, no matter how tired she was, she sharpened each before retiring for the night.

I have so many vivid images associated with my childhood, particularly the image of my mother working so hard, yet so happily. Still, the predominant emotion I hold is resentment toward my mother. Why did she treat my brothers with care and respect, but with me there was very little of that? Her daughters were treated differently. She would not even use the same water or bucket to wash our clothes. She had two separate clothes poles for drying—one for her husband and three sons, and the other for her and her six daughters. Of course, she was only following the tradition of Japan where boys were more valuable than girls. But it was always difficult for me to understand and accept this hierarchical system where boys were treated better than girls.

I don't know where my elder brother Hiroshi was while I was carrying out so many duties. He was the first son and should have been subject to his filial duty, too. I never thought to ask his whereabouts while he was alive. Colon cancer took his life in September of 2006.

There are many sad stories about girls who were sold by their father to geisha houses to sustain the family livelihood in Japan.

My father never sold me as a geisha. I was given a gift to search for knowledge, and I wanted to know the practical as well as the philosophical. He helped me develop that part of my life, by being my mentor. My desire for knowledge allowed me to attain academic degrees. Without these degrees, I could not get a good paying job. I could not send money to help my father support his family and educate my younger siblings. I was determined to be an educated woman.

Yet, because I was not a male child, my father lamented my birth.

He would say, "Mottainai, onna ni umarete, mottainai," translated, "It is such a waste you were born a girl. What a pity."

Maybe he was prophesying that I would suffer; yet I sensed some sort of sadness in his tone of voice. I also sensed the world was a man's place, and a woman's place was outside of that world. A woman's place was in the home. Home was where women belonged. No matter how hard I tried, I would never quite make it to the top in this man's world, only to a second place.

For some reason, I could not accept that my place was limited to homemaking or the procreation of humanity. I decided that I would have to prove to the world the worth of my being in some other way, perhaps with my God-given capacity for learning. Still, the public teaching of *danson jyohi*, namely that a man is to be revered, while a women is to be held in contempt, said clearly enough how a woman's life would be in this world.

Chapter Four:
World War II

Would the men of the nation of Japan be satisfied being considered second place in the world? Never. The Imperial Japanese army steadily moved toward territorial expansion, beginning in the late 1800s in the Pacific Islands. It was all propagated in the name of "One Asia, Unified Asia." They fought in Korea, Taiwan, Sakhalin, Manchuria, Singapore, Burma, and ultimately the Australasian seas. There was excitement and pride throughout Japan. Every household that had a radio was encouraged to play the music and songs of military marches, so that the whole neighborhood could hear and be excited and exhilarated to be the subjects of the Emperor Showa.

But Japan could not endure the long war. "Although World War II lasted a short four years, Japan had been fighting for territory expansion for the previous fifteen years, beginning in 1931. By the end of World War II, financing the wars with China, Manchuria, and Russia devastated economic conditions in Japan. They could hardly feed their own people. By 1943, the tide had turned decisively. The public had not recognized the significance of Japan's defeat at Midway in 1942, and then Guadalcanal and Saipan. The basic economy could not support a long war. Military men had greatly overestimated Japan's capacity to convert new-won wealth into military goods."[15] Japan used all of its wealth, which they acquired from winning

15   George H. Kerr, "Okinawa-The History of an Island People," p.464

the territories, to support the war effort and its military might, rather than the citizens of Japan. We ordinary people lived on rationed food. The farmers and fishermen found themselves with new opportunities to acquire wealth, while ordinary people almost starved to death.

While women were compelled to subordination and subservience to men, men were likewise drilled to give up their own life to serve the nation of Japan. I have often wondered how Japan was so successful in forcing men to think that they had no life of their own—that their lives belonged to the nation. Young men, some of whom were from the elite universities of Tokyo, Waseda and Keio, were recruited into a special attack corps of suicide units known as Kamikaze Tokkotai during World War II. *Kamikaze* literally means "a divine or providential wind." A divine wind was supposed to save these young men from suicide and the providential wind would destroy the enemy ships. The true history of Japan tells us differently, and not even one man survived.

In fact, I knew some of those suicide bombers. We were renting part of a large house from a rich Taiwanese woman. It was during the time when my father had led a group of evacuees from Yaeyama to Taiwan in a voluntary evacuation to a place of safety. This was during the last period of World War II. These young Kamikaze Special Unit Corps men were frequent visitors to our landlady's house.

I don't know who gave my father permission to move from the refugee camps to this place. It may have been because he needed a place where he could readily find clean water, as my sister and I contracted hepatitis by drinking dirty water. Or perhaps we needed to be segregated from others. There was no medicine. There were no doctors to treat us. My father went to a river at dawn to gather *asari*, short-necked clams, to make a soup, which we drank.

Later, in my adult life, my mother told us the story about that rich woman and how we got to rent the apartment from her. She was the only one in town who would rent an apartment to a family with so many children, and to a Japanese man. Most Taiwanese were not willing to rent their houses to the Japanese, who the Taiwanese felt, had mistreated them during the occupied periods.

I read many history books on Okinawa of this particular time period, but could find no information about the Kamikaze being trained at Taiwan.

Kerr states, "The kamikaze corps were to swoop upon the American ships to save Lt. General Ushijima, who was confidently waiting for airborne help. On April 6, 1942 suicide planes did begin to come in from Kyushu bases."[16] There was no information about the kamikaze corps training in Taiwan. Yet I was able to find one line on a website by Domeisha, which said that during the latter part of World War II, kamikaze did come from Taiwan. There was confirmation that they were young Kamikaze pilots who brought us *onigiri* (rice balls), a much appreciated food in those days. They talked to my mother and us kids. They must have been very lonely, and we must have somehow eased their pains. One of the young pilots said to me (I was 14 at the time), that if he lived to ever come back, he would return to marry me. Of course, we never saw him again.

What were the last thoughts and words of the young men of Kamikaze Tokkotai? My heart breaks every time I think about the hearts, minds, and souls of those young men of Tokkotai. I was born and raised during this sad period of history.

---

16   George H. Kerr, "Okinawa-The History of an Island People," p.469

THE BATTLE OF OKINAWA

The world heard little of Okinawa until it was wrestled from Japan's control in 1945. The invasion began in late March. By a twist of fate, in June the modern USS 'Mississippi' moved in to train its guns upon the ancient walls of Shuri Castle. Within its walls, resided Japan's military headquarters for the raging Battle of Okinawa. This is where the Japanese resistance was broken by the Americans.

At the beginning of the end of World War II, the Battle of Okinawa saw the island turned into a battleground where everything was destroyed or burned by B-29 aerial bombings from above. The Island was "...surrounded by twenty-thousand Americans from warships who plunged ashore and crossed the beach near Kadena. The Okinawan campaign [of the Americans] began on Easter morning, April 1, 1945."[17] "After eighty-two days of bitter fighting, the island was in Allied hands. The Battle of Okinawa was one of the last major battles of World War II, claiming the lives of an estimated twelve thousand Americans and more than ninety thousand Japanese military men."[18]

"More than sixty-two thousand Okinawans perished. The great majority were civilians caught helplessly between opposing armies. Okinawa was the only inhabited part of Japan to experience a land battle during World War II. The physical heritage of the old kingdom vanished, and more than ninety percent of the population was adrift and homeless when surrender came."[19] Historical records in Okinawa show different figures: about two hundred thousand (200,000) dead, sixty-six thousand (66,000) Japanese forces, twelve thousand (12,000) Americans, and one hundred twenty-two thousand (122,000) Okinawans.

....

17   George H. Kerr, "Okinawa-The History of an Island People," p.468

18   Ibid, p.4-5

19   Ibid, p.5

The civilian populations fled before the combatants. No provision had been made by the Japanese high command to protect or segregate the noncombatants. Every Okinawan, old and young, was on his or her own. One might have preserved one's life if sufficient shelter was found. "On the evening of June 20th, American scouts pushed ahead toward the very edge of the cliffs at Mabuni. Early on the morning of June 21, Lieutenant General Ushijima and his chief of staff went to the ledges overlooking the sea, saluted the emperor in distant Tokyo, and quietly committed *seppuku* (suicide)."[20] The guns fell silent. The Battle for Okinawa was at an end.

It is my privilege to write about the brave young girls. Since my memories are waning, the following information is gathered from the periodical "Okinawa Tour Guide", published by the Bank of the Ryukyus International Foundation in 1993. The Japanese army recruited high school students to work with soldiers in the field hospitals as nurses. They would tend to the wounded, dispose of corpses, and carry water and provisions as they risked their own young lives. They all committed suicide or were killed. Only five students miraculously survived. One of them wrote a eulogy inscribed on a plaque at a war memorial site. I've tried to find the eulogy she wrote, but I was unable to find it. Perhaps I owe myself another trip to Okinawa before I die to read it.

It is also, my privilege to write about the 400 brave boy students of Teacher's Junior High or Senior High, who were summoned as student soldiers to form the *Tekketsu Kinnoutai* (Blood and Iron Corps). They joined the Japanese army and fought under their commander Ushijima. All were killed or committed suicide. My brother's life was spared because he failed the entrance examination to enter this school.

....

20   Ibid, p.471

I write this portion of my memoir about disturbing and gut wrenching historical facts in the hope to find a just understanding of the cruelties of war, and to finally realize the depth of man's sin. Young students of boys and girls chose to commit suicide because Japanese propaganda told us that unless we win, we would be separated from our families. Our fathers and brothers would be sent to one island, and our mothers and sisters would be sent to others. Japanese propaganda almost destroyed the entire Japanese nation. The Nobel Prize winning author Kenzaburo Oe testified at the Osaka Prefecture Court hearing on November 9, 2007. He testified that, "Mass suicides were forced on Okinawa Islanders under Japan's hierarchical social structure that ran through the state of Japan, the Japanese armed forces and local garrison."

There are many war memorial sites; all are located in the Southern part of Okinawa:

Shiraume-No-To: A Tower dedicated to the young Shiraume student soldier nurses and teachers.

Himeyuri-No-To: A Tower dedicated to the young girl student nurses and teachers assigned to Haebaru Army Hospital. American soldiers called this tower the "Pitt of Virgins."

Konpaku-No-To: A Tower dedicated to the unknown war dead.

Kenji-No-To: A Tower dedicated to the young boy student soldiers who fought side by side with real soldiers as the "Blood and Iron Corps."

Mabuni Hill and Okinawa Peace Park: On June 23, 1945, Lieutenant General Ushijima, and the chief of staff, Cho, committed seppuku on this hill. The Battle of Okinawa ended here. This site represents the center of the battlefield. The area was designated and named *Peace Memorial Park*.

Many memorials were constructed by the bereaved families and war comrades from each prefecture of Japan.

Truth lies within the hearts of the leaders of the Japanese Imperial Army. Why did Japan decide to declare war against the United States of America? Japan is but the size of California. My heart wants to know. Why was Japan so desperate to lead the nation to commit suicide? We must never be blinded by propaganda in order to find the truth.

EMPEROR HIROHITO SPEAKS

After the first atomic bombings of Hiroshima on August 6, 1945 and the second on Nagasaki on August 9, 1945, Emperor Showa (Hirohito) on August 15, 1945, announced the defeat of Japan on national radio. I am not sure which news affected the Japanese citizens more—the defeat of Japan or hearing the "divine" voice of the Emperor publicly state that he renounced his divine authority. I heard from my mother that on the day, when the citizens of Japan heard the Emperor's announcement, the country was filled with the wailings of its citizens. Many committed suicide, unable to live with this reality. With his announcement of the Japanese surrender, the Emperor called upon the nation to 'bear the unbearable and endure the unendurable.' It was a dark day for the nation when the empire fell. So ended the reign of the Japanese Emperors, the most ancient hereditary monarchy in the world. I heard his voice, but like many others, we could not understand the words he was saying because he spoke in a court dialect only the Emperor, his families and his court members could understand.

A new chapter of Japanese history had begun.

The following is his speech, which was translated from Emperor Hirohito's "court dialect" to the national Japanese language.

Emperor Hirohito accepted the terms outlined in the Potsdam Declaration. He began his announcement addressing his people "Our good and loyal subjects",

"After pondering deeply the general trends of the world and the actual conditions obtaining in our empire today, we have decided to effect a settlement of the present situation by resorting to an extraordinary measure.

We have ordered our Government to communicate to the Government of the United States, Great Britain, China, and the Soviet Union that our empire accepts the provisions of their joint declaration.

To strive for the common prosperity and happiness of all nations as well as the security and well being of our subjects is the solemn obligation which has been handed down by our imperial ancestors and which we lay close to the heart.

Indeed, we declared war on America and Britain out of our sincere desire to insure Japan's self-preservation and the stabilization of East Asia, it being far from our thought either to infringe upon the sovereignty of other nations or to embark upon territorial aggrandizement.

But now the war has lasted for nearly four years. Despite the best that has been done by everyone—the gallant fighting of our military and naval forces, the diligence and assiduity of our servants of the State and the devoted service of our 100,000,000 people, the war situation has developed not necessarily to Japan's advantage, while the general trends of the world have all turned against her interest.

Moreover, the enemy has begun to employ a new and most cruel bomb, the power of which to do damage is, indeed, incalculable, taking the toll of many innocent lives. Should we continue to fight, it would not only result in an ultimate collapse and obliteration of the Japanese nation, but also it would lead to the total extinction of human civilization.

Such being the case, how are we to save the millions of our subjects, nor to atone ourselves before the hallowed spirits of our *imperial ancestors? This is the reason why we have ordered the acceptance of the provision of the joint declaration of the powers.*

We cannot but express the deepest sense of regret to our allied nations of East Asia, who have consistently cooperated with Empire toward the emancipation of East Asia.

The thought of those officers and men as well as others who have fallen in the fields of battle, those who died at their posts of duty, or those who met death and all their bereaved families, pains our heart night and day.

The welfare of the wounded and the war sufferers and of those who lost their homes and livelihood is the object of our profound solicitude. The hardships and sufferings to which our nation is to be subjected hereafter will be certainly great. We are keenly aware of the inmost feelings of all of you our subjects. However, it is according to the dictates of time and fate that we have resolved to pave the way for a grand peace for all the generations to come by enduring the unavoidable and suffering what is un-sufferable. Having been able to save and maintain the structure of the Imperial State, we are always with you, our good and loyal subjects, relying upon your sincerity and integrity.

Beware most strictly of any outbursts of emotion that may engender needless complications, or any fraternal contention and strife that may create confusion, lead you astray, and cause you to lose the confidence of the world.

Let the entire nation continue as one family from generation to generation, ever firm in its faith of the imperishableness of its divine land, and mindful of its heavy burden of responsibilities and the long road before it, unite your total strength to be devoted to the construction for the future. Cultivate the ways of rectitude, nobility of spirit, and work with resolution so that you may enhance the innate glory of the Imperial State and keep 'peace with the progress of the world."[21]

21   http://Conservapedia.com/Emperor Hirohito

Personally, I am grateful to Emperor Hirohito who stepped away from his divine role and took the political initiative to surrender even when his ministers were divided on that issue.

Emperor Hirohito accepted the implicit bargaining of General MacArthur, Supreme Commander of the Allied Powers. MacArthur said, "help me and I'll keep you from being tried as a war criminal". Emperor Hirohito agreed. He then did his part to remake Japan under the American model, backing the new constitution, renouncing his divinity, and trying humbly to play the part of Japan's first democrat. The Emperor thus ultimately helped unify and transform a shattered country into a thriving democracy with economic prosperity.

At the end of World War II, the Japanese were to return to their indigenous land. They were no longer able to live in occupied countries such as Taiwan, Korea, and Manchuria. We took what we could carry within our hands and on our backs. We boarded small boats at the Kyurin seaport of Taiwan bound to Yaeyama. I am not sure how my parents were able to bring all their children alive back to Yaeyama, but I remember how sick and weak I was.

Not completely cured from hepatitis, my sister and I contracted malaria shortly after we arrived because, at that time, Yaeyama was infested with malaria. We found my uncle and my cousin dead when we returned to my paternal grandfather's house. Even today, my blood tests show the traces of those two diseases. Nobody wants to take my blood on blood-drive day.

JAPANESE WAR BRIDE

When American soldiers landed in Okinawa during the occupation, the old and the young, the men, the women, and the children all came out of the caves where they were hiding. They were wearing rags, and most of them were emaciated from starvation. There was nothing for people to eat. Most people survived by eating the roots of Sago palms, which if you fail to prepare it correctly before cooking, would kill you.

I remember that on all the street corners, G.I.s who were once our enemies were distributing foodstuffs: corn meal, powdered milk, long grain rice—which we were not used to eating within our diet—candies, flour, and fatigues (G.I. uniforms). We were very surprised to receive such humane treatment from our enemy. They were not the cruel monsters our Japanese military officials had warned us about. We were told women would be raped and men tortured. And while it is true there are some records of rape—by both American and Japanese soldiers— these G.I.s were, for the most part, kind and humane.

My mother and other women graciously accepted whatever food they were given. They took American fatigues apart to make into blouses and skirts for girls and women, and pants for boys and men. Women also made school bags out of fatigues for their children. My mother learned to make noodles with the flour we were given and to cook long grain rice to feed her children.

My husband remarks, even today, about what he saw when he landed on Okinawa in 1951: "...men and women, dressed in G.I. fatigues, working in the biggest junkyard in the world."

With the beginning of the Occupation of Japan, American military bases provided various working positions in Okinawa and other parts of Japan. Since men as young as fifteen years old were conscripted into the Japanese army, the home front became the responsibility of women—mothers and daughters. At the end of the war, the eldest surviving girls had to look for any employment; positions as maids washing and ironing G.I. uniforms, housekeepers, clerks, waitresses, typists, interpreters, and even security guards on military bases.

Others not lucky enough to find a job had no alternative but to steal or to sell themselves to feed their family or starve to death. No one knew whether his or her fathers and brothers were wounded, dead, or alive. I remember when the army forcefully recruited my brother to be a soldier. He was to become a member of a battalion of student soldiers. The student soldier's duties were to clean, wash or to cook for the real soldiers. We did not know my brother's fate, but later, I don't remember exactly when, he came home completely emaciated.

Not only did the American Occupation Forces provide jobs, but the occupation period also ushered in the spread of democracy, the emergence of the Japanese war bride, and the legalization of abortion.

In this chapter, I will only address the topic of the Japanese war bride.

According to Miki Ward Crawford, "This time frame 1947–1965 is often used as an historical marker for the immigration of Japanese War Brides."[22]

At the end of World War II, American soldiers began to marry Japanese women. These Japanese war brides were the second substantial group of Japanese women to ever immigrate to America.

I want to tell you something of the plight of Japanese war brides, because they suffered for it. Something is very wrong about being called a war bride; although it is a historic fact that some Japanese war brides sacrificed their own dignity to help their families survive, or they all would have starved to death. The nation of Japan has forgotten, or is unable to face, those tragic and horrific days of suffering during the battle of Okinawa; and, toward the end of World War II, when people had nothing to eat except the Sago palm, if they could find one.

Japan still does not acknowledge this group of hidden women. Is it not the nation of Japan's fault that this horrific

---

22   Miki Ward Crawford, Katie Kaori Hayashi, Shizuko Suenaga, "Japanese War Brides in America: An Oral History," p.61

social situation was created? Don't we call it a social sin? Is it right for us to let an individual who sacrificed her life to save her family carry a man made stigma—Japanese war bride?

Some of the Japanese war brides had lost their fathers or bothers. Some might have been only children themselves—as young as 15 years old—who bore the responsibility of caring for their siblings and/or mothers. No one wins a war, and women and children suffer the most because of it. My only hope for the readers of this section is that they recognize that I am neither making all war brides martyrs nor am I making them prostitutes. I am merely stating the reality of some Japanese war brides. I am not sure of the experiences of European women as war brides, but I hope their experiences were not as harsh as that of the Japanese war brides, especially those who came from Okinawa.

I know because those war brides are my friends, and they are the first friends I made in Pontiac, Michigan and in Chicago, Illinois through Mr. & Mrs. Asato. Mr. Asato was one of the first immigrant farmers to enter America during the early 1900s from Okinawa, and Mrs. Asato was one of the first women immigrant wives who entered the United States from Okinawa. When I met them, they were storekeepers who owned a Japanese grocery store in Chicago, where they opened their house to anyone who came from Okinawa. We gathered there at least twice a year and reminisced about the country we had left behind. We shared stories of hardship around bearing the name of war bride. We cried and encouraged each other.

I know, too, some of the children of war brides who have earned academic degrees as high as a doctorate, such as Dr. Miki Ward Crawford, co-author of *Japanese War Brides in America: Oral History,* and Ann Curry, a famous journalist and an anchorwoman of the NBC Today show.

Japanese war brides overcame the language and cultural differences with the strong love they felt for their husbands, and together they have built strong roots in the new world they found.

I would like to quote another Japanese war bride who experienced discrimination similar to my own. When interviewed by the authors of *Japanese War Brides in America: An Oral History*, she said: "While living in the United States, I was discriminated against by the Japanese and Japanese-Americans because I was a war bride. I asked myself whether the term (戦争花嫁) (war bride) was a derogatory term or not. I would be angry if somebody said, "*you are a war bride*," but I *was* a war bride. I could not change that fact."

Another Japanese war bride who was interviewed states her experience this way: "In Japan, especially soon after World War II, the Japanese women who spent time with American soldiers were seen as prostitutes. The 'promiscuous relationship' between American soldiers and Japanese women was well publicized in the United States and Japan.

After the war, some women lost shelter and almost starved to death. To survive, they made their livings as prostitutes for foreign soldiers. Many were desperate, but in the war-torn country of Japan, not all Japanese women who spent time with American soldiers were prostitutes. Many Japanese women who married American soldiers were tormented by the image of the war brides, especially in Japan."[23]

I remember using that simple proper noun 'Japanese War Bride' to identify myself shortly after being employed by Japan Airlines. It created unexpected havoc in my life in Chicago. At that time, every new employee was sent to an orientation class. I was sent to San Francisco. I met many new employees. During

---

23   Miki Ward Crawford, Katie Kaori Hayashi, Shizuko Suenaga, "Japanese War Brides in America: An Oral History," p.67

the introduction period, I referred to myself as a war bride since that was a part of who I thought I was at that time. I don't know why I introduced myself that way. I had no need to. I knew the term war bride had a stigma associated with it. When I think back about that incident all I can say is "it was a mystery." Was I invited to experience the mystery of suffering to carry the cross Japanese war brides everywhere unfairly carried? I did not think I would suffer so much humiliation because of it. That simple declaration meant that I was treated differently. I was treated as one who sold her body to a G.I. This unfair treatment did not come from only American employees, but also from Japanese employees, – my own people.

For now, I don't need to detail my painful experience, except to say that it was difficult and that I should never have identified myself as a Japanese war bride!

Technically speaking, I don't belong to this group of women because in 1953 I married a former American soldier who was a civilian. Yet, I identify myself with them, and this identification carries a stigma that brings shame to all women in Japan.

Like any war bride, I went through various physical and mental tests, as well as a test showing that I did not belong to a group of Russian spies or the Communist Party. Only after I passed these tests was I granted permission to immigrate into the United States of America as the bride of Carl O. Streling.

Years later, another incident happened to me when the members of the Okinawa Kyoyukai (association) gathered at a park in Chicago, each bringing a favorite Japanese or Okinawan dish to share. A visiting professor from a university and his wife were guests. He was studying at the University of Chicago for the summer. The wife of the professor approached me and asked, "Are you Masako Streling?"

I am not sure how she found me but I could guess. I replied, "I am."

She continued saying, "I heard your story that you are attending Loyola University Chicago studying theology. I would like to know more about you."

We got to know each other, and thereafter I made an effort to meet her every time I got a chance to visit my parents, my siblings, and friends in Okinawa. On one occasion, when she took me to an elementary school in Okinawa and asked me if I could speak to them, she said sternly, "Do not make any mention of being a war bride because you are not a war bride."

She then explained to me why. I knew her intentions were kind, but I got her message for the first time and understood why Japan Airlines treated me differently than others. As I mentioned, the term *war bride* carries a stigma of some shame or immorality. When I heard her saying to me the very thing I did not want to hear, I no longer desired to continue the same relationship with her. My self-esteem was obviously still quite wounded from the stigma attached to being called a Japanese war bride. Ultimately, it was my issue to come to terms with.

What I wanted to hear from her were the words of her understanding and compassion, maybe a word of praise for those women who were here in America trying to assimilate into American culture while they tried to be a wife and mother. Being a mother and wife in one's own culture is difficult enough. Just imagine adding to that the responsibility of learning a completely different culture, language, and religion.

I began to realize that higher education does not necessarily make a man or woman a compassionate and understanding person.

Intellectual knowledge can in fact be a hindrance to spiritual knowledge at times, even though they should work side-by-side to help see things clearer. Sometimes higher education makes people separate themselves from their origins. We divide the world into neighbors, and enemies, good and evil, just and unjust and educated and uneducated.

Later I realized that it was time now to stop condemning the professor's wife who told me not to identify myself as a war bride. The way she thought was different from mine. I had no right appointing myself to be a judge or juror. Eventually, I realized it was time that I try to get in touch with her again. Who knows why she advised me to do that? All I know is that it had been too long since I heard her voice and I missed her.

I took the first step by calling her to help me construct that part of my story, especially when I speak about people of Okinawa. She promised that she would devote her time writing about Japanese war brides to help them recover their human dignity.

HOW DID WE SURVIVE?

The more I think about how fortunate modern parents are, having books and television readily available for them to learn about raising happier children, the less anger I feel toward my parents' inadequate or inept ways of raising their nine children. My mother was too busy making both ends meet. I doubt she had time to even think about whether or not her children were happy. She also had another burden to carry. She had a sick husband suffering from chronic asthma to care for at home.

I wonder how we got through those stages of our lives without any help. Some people believe that it is important for a child to live out each stage of life fully, or face a negative consequence sometime in later life. This theory confuses me. No one in my family became a murderer or a thief or a prostitute?

Let me talk about something else for a moment—food. I love food! I love to cook! I love to eat! I don't remember ever having three meals a day. In fact, the pain of hunger was with me throughout most of my young life. Obviously the pain of hunger not only affected the physical condition of my body, but also affected my psyche—anything to do with food. Do you know what the pain of physical hunger feels like? My pain of hunger for food did not leave me until quite recently. I cannot describe what that hunger pain feels like. There is no adequate word to describe it other than to say that the area where it hurts is in your gut, above your navel but below the rib cage. *There.* There I felt a dull pain for many years.

I was the oldest child remaining at home toward the end of the war in Taiwan, when my elder brother, Hiroshi was recruited into the Student Army Battalion. He was only fifteen years old.

Every day, when the B-29s attack ended at dusk, Chiyoko, Takako, and I crawled out of the air raid shelter in the underground. We went out to the farmers' fields to find any sprouts of sweet potatoes, which were an indication that there were potatoes underneath, or green vegetables that were edible. What we were doing then was gleaning the field for God's gift of food for the poor. One night, while looking for something to cook, I overheard the women saying that one of them saw a dog with a Taiwanese woman's bound-foot in its mouth. We were so afraid we might encounter the same fate.

My mother used our gleanings as best she could to feed us. Usually, she made soup with all the things we gathered in the evenings. It was more of a liquid than what teeth could chew and our palates could taste. Although we could go out at dawn to gather snails, as many other children and women did, my mother would not think of eating them, much less feeding them to her children. During my trip to France years later, I learned that *escargot* is a fancy name for snails served in high-end restaurants.

I never felt my stomach was full or satisfied until I came to America. It seems what I describe in those days of darkness was a bad dream. The word of Scripture comes to mind:

Jesus said in reply, "It is written: 'One does not live by bread alone, but by every word that comes forth from the mouth of God" (Matthew 4:4).

Then how did I satisfy the hunger of my soul? How did I survive physically and emotionally? How did I survive spiritually? I honestly don't know if I have ever been a child, as my childhood was one of responsibility and duty.

I am more neurotic than I like to admit. Yet the stories I've heard from my contemporaries who were raised in an affluent culture, such as America, assure me that I am not much more or less neurotic than they are. We all have our issues.

I did survive, but as a different person. I thought — I am not quite sure if I like this person I am living with, because she seems so unlike the person I once was. I lost the child's gift of wonder, spontaneity, and trust. Maybe I learned to be cautious living the life that was given me?

Eventually, I felt I became a cautious and unspiritual person. I was once kind and spontaneous, always ready to help one who was in need. I was a typical product of Japanese upbringing. But one day I was forced to see the world differently. One may say it was a process of learning how to survive in the world.

I remember when I lived in Chicago. Every Saturday and Sunday, I took my pet dog, a poodle, named Hics, to Belmont Harbor near our apartment. There, I used to meet homeless people wandering around the Harbor. I brought them home occasionally because they were begging for money, which I did not have. But I invited them home to make sandwiches for them. One day I brought one homeless man home and asked him to wait outside of the kitchen while I was making a sandwich for him. I did not realize my husband Carl was home from work.

Carl came to the kitchen and asked, "What are you doing?"

I replied, "I am making a sandwich for that man outside."

He said, "Don't bring strangers home again. They could hurt you. You might not be that lucky the next time." I guess I was quite naïve about bringing strangers home. I felt humiliated. Feelings of fear and humiliation invaded my soul. Regardless of what I thought about homeless people, this experience shook me.

Chapter Five:
Turning Point

I THOUGHT THE SUN WAS GOD

When I was a child, I felt I heard God talking to me. I thought and felt that I could talk to Him.

I began praying at age seven or eight. I felt I heard God saying that I was just as smart as my male classmates, and just as good as my brothers. These words of God that I heard were also the words of my mother.

I wanted to know why I had to settle with being second place? I needed to know. Was it because I was born a girl? Why did I have to carry a box of chalk instead of my teacher's school-books when the class began? Miyara Shinken, a male classmate was the one who carried my teacher's books, not a box of chalk.

As I grew older so did my question to God: *How can I, a thirteen-year-old girl, fight with Japanese society?* God was silent.

Japan was strongly patriarchal when I was growing up. I was continually given the message—*You are inferior because you were born a girl. The only salvation of your life is to find a good husband so that you will be well taken care of. For this reason you are to be his servant, and your husband your master.*

I was deeply aware then that the world was an unfair place. Despite what society says about the female gender—with God's assurance deep in my heart—I never thought I was inferior because I was born a girl.

But even though society measured the worth of humanity according to gender, and no matter how much my father lamented my being born a girl, I never thought it was unfair that I was born a girl. I just wanted to be treated the same as a boy. I wanted to have the same rights. But, I did not know who God was. I thought the Sun was God.

I often chose a small path instead of the main road to come home from school, because the path took me to a farm. There I could be alone and nobody would be watching me when I prayed to my Sun God. Standing in my bare feet, I asked many questions: *Why is the world so unfair? Why does my father have to suffer every day from this terrible chronic asthma?* As always, pleading to my Sun God ended my prayer.

I would ask, *"Please make my father completely cured."*

I prayed to the Sun God and asked that when I got home that day I would find my father breathing better. I prayed that he would be up and around. Oh, how I wished he were well! When he was well, he would ask me to gather up the neighborhood kids, especially when the moon was full. We would sit on a straw mat outside and underneath a luffa-gourd arbor, letting the moonlight filter through upon us as we listened to my father tell stories. We huddled together in case it was a scary story. My father's stories were so scary, that sometimes he would have to walk the kids home afterwards.

In our household nobody talked about God. There was much talk about right and wrong conduct to honor or dishonor our ancestors' names. Saving one's face was tantamount to a religious tenet. We were told that our dead ancestors, whose name tablets were honored on our family altar, were our gods. I decided my god would be the sun. I don't know why. I knew this much though, even as a child—just because you die, you cannot become a god. I knew, too, that my grandfather could not possibly become a god when *he* died.

One day I would learn that God was the creator of heaven and earth, including the sun. I learned that God is the only one who will judge us when we die. He will judge us according to how we did or did not conduct our lives according to his will.

One afternoon my father's chronic asthma was healed suddenly. When I came home from the school, I saw the pool of thick yellow phlegm on the vestibule with Unme assisting him to breathe. I wondered often, even today, if this miraculous cure of my father's chronic asthma was a result of my prayer. Did God the Father hear the child Masako's prayer?

AMERICAN DREAM

As I grew older, so did my worldview. I marched to different music than my father. My prayers changed. I complained about social, cultural, and women's issues. My search for the true God took many years. It was a difficult journey.

My life did not belong to me then. My father allowed me to finish my 12th grade but denied me further education.

There was a full moon on the night when a group of my classmates and the Yaeyama High School principal visited my father. They tried to persuade my father to let me be included among the candidates who would apply for a scholarship in an American government-sponsored exchange student program. He refused to accept the invitation from the Yaeyama High School principal. He agreed only that I would finish the 12th grade. I was brokenhearted and became very defiant toward my father. The harder he fought against my desire for a higher education, the more time I spent researching and studying how I could find a way to get onto that list of candidates.

One afternoon, when I came home from school, I found all of my schoolbooks had been thrown into the pig house where they were dirtied by the pig's dung. When I went into the pig house to gather my books, crying my heart out, my mother and younger sister Chiyoko came to help. We collected the books and washed them as clean as possible at the well. This horrible incident prompts important questions. Why do I not remember the details of that day? Where was my father when I was crying my heart out, trying to rescue my books from the pig's dung? Why did I not run away from home? Could it be that, despite being brokenhearted, I knew in the depth of my heart he was desperate for my help?

My plan to study in the United States of America under any program was shattered, yet I dreamed that someday I would get to America. I also dreamed that someday I would become a lawyer. I wanted to help build a society where men and women would be treated equally. A society where gifted children like me could get some help. How little did I know my dream would come true, but instead of studying human law, I chose the study of God's Law, Theology.

I read every book I could get hold of, including school text-books, magazines, and newspapers about America. The U.S. Constitution fascinated me because it was based on an idea that we are all created equal. I was inspired by the American system of government, its judicial system, democracy, freedom of speech, and responsibility. I was inspired by the idea of America as the land of opportunity.

I dreamed that someday I would find employment with the U.S. military, but I first had to graduate from Yaeyama High School then go to Naha, the capital city of Okinawa Honto. Naha was where the most jobs existed. Soon after graduating from Yaeyama High School in March of 1950, I went to Naha.

I found a job working at the Horticultural Department of Naha as a bilingual sales person. I realized then, that I needed to learn how to type in order to get a better job.

I continued to dream that someday I would have an opportunity to go to America. My dream came true when I met my husband Carl, an American soldier in the 29th Infantry stationed at Camp Noborikawa, Okinawa.

When World War II ended on August 15, 1945, the U.S. Occupation Army arrived in the defeated country of Japan. The occupation provided various working positions that brought many Japanese men and women necessary employment. Also, any native of Okinawa could acquire a practical skill such as typing, cleaning houses, ironing, or learning English, by applying at any U.S. Military base. I applied at the 29th Infantry, Camp Noborikawa and was selected from the many applicants to learn how to type because of my knowledge of English. My above-average English knowledge was the main reason that the Yaeyama High School principal used to try to persuade my father to change his mind.

The instructor's name was Lt. Robert Taylor. I heard later, that he was sent to the Korean War where he was killed. Every student who finished the course received a certificate of proficiency in typing skills. We also received a photo. In each photo, you can see a recipient who is receiving a certificate from Lt. Taylor. I wanted an additional photo so that I could send it to my parents, but we were not allowed to enter a store called the P.X. (post exchange) to purchase one. I asked the first soldier who looked at me kindly if he could get me a second copy of the photo at the P.X. That soldier was Carl Oscar Streling, my husband today.

That must have been in the spring of 1951. Our relationship began to grow from that day forward. One December morning in 1952, he told me that he was going home to the United States where his brother Vern was waiting to start up a trucking business. We exchanged addresses and parted. I wanted to see him one more time, so I took a bus to White Beach, Okinawa to see him off. There were many soldiers on the five-story high troopship. I could not find Carl. Suddenly I saw him waving and I asked a M.P. who was guarding the ship if he could take a love letter I had written to Carl. The M.P. said he would, but Carl never received my note. We corresponded to each other from that day on.

MARRIAGE

One year later, Carl returned to Okinawa for one week as a civilian to marry me. He then returned to the U.S. Lawrence C. Mitchell, the Vice Consul of the American Consular Service in Tokyo, Japan, stationed in Naha, Okinawa, signed the Certificate of Marriage. Our witnesses were Mary Jean Davis and Cheei Taira. We were married on November 5, 1953.

I did not tell my parents that I was married to an American for many months because it was seen as scandalous. I did not want to shame our family name. I knew though, that I must face up to the fact that I was married, and that my parents had the right to know. One day, I received a letter from Carl telling me that he would like to dissolve our marriage if I was still ashamed to be married to an American. I had to choose.

His request was justifiable because I was giving him various reasons why I could not leave Okinawa to join him sooner in America. I was torn between my love for him and my duty and devotion to my family, friends, and my country. To leave the familiar and travel to an unfamiliar place called America to be with Carl, as his wife, was the most difficult decision I ever made.

The dreaded day came when I had to announce our marriage to my parents and tell them I had been married since November 5, 1953. Carl sent me a ticket to travel. The date was for July 24, 1954. A couple of months before I left Okinawa, I quit my job where I worked as the head of a bilingual sales department in a horticultural office at Naha, so that I could return to my parents' house to announce my marriage to an American. Not only that,

I said I was leaving Okinawa in several weeks to be with him in San Francisco, California. This shocking news brought tears to my father's eyes. He asked several questions about Carl, but I could not answer most of them. The only thing I knew about Carl was that he was a decent man, kind, handsome, and that he had a brother, Vern, and a sister, Beverly. I knew nothing of his heritage.

My father said to me, "You will suffer because your marriage, like mine, is retribution. You will suffer."

The Japanese word for law of retribution is *Inga Oho*, meaning that it is according to the law of cause and effect. My father's remark was because of his pain, I would inevitably suffer as a consequence. Ironically, my father suffered the broken dream of coming to the United States to study; while I suffered the broken dream of helping my parents raise their nine children. I too married a man not knowing very much about him, just as my father married my mother about whom he knew very little. The only thing he knew about her was that she was beautiful.

My father told me that the only thing I knew of Carl, was that he is handsome and kind. I had married a man I didn't know very much about. But he also told me I would succeed because I had an unusually strong character, like a man that was born as a woman.

VOYAGE TO AMERICA

I left Okinawa by ship on July 24, 1954 bound for Yokohama on the main Japanese island of Honshu. Upon my arrival I met my friend Yoshiko Takamine at Yokohama Harbor. She had been my best friend since high school and was studying in Tokyo to be a seamstress. In high school we had often talked about how unfair life seemed, and how money seemed to control the world, including the teachers and our principal. At that time we could not see any consistency in their teaching or the examples they set. We had shared whatever money we could pool together between us to buy something to munch on as we discussed life issues. We were simply two student idealists who sought perfection in an imperfect world.

We traveled by bus to Yoshiko's apartment in Tokyo. I spent about a week with her there. The night before I left Yokohama onboard a ship bound for San Francisco, we visited Ginza, a nightspot nobody should miss. At a crossroad, under a dim light, a fortuneteller beckoned us. She took my hand and studied it.

"You are going to a far-away place," she said. "Your life will be challenging, but it will become more fulfilling after you reach the age of fifty."

I often wonder about her pronouncements. How did she know?

Yoshiko wanted to see me off, so we traveled by bus to Yokohama Seaport. Before I boarded the S.S. President Wilson on August 1, 1954, Yoshiko gave me a Bible and a Japanese doll to remember her by. I still have both of these gifts. The enormous engines rumbled to life and the ship left Yokohama bound for America. The vastness of the ship overwhelmed me. This was the second largest ship I had ever seen. The first being the troop ship Carl was on when he left Okinawa in December of 1952. Suddenly, the reality hit me—the fear, the loneliness, the uncertainty. Would I see my parents, my siblings, and my friend Yoshiko again? I walked numbly toward my cabin as a steward led me, holding the Bible and the Japanese doll in my arms. How little did I know that the Bible Yoshiko gave me would change my life in the future. I wept bitterly. I tried to read the Bible during my sea voyage, but it was written in classic/ancient Japanese. I could hardly get myself interested.

The twelve-day sea voyage from Yokohama to San Francisco was very difficult. I was seasick the entire time. Despite that, every day and night I managed to go up to the top of the deck to gaze at the vast Pacific Ocean and observe its breadth separating my past and my future. I saw a calm, cobalt blue ocean as far as my eyes could see. The ship steamed toward the Hawaiian Islands.

I saw the most beautiful sunsets and sunrises while I wondered if what I had chosen for my life was right. Would my parents ever forgive me? I promised every night that I would someday repay them. I did not know I was praying then, but I know now — in fact I was.

The ship seemed to swallow the ocean between Yokohama and the San Francisco Bay. How powerful a sight that was! I often thought how the water separated me from my beloved country and my family whom I loved, and my husband. My heart was divided between my husband waiting for me in San Francisco and my family, whom I had just left behind. I looked around me. There was nothing but the President Wilson and the sea below.

The ship plowed the water like a farmer plowing a vast field that stretched to the horizon and beyond. I looked up and saw a new moon. I wept. When would I see my family again? Deep fear overtook me, yet I never doubted that I had a new, exciting, and challenging future awaiting me. And I never doubted that my husband, Carl, would be waiting for me in San Francisco to start our new life together.

I lay on my bunk most of that ocean journey eating only the fruits that were brought in daily by my cabin steward. My roommates were two *nisei* (second generation Japanese) sisters, Hazel and Judy Sato, who boarded ship at Yokohama Seaport, One evening they asked me whether or not I was sick.

"No, I am not sick," I said. "If you are not sick," Judy asked, "Why do you not go to the dining room to eat?"

I confessed that I didn't know what to order and how to handle a knife, fork, and spoon. I never used these eating utensils. I used chopsticks to eat with all my life.

Hazel said they both would help me. They told me to sit in front of them and instructed me that when they picked up a fork, I should pick up the same one and so on. With some fear, I decided to dress up for the occasion. I made my way down to the dining room with them.

When I picked up the knife and cut into a piece of steak, everything on my plate flew off onto the table. I was embarrassed and felt so stupid, but the Sato sisters said not to worry. With practice, I got better. Eight days later we arrived at the Hawaiian Islands where I said farewell and cried as the Sato sisters disembarked.

A couple of days later, the ship sailed toward the San Francisco Bay. I met my new roommate, who was returning home from Honolulu to Detroit. Her name was Dorothy Hess. She also became one of my teachers and mentors during the early days of my life in America. She took me to the Ford Museum, introduced me to the history of the Ford Motor Company, and showed me how automobiles were made. She also introduced me to her parents. Her father owned and operated one of the neighborhood gasoline stations. She encouraged me to take an English course offered by a nearby college. I eventually enrolled myself in a business college by our neighborhood, taking Business English with the hope that I would be better qualified to find a job.

I was a stranger, but the Sato sisters and Dorothy Hess treated me as though I was one of their own. I was deeply touched by the kindness of these strangers. For the first time in my life, I felt something other than my own assurance that I would be all right in America.

I was ready when the loud speaker announced the time we would arrive in San Francisco. Dressed in a yellow suit and hat, I went up on deck to watch the ship sailing under the San Francisco Bridge. It was a magnificent sight that I can still see in my mind's eye. It was early in the morning on August 12, 1954, when the ship docked at San Francisco Bay for us to disembark. I saw my husband Carl in the distance waving at me. With one brown trunk, I left the ship to begin my new life in this vast new world of America with Carl.

Carl Oscar Streling, my husband, was the sole person I knew and trusted. I had traveled alone from Okinawa to San Francisco Bay to spend the rest of my life with him. On a deeper level, I met God through my cabin roommates' kindness and compassion to me — a stranger. It was indeed a sign that I would be taken care of.

Years later, Carl shared his thoughts about his drive to San Francisco from Pontiac, Michigan. He prayed that his 1951 Chevy convertible would make it on time to meet the ship's arrival. I remember that beautiful green convertible. It took us safely back to Pontiac. The hope of starting our new lives together and our trust in each other replaced the pain of separation from my country, my family, and my friends.

LIFE IN AMERICA:
SAN FRANCISCO–PONTIAC, MICHIGAN

Although Carl looked different, more mature and tired, he was very happy to see me finally arrive in San Francisco to start our life together. I too, was very happy to be united with him as his wife.

The first thing I asked him after we were settled was, "When will I get to meet your family?"

I was a little nervous about meeting them. He told me I would meet them in a week. I had no idea of the vastness of this continent of America. Even the birds seemed larger — the crows, the sparrows, the swallows. The size of all of the Japanese islands equaled the state of California.

Frankly, I remember very little of the sights and sounds of that trip from San Francisco to Pontiac, except the mountain ranges of Colorado. I was amazed to see the depth of the canyons, the rock formations, and the heights of the mountain ranges as we climbed them and then descended to sea level. Some place in the mountains, Carl took me to a restaurant where I could order a fish dinner. He told me it was fresh water fish called trout. I thought it had a fishy smell, but then he said Okinawan fish had a fishy smell, too. I guess fish have a certain smell from the waters in which they are raised. I enjoyed the dinner.

One week later we arrived at his parents' home in Pontiac. I asked him to just drive around until I could calm myself enough to meet my new family. Waiting in the dining room were his parents, his brother Vern and wife Lois, Carl's aunt Margaret, his uncle Otis and his wife Marge, and his youngest sister, Joan. After a brief introduction, we all sat down to eat.

I knew nothing about the "passing of the food" around the table, so all the dishes stopped at my side of the table. Finally, Carl helped me out so that everyone could have whatever they wanted when the dishes were "passed." The only thing I remember vividly that day was that I took a dish of cottage cheese, mistaking it as mashed potatoes. What I tasted was not the mashed potato that I had learned to eat on the ship, but rather the sour taste of cottage cheese. I managed to swallow it, but to this day, I don't care for cottage cheese. I don't know what dishes were served that day. It was not steak they served. I had eaten steak for the first time in my life on the ship and remembered how it tasted. Frankly, I did not care for it. Besides, the size of the steak scared me.

At the end of the dinner, we celebrated our wedding with my new family. We all had a piece of wedding cake as dessert. I could not eat the cake that day because it was too sweet. Almost sixty years later, I would rather have dessert than dinner. It is incredible how time changes one's palate. A steak dinner has also become one of my favorite American dishes.

One day, shortly after my arrival at Carl's parents' house, I walked to a neighborhood Catholic Church. All the trees were bare. I walked on the wet and colored leaves toward the church. I had not seen the sun for some time now, and it was the first time I had ever seen the trees without leaves on them. I did not know, of course, what brought me to this church any more than I knew it was a Catholic Church. I was told not to go there by my mother-in-law. For some reason, she did not like the idea of me attending a Catholic Church. I asked my husband to take me to a church, any church. I wanted to find one where I felt comfortable in praying. He took me to every church he could find, including a Pentecostal Christian Church as they called it, but I could not find one like the neighborhood Catholic Church where I was asked not to go.

Why was I attracted to a Catholic Church? I don't have any specific reason to tell you except my friend Yoshiko, who gave me the Bible as I left Yokohama harbor, told me she was a Catholic.

Every Monday, I received a letter from my father. He never failed since my arrival in America. His letters comforted me. I longed for a day when I would see him again. I worked toward that opportunity.

Life in America was not easy, but I believed in the American system.

I was faced with many things. I needed to learn how to cook American dishes, how to use a knife and fork, how to eat soup with a spoon, how to speak English more fluently, and how to greet people. More importantly, I needed to find a job. I needed to meet people who could help me practice and speak English at the same time I could help Carl earn our living. For one thing I knew, if I would work hard and persevere enough, there would be someone who would recognize my talents and ambition and I would be given an opportunity. It happened, but not without hurdles.

The first job I applied for was a clerk, but the interviewer said that the position was filled. I kept looking, but no luck. These repeated experiences told me that I should lower my standards, so I applied as a factory worker where I would operate a small machine making small precision parts for automobiles. The factory was in a man's three-car garage and the workers consisted of himself, his wife, and me. My hands became oily and torn by sharp steel parts flying around the machine.

Eventually I left that job and applied for a position as a *tray pusher* working in a fountain in Ted's Trailer Drive-In Restaurant in Pontiac. A tray pusher's job is to make ice cream cones, ice cream sodas, floats, and banana splits. I worked with Pat Misegan, a Native American girl, who taught me how to make a beautiful banana split.

One day, in the restroom, Shirley, a dining room waitress told me that she was quitting because she was pregnant. She told me that I should apply for the position because I would make a lot of money in tips. So I went to see Herb, the manager, a stocky man with a cigar in his mouth, and asked if I could talk to him. He yelled at me when I asked about the job opening.

He said, "I can't afford to put you in the dining room."

"Why?" I asked.

He replied, "I just can't."

"I don't understand," I said. "Look," he said, "I can't let you work in the dining room because I will lose too many customers."

"Why will you lose too many customers?"

"It is because you are Japanese," he said, "I cannot have you in the dining room. I will lose tons of money."

So I took off my apron in front of him and resigned.

ASK FOR BETTER OPPORTUNITIES

While going home on the bus, I thought, "Is this the America I believe in, where I read that everybody is equal and the color of one's skin does not matter?"

I was bitterly disappointed. How could I, a Japanese war bride, get an equal opportunity and get a better job?

With this simple quest, I wrote a short letter, took it to the Pontiac Press Newspaper office and asked to see an editor. A young woman appeared, took time to talk to me, read my short letter very carefully, and promised it would be in that evening's edition. That was January 19, 1957, more than fifty plus years ago, three years after my arrival in America. Perhaps, that courageous act was a part of my samurai spirit defending the honor of my ancestry. Or, was it Jesus who was leading me to defend my position publicly?

The first letter was condensed due to lack of space in the newspaper.

Japanese War Brides Ask for Better Opportunities

Pontiac Press "The Voice of the People" January 19, 1957.

I am one of the Japanese war brides. That is what they call us.

One thing I really would like to know is why this country does not give us an opportunity to have better jobs or give us the chance to prove our abilities. They require that we have experience in this country.

If nobody gives us a first chance, how can we build that experience?

After all, we are willing to learn everything and help to earn a better living with our husbands, as well as other wives. Maybe we are even willing to work harder.

Please do not let us down; give us a chance to share responsibility. We worked for the Armed Forces as office girls and waitresses, and our knowledge of English was quite satisfactory.

I have been working at a restaurant as a fountain girl and have been asking for a better position, but have been unable to get one, even though I am qualified for office work, having trained in Japan and at a Business Institute here.

Masako Streling

The night of January 19th the telephone rang steadily. Some called me Jap and told me to go home. Some offered me a job. The first person who called me was Mr. Ralph Robinson, the owner of Robinson Photographic Studio. Then a law office called, a bank, and many other businesses. In spite of Carl's suggestion that I should take a job at a law office, I took the job as a receptionist at Robinson Studio because I felt grateful to Mr. Robinson. He called me first. He did not really need me as his business was slowing down, so I cleaned his office and straightened his files in order to keep my eight hours occupied.

On March 2, 1957, I wrote a second letter, this one was a letter of thanks. I marveled at the different views American people had regarding the Japanese. I was a stranger, an immigrant, a Japanese War Bride, yet many people offered me a job.

This eye-opening experience confirmed my strong hope and trust in America.

War Bride Now Understands U.S.

Pontiac Press "The Voice of the People" March 2, 1957

I am the one who asked for better opportunities for Japanese war brides. Now I clearly understand the difference between people in this country and in mine. My country has been adopting America for its future. I may have been thinking a little selfishly about the freedom, etc., but I had expected it to compare with that in Japan.

I have discovered, and not only because I have been offered a job and so forth, that there are many people who are interested in helping us and treating us equally if we try hard enough to have faith in this country. I appreciate very much the help of The Pontiac Press and my employer.

Masako Streling

That summer, Carl decided to move to Chicago to look for a job. The trucking business with his brother Vern did not work out. We moved to Chicago on July 4, 1957. Though we moved to Chicago, I received a Christmas card every year thereafter from Mr. Robinson. After his death, Mrs. Robinson continued to send me a Christmas card. In 1961, I received a Christmas card from their daughter with a note telling me that Mrs. Robinson had also died. We went to Pontiac for the last time to visit Mr. and Mrs. Robinson's daughter and her parents' gravesites. We thanked her for her kindness in letting us know about her mother and expressed our sympathies and gratefulness to her parents for being friends all those years, especially during those first few years of my life in America when I needed friends so badly. The Robinsons and Dorothy Hess were among the first friends I met in America. Thereafter, I was blessed with many mentors who helped me.

It was through the kindness of people like the Robinsons that I began to realize the differences between the people of America and those of Japan. I was puzzled and sought the answer as to why Americans were so compassionate and willing to include strangers in their circle. You see the Japanese are compassionate people only to those who already belong to their circle.

CHICAGO

After we moved to Chicago, Carl left me with piles of boxes to unpack while he went to work. His trucking job took him away from home a week at a time. Alone with all those boxes in front of me, I longed for something familiar. I reasoned that, as Chicago was a big city, there must be a Japanese restaurant nearby. I took out the telephone directory to look for a Japanese restaurant, but the first thing after the word, *Japanese* in the telephone book was a Japanese American Employment Agency.

Curious, I dialed the number and a young woman answered. I stated my business, made myself clear that the reason I was calling was not for employment, but a name, telephone number, and address of a Japanese restaurant.

She said that her name was Mrs. Nishimura and gave me the following instructions:

"Come out of your apartment, turn left and you will be on Barry Avenue. Turn left again and you will come to Broadway Avenue. Stand on the west side of the street and take bus number 36. Ask the driver to let you off at Clark and Division. I will be there waiting for you."

I followed the instructions as given and got off at Clark and Division looking for a young woman. But it was an older woman in her sixties who approached me. I was shocked because I was looking for a young woman, though her voice sounded exactly the same as it was on the telephone. She took me to a Japanese restaurant where I ate until I was full. I had not had any authentic Japanese food for three years. Next she took me to a Japanese grocery store. I bought a large bag of rice, Kikkoman soy sauce, miso, some fish, and two boxes of tofu. I thanked her for her kindness and tried to leave.

"Masako," she said, "now I want to ask you a favor. I want you to have a job interview. My client needs a typist urgently."

"But I am not dressed for a job interview." I replied.

You look just fine," she said.

She took me to an advertising agency named Altheimer & Baer, near the Merchandise Mart in Chicago. While I was waiting for the interview, I heard a loud voice yelling and screaming. I was wondering who that man might be. The loud voice stopped, and a man appeared in front of me.

He took me to his office and asked me, how much do you want to be paid for the job?

Nothing else was asked. Naturally, I was not at all prepared to answer any questions, particularly that one. Besides I was not sure what I was worth.

"Please pay me whatever you think that I am worth," I said.

I started as a clerk typist, working for his assistant manager, Mr. Merrill Natker, for $50 a week. As a clerk typist, I was to type Mr. Natker's handwritten letters.

One day after I typed up a handwritten letter and put it on his desk for his signature, something strange happened. I went back to my desk. I heard him laughing. I knew that the letter I just typed was not a funny one. I thought, "Why is he laughing so hard?" Puzzled, I went into his office. He asked me to take that letter and show it to my husband.

"Your husband can tell you why it is so funny," he said.

I took the letter home and showed it to Carl. He laughed too.

"You called him an ass manager," Carl said.

"Ass?" I said. "What does it mean?"

He said that I should consult a dictionary. I did and learned one more word, which was added to my English vocabulary. I learned the literal and colloquial meaning of ass.

The next day at the office, I apologized to Mr. Natker for my ignorance and promised that I would never call anyone ass any more.

Mr. Natker was good-humored and very kind. He was an angel sent to me from heaven. He told me I should not stay there too long, and I should go to night school to better myself.

I suggested to him that I could learn to be an accountant or a bookkeeper because numbers are universal.

He enrolled me in twenty weeks of night classes, accounting courses, at one of the business schools in downtown Chicago. When I got the certificate showing the completion of the courses, he found me a job working as a bookkeeper at the Methodist Conference of Chicago on LaSalle Street. I called Mr. Natker often after I finished working for him. But one day I called and he was no longer there. I often wondered what happened to him.

I changed my jobs four times during 1959 — 1964: From a clerk typist at Altheimer & Baer Company, to a bookkeeper for the Methodist Conference of Chicago, the William Greiner Company, then the Interstate Steel Company. By 1964 I had built my résumé as an experienced bookkeeper, and a very good one at that! At Interstate Steel, I met many famous people such as Ed O'Bradovich (1962-1971), a former NFL football player. Ed played defensive end for the Chicago Bears. I met

Carol Kleiman, the prize winning columnist of the, "Woman at Work" column from the Chicago Tribune. Carol Kleiman interviewed me around 1965-1966. I still have her article in a frame. The date is hidden inside. In the article, I was praised for the method I developed to collect overdue/outstanding accounts when I worked for Interstate Steel. Under my supervision of the Accounts Receivable Department, I handled millions of dollars of business and collected outstanding invoices, which apparently, my employer said, never happened before with such success. They were very happy with my work. Their approval of my work brought me joy and satisfaction because they were such productive years in my career.

My new life in the United States, in general, was very good. People were tremendously kind. I had not suffered finding a job. A job found me. However, I was terribly lonesome for my husband, my parents, my siblings and friends in Okinawa. I hungered for seafood. Okinawa serves the best Sashimi in the world. Sashimi is like sushi but without the rice. Somehow, the friends and American cuisine I found in America did not seem to assuage my feeling of emptiness and hunger.

While I worked at the Interstate Steel Company in Des Plaines, Illinois, I went to night school to learn to become a travel agent. I did this because I knew that working in a travel agency would give me travel benefits to visit Okinawa. As soon as I got a certificate to show that I was now qualified to be a travel agent, I applied for a job at one of the largest travel agencies on Michigan Avenue.

It was the early 1960s. The airline business was at its height. Airlines entertained travel agents at very expensive hotels in those days with the hope that travel agencies would sell those particular airlines. I was at the Continental Plaza hotel on Michigan Avenue as a guest of Northwest Airlines. A man working at Japan Airlines approached me and mentioned that he would like me to apply for a position as a bilingual Japanese secretary. I declined because I was very interested in learning about the travel agency business with the hope that someday I could own one. However, he was not satisfied by my answer and had his secretary call me.

I then discovered that he was a regional manager sent by the Japan Airlines headquarters in Japan. After much debate, I accepted the position because travel benefits extended not only for me, but also for my husband Carl, and for my children if I had any, and for my parents. My desire to work at O'Hare Airport near our house instead of driving all the way to downtown Chicago was also granted. So while I was under the jurisdiction of the administration department of the downtown Chicago office, I was to work at the airport. My position was to be a bilingual Japanese secretary of the Cargo Sales Department, and to also handle the accounting duties of cargo sales accounts. There was no passenger sales office at the airport office at that time. JAL celebrated the inaugural flight number 009 from Chicago via Anchorage, Alaska to Tokyo/Narita Airport three times a week in 1983. While the deal was made, the wind had shifted decisively and started to blow unfavorably in my direction.

Up to this point in my life in America, I was treated quite warmly wherever I went. However, the unfavorable wind blowing was discrimination. The only place I experienced serious discrimination in America was by this employer, Japan Airlines. I endured a unique form of discrimination for what felt like an eternity. It was in fact sixteen years of humiliation and discrimination from my own people who worked at the airlines. To them I was a Japanese war bride — a loose woman, a prostitute.

This burden became heavy to bear. The perception of a Japanese war bride was unfair and manmade. It was scandalous tableau that judged me, and many, many other women like myself, who married out of love, but were perceived to marry for money.

The following story I share publicly for the first time. For many years, not even my husband knew of this story. The experience was that painful. I kept it in the depth of my heart, until our friend and the final editor of this memoir, Matthew Ferraro, said my story needed to be complete and truthful, even if it was painful for me to speak of. He said others needed to hear and understand my experience. I felt I heard God's voice through him.

During the sixteen years of my employment with Japan Airlines, I helplessly watched the dirty politics played against me because I was a bilingual secretary who was recruited by the Regional Manager. Regional Managers are part of the top management sent from Japan. Many times when I was talking to the Regional Manager in the Japanese language, my co-workers thought I was talking about them. I understood my co-workers concern, but I was never a woman of gossip or malicious intention. I also understood their concerns. I never turned any of them in because I knew they all needed jobs. I was also proud of my name. My name was a name that embodied honor and dignity through hundreds of generations of the Samurai tradition. If I spoke of gossip, then where would my name be? I am a descendant of the Satsuma Samurai. I was taught to be obedient to my duty and to defend my honor. Other employees did not understand that I was answering my manager's questions about cargo sales accounts mostly held by Japanese freight forwarding companies such as Nippon Express, etc. I was a bilingual secretary, answering my boss's questions to facilitate his ability to work in America. Questions like: What is the name of the grocery store closest to his house? Or what store should they go to get certain things? Or where was the closest Department of Motor Vehicles so my boss could get a driver's license. I provided information to make my manager's work life easier. After his tour of duty was completed, my first Regional Manager returned to Osaka, Japan. I saw three other regional managers come and go. Their needs were the same, and I was privileged and honored to help them.

However, there was one manager who caused many of us much pain. My immediate manager who was locally hired betrayed me, and his wife. An immediate manager is a manager hired locally in the U.S. rather than from Japan. I knew this manager was running around with my co-worker, but I did not know that I was the one who was accused of running around with him until his wife told me. She called me often at nights when he was away on so-called business trips. It was strange. One night I asked her, "Why are you calling me?"

She said "My husband told me that you are the one who is having an affair with him."

Her statement shocked me! The next time I saw my immediate manager, I told him strictly, "Leave me out of your affair!"

After I confronted him, I went back to keeping my head down and working at my job.

Eventually, my co-workers convinced him to remove me from my position from the Administration Department to the unfamiliar section in the Cargo Reservation Department, as a cargo reservation agent. A Chinese girl who did not speak Japanese replaced me.

I watched helplessly as my co-worker became promoted to my supervisor. Under his supervision, I was never evaluated fairly. To him, I was not worthy of any promotion. Junior employees were promoted ahead of me. I often thought that it was my responsibility to let the top management know what was going on, but I could not. It was not my responsibility. Instead, I tried to indict Japan Airlines for discrimination, but

I withdrew my complaint. I did this mainly because I could not allow my beloved Japan Airline's name be ruined because I was mistreated by those who were jealous without cause. Eventually my health became an issue. Everything I was in my DNA cried out to stand up and defend my dignity — but for some reasons, I could not. I could not even pray. Instead I stoically endured the pain, which I was expected to do, as I am a descendant of the Satsuma Samurai. My soul must have prayed for me. I was defeated and lost my self-confidence. It became the darkest day of my life. What happened to my courage — my 'will to prevail'?

I was not always the dud I allowed them to make me. I was known as the best accountant who collected overdue money according to the accounts receivable ledger. But co-workers spread the rumor that I could not even balance the $100.00 petty cash fund. The truth was that they did not even know how to read the general ledger, or the accounting records for that matter.

I worked hard those years because I did not want to fail the Regional Manager who did not give up until he was able to recruit me. He knew my record when he hired me. I have his gift of appreciation displayed on my desk. It reminds me of him, a hard working and generous manager. He visited our office often. Under his watch, the Cargo Sales Office transformed from a chaotic office into a somewhat organized office.

After sixteen years in a stressful corporate environment, Japan Airlines introduced the first retirement program in 1985. I took it. Then, top management called me and told me to reconsider because the offer was intended to get rid of the corrupt mid-management people and the old non-productive employees. But I declined and retired from Japan Airlines. Fortunately, they knew all about the conditions I was working under. I did not need to be "tattling".

There was one positive note. I was paid well. Japan Airlines still pays for the major portion of my health insurance, and I am able to travel all over the world via the JAL system, for which I owe a debt of gratitude.

How little did I know that I would be challenged again and again to stand up and defend what is just? I often think of scripture — "A time to keep silence and a time to speak" (Ecclesiastes 3:7).

I wish I had known then how the ancient women in the Bible handled themselves in order to accomplish God's work. I did not know the difference between knowledge and wisdom then.

Carl's work flourished, and between our two incomes, we lived quite comfortably and traveled together quite extensively—as often as Carl could take time off. I traveled on my own a great deal. I would go to France and England every time a national holiday fell on a Friday or Monday. I took a couple of vacation days to make it a full week. I loved to visit the Louvre Museum in Paris where I saw Da Vinci's Mona Lisa and the art works of Monet, Van Gogh, Renoir, Picasso, and hosts of other artists. The Mona Lisa's haunting, enigmatic smile is still in my heart. What a woman she must have been!

I remember one trip, stopping in England on my way home to shop at Harrods. I felt empty. I kept asking, "Is that all there is to life?" I remembered there was a song at the time lamenting a similar theme. I just don't remember the song's name.

I kept asking, "What is there left for me, now that I have helped Carl accomplish financial security? I have traveled the world, not entirely, but enough. I am about to finish my filial duty. What is there left for me?"

I began to feel useless. Everything that gave me the status of being the first daughter of my parents simply disappeared. My sisters and brothers had graduated from universities and had good jobs. They didn't need my help any more. In fact, they avoided my advice because they said I sounded too authoritarian. Clearly, my role as the first daughter of my parents was finished.

I felt what my parents had said about me was little more than a bunch of pumped-up ideas. It was a tune to which I'd been expected to dance. I had become a person with a cumbersome Messiah complex. I had lived long enough to realize that I was not that smart, courageous, or a kind person. Far from it. I felt everything around me was falling apart. I even felt used by Japan Airlines executives.

"Where is my reward, Mother?" I cried out often, and I pondered and pondered why was I so unhappy. Then I realized that the cause might be the old teaching of the Japanese: Retribution. This theory does not always make sense to me. A person who does good will not always be rewarded. A person who sins will not always be punished either. I was not a Christian then, so Jesus' teaching of this paradox obviously had not sunk into my soul.

Also, I had not yet become familiar with the wonderful story of Job. With the help of Scripture, I would eventually discover the teaching of St. Paul, which helped me to find the way to love again.

"Owe nothing to anyone, except to love one another;
for the one who loves another has fulfilled the law"
(Romans 13:8).

Although it costs very little to travel as a Japan Airline employee, my trips to Japan became less frequent over the years because I felt a sense of failure. My friends were now judges, professors, principals, and successful merchants. I was every bit as capable as they were, but had been born into a poorer family. Money can talk loud and clear.

Though I could rationalize intellectually, I still felt cheated and bitter. The treasures I had collected on my journeys did not make me feel rich or happy. I hardly wore my fur coats or my diamond ring. I felt that I did not have anything to be proud of.

Chapter Six:
My Spiritual Journey

PAIN OF LONELINESS

The most difficult thing I dealt with living in America was lone-liness. I decided to go to the neighborhood Catholic Church, Mary Seat of Wisdom in Park Ridge, where I wanted to spend time with God. I thought that perhaps I could find something or somebody to ease the pain of loneliness and hunger for human words of comfort. Perhaps I needed to be with people and the warmth of human beings, if not God. For some reason, I had never had the desire to develop friendships with others on a deeper level. My friends were neighbors and co-workers. Carl's family was scattered all over Illinois, Michigan and Pennsylvania, and mine was in Okinawa Japan.

I began going to the church regularly right after we moved to Park Ridge in 1964. For twenty years I never missed a Sunday Mass or holy days, and I always sat in the same pew. I tried to decipher the meaning of homilies and the stories of the Paschal Mystery. All the while I wondered how God could let His only Son be hung on the tree to die.

QUEST FOR JESUS

> *"For God so loved the world that he gave his only*
> *Son,so that everyone who believes in him might not*
> *perish but might have eternal life" (John 3:16).*

Every time I hear this Scripture reading during a Mass, or during my own meditation, my heart almost breaks, not because I understand God's love for His only Son, but because I understand Jesus' love for His Father in some measure. His Father asked for Jesus' sacrificial love to save the world, which, according to the text, seems to imply that He loved His world more than His only son, Jesus.

I was reflecting on my life over the stories I heard. How else did I find life's meaning then? To find my life's meaning, I kept coming back to the Church to listen to the stories of Jesus. The stories of Jesus comforted me though I did not understand them fully.

My father asked for my filial duty and sacrificial love to save his eight other children. What am I saying? He told me that as soon as I finished high school, I was to go to work to help him support the family. That meant I had to give up my self-interests. I became his instrument to support his family. I even placed my husband Carl in second place all those years. I served my father's children for thirty years of my life by sending my family money. In addition, I was dealing with the unfair treatment I received from management at Japan Airlines for sixteen years, as I described in the previous pages.

It is no wonder that, for twenty years, I sat at Mary Seat of Wisdom Church all alone trying to search for the meaning of *agape* ('Christian' love/charity) without any results. God's agape is given and felt. I was looking for it in the wrong place. Seeking knowledge of him did not satisfy my heart's deep desire to understand that God loves and that God is love.

My heart seemed to feel comforted when I found the following commandment to His disciples:

"This is my commandment: Love one another as I love you" *(John 15:12)*.

It is easier for me to follow this commandment because I don't find the text saying that we must love God. He tells us we must love one another. If we do this, He will be in our midst.

For twenty years I tried to figure out how it was that an ordinary person like myself could have committed sins grievous enough to warrant Jesus' death on the Cross.

Why, could I not be invited into God's family? I needed a new family so desperately. I told myself that I was too imperfect. But I was wrong. My imperfection was precisely the reason Jesus was inviting me to join Him. It was through the RCIA (Rite of Christian Initiation of Adults) meetings at Mary Seat of Wisdom Church, and theology courses years later at Loyola University, where I gradually came to understand. It was through the glimpse of Him and His teaching, intellectually and emotionally, that I began to comprehend God the Father, the Son and the Spirit. It was a comprehension that had been hidden from me all those years of my life.

Everything I learned about the values of human life, about my worth, about duty and responsibility; and, everything I was taught by my parents, grandparents, schools, and society was contradictory to what Jesus taught. For example, Jesus preached: *"Blessed are you who are poor..." (Luke 6:20)*, and yet the poor in Japanese society are considered a shame or a curse. The blessed are the rich, with fame and long life, as my ancestors taught me. And the first step to achieve riches and fame is to compete and excel as a student. In Japan, to be successful in all areas of your life, students are encouraged to be well educated — as much as their parents can afford. The education not only includes intellectual disciplines, but also inner strength, which help development through many forms of discipline. In Japanese, we call this *'Do'*, or in English, 'way': *Kendo* is Japanese swordsmanship; *Judo* is the Japanese art of self-defense; *Shodo* is Japanese calligraphy; *Bushido* is the way of the Japanese warrior/samurai spirit.

It is not enough to be a good student; you must strive to be the best student.

I need to explain what a Japanese student thinks of as the best. When I was at Loyola University, I met a young male student. One day we were discussing how we thought we did in our test.

"I don't think I did well," I said, "perhaps a B+."

He looked puzzled, and then he shook his head and walked away without sharing his thoughts on his own grade. What does good or the best mean to a driven Japanese student? It has to be either a perfect score or in the range of an A.

The root of teaching these disciplines comes from the idea that the Japanese nation considered itself a superior race, a very proud race of (Yamato). Showing human weaknesses such as emotional and physical pain were not for a disciplined person. We were trained to be like a god and to adopt a driven state to achieve perfection. Not too many people achieved this goal. Because of this demand, many young people committed suicide. The achievement of these goals was expressed as humility, not as pride. The teachings of true humility in this proud race—which I have seen in my grandfather, Kimura Naotaro—did not impress me. When he met his subordinates or workers in his factory, he bowed his head lower than them and spoke to them with respect. His treatment of his own family was different, of course.

We saw a display of humility in our yard one early rainy morning. We were finished with our morning walk and came to our kitchen to have breakfast. Carl told me to look outside.

There sat a hawk drenched with rain, just perched on the edge of our fence letting little birds attack him, never moving an inch or reacting. Then I remembered a Japanese saying that an eagle never shows his claws until he is challenged with an equal. True humility suggested that the more you have achieved in this world, the more humble you ought to behave.

What about forgiveness or forgiving your enemy? In Japanese culture if one shames you, you must avenge yourself because you have been put down. You can no longer hold your head up. In order to hold your head up once again, you must avenge. Vengeance is a virtue. If anyone has ever read a story about the Samurai, you will notice one of the themes is the seeking of vengeance on the avenger, or *Katakiuchi*. Thus, you are never to shame anyone's name. But if you are the one who has shamed others, you must ask their forgiveness with your life.

To speak about God as a person is so hard for me to comprehend, and I am sure for most Japanese as a whole, to understand. It took me many years to understand the concept of God. For most Japanese, God is not a person with a body. For them, God is spirit.

In a mysterious way, the silence of Jesus teaches us about trusting the inevitable justice of God. In contrast to Jesus' teachings, silence teaches a different discipline in Japan. Since I am not versed with the idea of discipline, I will only mention what I learned from my own household. In our family, there was no word for *no*. Silence meant no. When you asked about something from my father or my grandfather, if they did not say "yes" and you received their silence instead, it meant your idea or your plea was rejected.

But I failed to learn, and my quest for the meaning of silence pursued me.

Thus, my conversion with the Catholic faith took many long and difficult years. It took many years before I could truly claim that Jesus Christ was my personal God, whose bodily scars indicated how much He loved us, who died for us so that we will live in eternity with Him. I know He is with me now, guiding me as I write this memoir.

ONE LENTEN SUNDAY OF 1984: THE SAMARITAN WOMAN

I remember all those years I sat at Mary Seat of Wisdom Parish seeking before I decided to call on the pastor, Father Ronald Kalas. It was on one of the Lenten Sundays of 1984 that I heard the reading of the Samaritan woman. I was fascinated by the story, not because I understood it, but because the woman reminded me of myself. She was very spunky, not always understanding the subject, and often talking in parallel. I have no idea why the story of the Samaritan woman caught my ears that day. I heard the words describing the time of day: "The hour was about noon." That was the time I prayed to the Sun God as a child.

My grandfather had two wells—one for his family and the other for his workers. Many peasant women came to draw the water. They never came alone. They came in twos or threes and never during high noon. Samaria must be like Okinawa — very hot and humid. You could hear the women coming from far away because they would be laughing, gossiping, and making lots of noise.

I heard enough for me to call Father Kalas for an appointment.

Father Kalas was the fourth pastor since I had begun going there. He received me very cordially but very curiously. I told him I was not a new parishioner. In fact, I was not even a Catholic. I told him I had been coming to this church for the last twenty years, sitting in the same pew, trying to decipher the teachings of the priests and the church by myself. It was difficult to express my desire to learn more about this person Jesus, who was silent all the while people were plotting to kill Him.

The first words Father Kalas said after hearing my brief introduction were, "Was there not anyone who approached you during the twenty years?"

I said, "No sir."

At the end of our meeting, he said that what I had asked him was very theological. He asked me to make an appointment later in the following week so he could help me answer some of my questions.

I asked him what he meant when he said my question was a "theological question?"

At that time, the word, "theology" was not in my ordinary vocabulary. After a couple of meetings with him, I felt something like a flame burning inside of me. I could not stop thinking about this person, Jesus.

RCIA (RITE OF CHRISTIAN INITIATION FOR ADULTS)

I came to Mary Seat of Wisdom Church shortly after we moved to beautiful Park Ridge in 1964. Prior to the completion of my initiation rites, I was attracted and drawn to this parish, and I felt there must be something more to explore. I had had no formal religious affiliation. I sat in the same pew for twenty years trying to grasp the core of Catholicism, but I could not.

Soon I attended a meeting and enrolled in the RCIA (Rite of Christian Initiation for Adults Program) as advised by Father Kalas. That was the fall of 1984. My journey was long in getting to this point — more than twenty years long. Indeed, I was in search of Jesus. In the first meeting, I started with the story of my search for the true God, which I had shared with Father Kalas, Before I knew it, my story spread all over the parish. The community welcomed me with open arms. At first I was fearful and uncomfortable sharing my story. Sharing my own vulnerability with people I never met before was not an easy thing for me to do, maybe because it violated my upbringing. I was taught that I must always be in control and be strong: *You are a Kimura, a descendant of the Samurai clan, and you are the first daughter. You are one of a superior race.*

Yet my time at RCIA was an exciting period of my life. In my vulnerability and fear, in my shame of not always being able to live up to my grandparents' standards and my parents' expectations, I met my true, fragile self.

Gradually and surely I began to give myself permission to open up to others—to be me. Fearfully, I faced my own darkness, my brokenness, and myself. I had to let my old self essentially die. I wept. I shed a river of tears. The change I experienced in myself I owed to my sponsor Father Theodore Stone and the RCIA team who took me literally by my hand and walked with me. I came to know them and trust them. I discovered how this group of strangers became the face of Jesus for whom I was searching for so many years. Through them, I found life-giving and nourishing words of comfort to walk with other catechumens whom I called my brothers and sisters in Christ.

BAPTISM — NEW LIFE

> *Jesus answered and said to him, "Amen, amen,*
> *I say to you, no one can see the kingdom of God*
> *without being born from above" (John 3:3).*

At the Easter vigil of 1985, I was washed clean by baptismal water and breathed deeply of Christ's gift of new life. I celebrated my Baptism and Confirmation into the Catholic Church. My husband enrolled in the RCIA Program in September of 1985 and was baptized at the Easter Vigil of 1986. I will never forget that day in September 1985. The Director of RCIA called and asked to speak to Carl. I said he was out. I asked if there was any message. She said that the next RCIA meeting was cancelled. I was shocked. I didn't know he was attending the meetings. I was too busy attending evening classes at Oakton Community College in Des Plaines. I felt so embarrassed because I was so selfish not knowing what he was doing in the evenings. When he came home I asked him why he did not tell me. He said you have never asked me to join the RCIA with you, so I did it myself. That is my beloved husband of fifty-eight years. I will forever be grateful to him for not only loving me, but for forgiving me for my selfishness.

I was given my physical life in Okinawa, Japan, but I chose to receive the gift of my spiritual life in Christ, in Park Ridge, Illinois in the United States of America.

I ponder this often: If I had chosen to stay in Okinawa, would I have become a Catholic? Most likely not. None of my siblings are Christian, much less Catholic. The practice of their religion is rare. Their god was the emperor of Japan until the end of World War II. Even, the word 'God' is hardly spoken among my siblings.

I am a Japanese immigrant who came to the United States of America for a better life. Today, with the eyes of my faith, I know in my heart and mind that it was our loving God who invited me to the United States of America, the Promised Land. However, my journey has not been very easy.

I will always remember most vividly, my Baptism when I celebrated the Easter Sacrament with my husband and the community of Mary Seat of Wisdom Parish. When the cool water ran over my forehead, I experienced rebirth. I can still feel that sensation and the simultaneous feeling of grace and love of the Lord in my heart. I finally became a member of His family. I publicly declared that I would carry on my duty as a Christian. The Lord was very patient with me. He called me to join in His discipleship and walked with me for over twenty years until I accepted His invitation to join His family.

DISCERNMENT — CATHEDRAL QUILT

On July 26, 1985, I decided to take early retirement from Japan Airlines to pursue my dream of someday graduating from a university. But there was tuition to be considered. How could we pay this unexpected sum? I made a couple of attempts to get various scholarships, but was denied. Was I right to take money out of our retirement funds to pay for my education? It cost money to be educated, and I was not a young enough person to think about borrowing money to pay for it. Looking back, I realized I should have thought about this unexpected sum of money for tuition before taking early retirement. Also, how selfish was I to think about entering a university as an undergraduate student when my husband was thinking about retiring from his job to be with me?

During this discernment period I was led to create a cathedral quilt. Who am I? Who am I to God? Who is God to me? During my transition period, 1985–1987, shortly after my retirement from Japan Airlines, I suffered from an identity crisis. Nobody, including the restaurant staff where we regularly used to have lunch, knew me without my uniform. I was known as an employee of Japan Airlines and the wife of Carl O. Streling. During this period I came across some obscure instructions on how to make a cathedral quilt. They were given to me by my husband's aunt, Mamie Crenshaw. The cathedral quilt was created and hand sewn by me with the collaboration and dedication of my beloved husband Carl, who washed muslin, ironed, measured, and cut all of the materials for this work of love. When we finished the quilt and looked at it, I heard a quiet voice saying: "You are looking at the church. You are a beloved daughter. You are the church, the people of God."

It is the Church because our neighbors gave the materials used to make the quilt. It was a product of the community. I went to them and asked for donations of any materials they did not want. My only purchase was the muslin used to make up the background materials. For two summers, I spent about four to five hours every day hand sewing little sections together to complete the quilt. I took the quilt with me when Carl and I were commissioned to serve a priestless church in Japan beginning in August of 1993. I wanted to show the community what a church might look like.

During this discernment period, Carl and I spent one summer watching Lieutenant Colonel Oliver L. North testify before the Congress about his role in the political scandal of the Iran-Contra affair in 1987. Watching Lt. Col. North testify was quite fascinating and educational. It felt worthwhile to spend a summer learning about how America's judicial system works, while sewing every stitch of the quilt. Lt. Col. North fascinated me. Maybe I was fascinated because his record included service in Okinawa as commanding officer of the Marine Corp. In 1988, he was sentenced by a US District Judge to a three-year suspended prison term, two years on probation, one hundred fifty thousand dollars ($150,000) in fines, and twelve hundred (1,200) hours community service. In the end, the Supreme Court declined to review the case, and on September 16, 1991, Judge Gesell dismissed all charges against North.

LOYOLA UNIVERSITY CHICAGO

After years of thinking, Carl and I agreed that I would enroll as an undergraduate at Northwestern University. I would begin in the fall of 1986 to study pre-law. But that summer, I found a book in the Parish Library. The book was called *Love*, written by John Powell, S.J. On the cover of the book, I discovered that he taught Theology at Loyola University Chicago. I signed the book out and read it carefully. After I finished reading the book, I went to Webster's Third New International Dictionary for the definition of *theology*. Among many definitions, the following caught my eye—*the study of God and his relation to men and the world*. That definition of theology, and my friendship with Ann Filkins, who was also teaching at Loyola as a part-time professor, led me to my decision to enroll as an undergraduate at Loyola University Chicago, instead of going to Northwestern University to study human law.

The first course I enrolled in was Theology 101 because Father John Powell, S.J. was teaching it, and I wanted to begin my undergraduate study with him. However, the course was filled.

There was another professor listening to my plea with a student clerk helping at the registration tables. His name was Richard F. Costigan, S.J. He instructed her to accept my registration. Thus, I finally began my undergraduate study under Father John Powell. Little did I know then that these two professors, Father Powell, S.J. and Father Costigan, S.J. were world-renown professors and theologians. It was a privilege to study under them.

I started my study in the fall semester of 1987. I was 56 years old. Through Ann Filkins, I met Justin Spina who was several years older than I, and also an undergraduate majoring in theology. I later discovered that younger students called us *the trinity* because we were always together.

AWAKENING

It was a typical dark, drizzling fall day in Chicago when I began my second year of undergraduate studies. I was driving my little VW Rabbit home from campus when I noticed the windshield wiper was not working quite right. Luckily I made it home safely. Carl looked at the wiper and tried to fix it but could not.

We took it to a repair shop. The cost of the repair was more than the car was worth, so Carl donated it to charity. Fortunately, I was able to use public transportation to get to and from campus. I attended the university five days a week. I walked one and a half blocks from home, and took a bus to the train station, transferring to a train that took me near Loyola.

During my daily bus rides to the train station, I noticed a group of adult men and women with Down Syndrome getting on the bus to go to work every morning. The first time I met anyone with Down Syndrome was at Oakton Community College in Des Plaines, Illinois. I was taking a couple of evening courses to accumulate enough academic credits to earn an Associate Degree in 1980–1985. I was very proud that Oakton Community College made the effort to help these adult men and women become self-sufficient.

Years later, when I saw a different group of Down Syndrome men and women, I found a difference in my own reaction, as though I had seen something I had never observed before. Then, at the train station, I saw homeless men asleep here and there on the floor. One man had Down Syndrome. Obviously the train station served as a shelter for homeless people, especially in the severe weather that Chicago experienced. Again, I saw God hidden in them. I had been looking for Him in the wrong places. I could not see the face of Jesus in the rich, famous, and learned people I was trying to imitate, as I had been taught by my grandfather, mother, father, and the society in which I grew up. These experiences were an eye opener. They evoked a painful sense of discomfort or guilt. I was almost ashamed of myself for living in a comfortable house in one of the well-to-do suburban areas. I had never thought about the less fortunate until then. They were outsiders and strangers, as I was for many years in this country.

In 1991 I earned a Bachelor of Arts degree, Cum Laude, majoring in Theology, along side a host of other graduates forty years younger. On January 15, 1994, I earned a Master of Pastoral Studies from Loyola University of Chicago. I didn't attend my graduation because I was working in a mission field at Kainan from August of 1993.

It was in my freshman year in Theology class when I realized the U.S. Constitution is actually based on the biblical truth that everyone is created equal.

For seven years I studied diligently. I don't know how to thank my husband Carl for all those years he supported me, not only emotionally but also financially. I had forgotten myself and forgotten my husband. I hardly slept and ate. Those were the most fascinating and mysterious years of my life. God did hear my prayers. He gave me a chance to earn a university degree with the help of my husband.

Chapter Seven:
Summary of a Call to Serve as the First Columban Lay Missionary

"...your journey to my people and back to your people delights me. I hope this book, Christianity Rediscovered, *by Vincent J. Donovan fortifies your experience of speaking the Good News."*
Eugene M. Geinzer, S.J. (inscription on a book given as a gift)

What if you were foreign born and told to go to your homeland as a lay missionary to speak about a New Belief of Jesus and the Good News? This is exactly what happened to me one day in 1992.

I was in my last year of graduate study at Loyola University Chicago, when my friend Joyce approached me during a lunch break. She said there was a place where a group of Japanese men and women met once a month to celebrate Mass in the Japanese language. It was very close to campus, probably a ten minute walk.

I was very excited to hear I could celebrate Mass in my native Japanese language. As a new convert to Catholicism, I never heard the Mass celebrated in Japanese. I decided to walk over to this place one afternoon after class. When I pressed the door-bell, a man came to the door and invited me in. I introduced myself very briefly and explained my reason for being there. The man said he was one of the St. Columban Missionary Fathers and that a group of Japanese men and women did, indeed, come to celebrate a Mass in Japanese. He told me the day and time of the next gathering and invited me to join them. I was delighted with such welcoming news and the warm reception I received from him.

After a few meetings and celebrations of the Eucharist, one of the Columban Fathers asked me what I was planning to do with my education, specifically, the Master's Degree I was working toward. Such an inquiry startled me. I had never thought about what I would do with my education. I was studying for myself. I could not get enough theology of the God Man Jesus. The study of Scripture became my passion ever since my first theology class with Father Powell. I was captivated by Jesus' question, "Who do you say that I am?" I hardly ate and slept. All I wanted was to study. I wanted to know who this Jesus was for me.

Jesus is still evoking my spirituality today. Like the Samaritan woman from the gospel of John, I thirst for the living water.

The Columban Father again asked me if I had any plans for using my education. I answered him, rather puzzled because I never thought I could use the knowledge I gained. I thought of my studies in terms of my own enrichment. He said it would be a shame if I didn't share that knowledge with others. He did not have to explain further because I suddenly knew what he meant.

So I asked him how I could share my knowledge with others.

He said Japan needed me. He told me there were many priestless churches in Japan.

The conversations I had with the Columban Fathers aroused my interest in serving in Japan. I was very excited to hear what I learned in one of the "Pastoral Studies" of the Second Vatican Council. In particular, the very gifts of the Second Vatican Council encouraged the beginning of more active participation by the laity, both in worship and in the life of the church in general. I felt I was called to be a full participant.

I said I wanted to serve in some way. Repaying God and others is a strong part of Japanese teachings, and it is exactly what Jesus teaches us: love both God and neighbor. It suggested a way I could repay all of the wonderful things I received, particularly during the last seven years through my husband's support. But I needed to speak to Carl first.

I don't think they were prepared to hear I was a married woman because there were not too many Japanese women who were married at the graduate level of Pastoral Studies. I am sure they thought I was another nun! That night I told my husband about the conversations with two of the Columban Fathers regarding the possibility of serving in Japan. I said to him, "According to them, I am well qualified, given my bilingual language skills and Japanese background."

To my surprise, Carl agreed to serve in Japan without any hesitation. The Regional Director of the Columban Fathers, Brendan O'Sullivan, and two other Columban Fathers, John Burger and Jim Hastings came to our house to interview Carl.

The night before they came to our house, I dreamed a strange dream of God. In this dream I saw God's face merged within a huge whitish grey thundercloud. He held a lightning rod, which looked like the figure Z. He was playing and rolling around on the clouds with a big smile on his face. The face I saw was the big fat and happy face of Buddha! I wondered, what was the message from God that night? I now have a vague and very pleasant idea of God's message.

Father O'Sullivan told us the Church would like me to go to Japan and administer to one of the priestless churches as a pastoral associate. Carl was invited as well.

He then asked Carl, "Do you need a contract?"

Carl said if we couldn't trust a priest, whom could we trust. Father O'Sullivan never spoke any further about the contract. In retrospect, we should have questioned him about the contract he mentioned, but we did not.

At that meeting, I offered to take a trip to Japan to meet Father Youngkamp, Regional Director of the Society of Columban Fathers, Tokyo Japan. I was planning to visit my parents and siblings in Okinawa. My travel benefits were still covered by Japan Airlines. The Columban Fathers agreed and made arrangements for me to meet Father Youngkamp. I would have an interview with him at Haneda Airport. At this meeting, Father Youngkamp briefly spoke of the Society of Columban Fathers as missionaries. His interest was in interviewing me— checking to see if what Father O'Sullivan had said about me was correct. I was interested in knowing the specifics of what my job entailed, but no concrete idea was given. Still, I felt good about Fr. Youngkamp.

After that meeting, I went to Okinawa to see my parents and siblings. A week later I returned home to my husband in Park Ridge, Illinois. Little did I know the Society of Columban Fathers were operating under the same system as any corporation—politically, socially, and economically. My meeting with Fr. Youngkamp marked the beginning of a dramatic change in our lives. A change that would ultimately test our faith in God and in the Church.

We left O'Hare Airport in Chicago onboard Japan Airlines Flight 009 on August 22, 1993, non-stop for Narita International Airport. Then we took a connecting domestic flight from Haneda to Osaka Airport. We never received or signed any type of contract. We trusted Father O'Sullivan. He was a priest, supposedly, a man of honor. All we had with us, besides the five suitcases, were two letters from Father Vincent Youngkamp, the Regional Director of Japan.

The first official letter from Father Youngkamp was dated December 14, 1992. It seemed to spell out everything we needed to know. The most important point of note was whether or not his colleagues accepted his proposal.

He wrote, *"At our December Council meeting we finalized our decision to assign you to the Wakayama District. Father Michael Healy, the Columban District Superior there, has been in dialogue with Archbishop Yasuda of Osaka about the matter, and the Archbishop has agreed that Carl and you may use the small, now vacant rectory at Kainan Church, as your place of residence."*

In terms of my duties he wrote, *"What we will ask you to take on hasn't been worked out in detail yet. However, the following is a resume of some of the areas in which we need help and hope you will be working."*

He suggested that I would be (1) providing follow-up care in the formation of newly baptized Christians, (2) participating in a supportive role (rather than a teaching role) for a process course of Christian initiation called *kirisuto-kyo Koza*. A course not entirely unlike the RCIA course Carl and I had taken, (3) helping parishioners enrich their community sacramental and liturgical celebrations, and (4) guiding them in Scripture and Gospel life.

I knew what I had learned at Loyola qualified me entirely to carry out these tasks.

He also wrote, *"At the Council Meeting, we arrived at the sum of ¥120,000 (about $1,000) as a monthly maintenance figure. Along with the utilities, travel, work-expenses, and insurance fees will be taken care of here. If, at some point, we see that adjustments need to be made, I'm sure we can work it out without much problem."*

There was no reason why we should have doubted his word or the consensus of the Council meeting according to this letter.

The second letter from Father Youngkamp was dated February 22, 1993. In it he mentioned an orientation program for people going to a foreign country with little knowledge of the language and culture.

He wrote, *"I never adverted to the need to bring it up with you in any of our correspondences or telephone conversations. These kinds of program are usually one-month long and seem to be geared primarily for people who have no knowledge of the language or culture they are entering into to be a missionary to prevent them from 'cultural shock'."*

Clearly the reason he did not mention the orientation program to us was because we were not going off into the unknown as missionaries. Rather I was going to serve in my native land, Japan.

However, he then wrote that Father Brendan O'Sullivan, Regional Director of US. Region—who had approved our mission to serve in Kainan—*". . . has sent me a brochure of the one which is held at South Holland outside Chicago and let you make up your own minds about it. I gather he feels it would be helpful for both of you, and said that the Columban U.S. Region would be willing to help you with the expenses. The program is in July but I think the application date is next month."*

Our feeling was that we could not, out of good conscience, allow the Columban U.S. Region to waste their money. So we notified them of our decision not to attend the orientation program. We were, after all, given permission to make up our own mind about it. We thought they could use the money for other good causes. Besides, our travel date was already set to leave in August that year.

Father O'Sullivan did *not*, at this point, reject our application to serve as their missionaries.

Father Youngkamp wrote in great detail about Father Healy, who had been doing the preparatory negotiations in Wakayama, characterizing him as *"your personal mentor."* He also wrote about the Kainan Church: *"...which has been without a resident priest for about two years. The parish community is small. Father Healy has been its official administrator for the past two years. The Archbishop and Father Healy would like you to take a kind of leadership role, sharing in the pastoral care of the people. This is recognized in Canon Law (#517:2). The term in English used for the role is 'Lay Associate'."*

He also mentioned in his letter that, *"... as far as I know, there has never been an arrangement for a lay associate to administer to a priestless church in Japan in accord with this canon."*

In short, at the behest of the Columbans of Japan, we were to test the waters as the first lay associates to administer a priestless church in Japan.

In his two letters, Father Youngkamp had told us everything we needed to hear. *"Come speak the Good News of Jesus in your native Japan, and everything will be provided for you."* That provision included a training session by the Columban Fathers of Wakayama before they turned us loose. He did *not* tell us of any age limit, nor, in either of the two letters we received, did he tell us that, unless we took an orientation program, we could not be accepted as the first Columban Lay Missionaries.

The Air Stewardess announced that it would take about fourteen hours before we reached Narita International Airport, Japan from Chicago. During the long flight we were reflecting on the solemnity of the commissioning Mass, which was concelebrated by Columban Fathers, T.P. Reynolds and Jim Hastings at our home parish, Mary Seat of Wisdom Church. The main celebrant was Father Ron Kalas, Pastor. The words I often heard in Loyola University Chicago echoed in my heart.

"Go forth and set the world on fire!"

ST. FRANCIS de SALES KAINAN
CATHOLIC CHURCH

Our missionary involvement with the Columban Fathers began on the morning of August 23, 1993. Our final destination was Kainan City, Wakayama Ken, Japan, where we were to serve a priestless church, St. Francis de Sales Kainan Catholic Church. Kainan City, Wakayama Ken is located about 37 kilometers (or 23 miles) south of Osaka on mainland Honshu.

As of May 2010, the population of Kainan, Japan was 56,813 people, and the total area is just over 100 square kilometers or just under 40 square miles. It is known mostly as an industrial center, producing lacquer wares. Wakayama Ken/Prefecture is famous for its historic sites, hot springs, and food. Winter temperature ranges anywhere from 32 to 40 degrees Fahrenheit with damp and very cold temperatures and snows that melt quickly. Spring visits Kainan very early. During the springtime, everywhere one turns, one sees the beautiful cherry blossoms, especially around the Buddhist's temples. Summer is very hot and humid, around 80 degrees Fahrenheit with humidity at 90 percent. It rains every day during the entire month of May. Immediately after the rains stop the heat comes with the sun.

The Kainan Catholic Church was a long one-story church. A common wall surrounded the church, our residence, the old rectory, and the Maria Kindergarten. Entering through the front walk-in gate, to the left was a very large arbor. Every spring, lavender-colored Japanese wisteria covered a trellis in a display of fragrant beauty. Beneath the arbor, the parishioners parked their bicycles.

The church stood where the wall turns. In front of the church stood the statue of Mary, Mother of God. There was a carport for one car, then our residence at the corner, and a back walk-in gate. The old rectory and the Maria Kindergarten finished out that wall. Near the last two walls were swings, monkey bars, and slides. A gate for cars was kept locked so none could come in during school hours.

Who were the members of Kainan Church? According to the official record of baptized Christians there were 150 members, but I counted only thirty (30) to thirty-six (36) people attending Sunday regularly. Strangely enough, only one-fourth of the total baptized Christians worldwide, actually live their faith.

The main pillars of the church were: Elder Kasai Mitsunari and his wife, Fumiko; his brother Imatsu Yoshiichi and his wife, Shizuko; Imatsu Yoshiichi's son, Imatsu Yoshimi and his wife, Kazue; and Elder Kasai's cousin, Maruta Yoshihiko and his wife, Setsuko, whom I call the Kasai clans; and Kodama Utako, non-Kasai clan.

Kainan is known to produce excellent lacquer ware products. All the Kasai clans were involved in the lacquering business. As a going-away present, we received a *Juubako*; a three-tier box used as a picnic box stained in wooden lacquer. It was one of their products from Yoshimi and Kazue Imatsu. Not too many wooden Juubako are found in Japan nowadays. They are mostly made with plastic because they are more durable, practical, and cost much less to produce.

The other Catholics, besides the Kasai clans and Mrs. Kodama, were few and far between. I am afraid that when all these church pillars pass away someday, there will not be enough of their children to carry on the faith of their parents. The aging church is one problem. The other is the young and educated are forced to leave their homes and towns to seek jobs that are more lucrative and prestigious in the big cities and towns. The biggest problem is the shrinkage of the Japanese population. They do not procreate. The Japanese government has been offering every possible award and merit to encourage young people to have more children.

FIRST TRIAL: CONFUSION

Now I shall begin the story of what exactly happened after we left Chicago to assume our responsibilities. I share this experience with you as logically and truthfully as I can recollect.

I would perform our assignment's major responsibility as an administrator at St. Francis de Sales Kainan Catholic Church. Carl, in addition to providing assistance and support to me in my endeavors, would be working on various duties. When I received my assignment to lead a priestless church, I wondered if this was the end for which God was preparing me. My mother's early words have echoed in my ears many times since: *"Masako, there is not a thing in this world you cannot do."* There I was, a woman assigned to lead a priestless church in Japan where men are leaders. I was quite anxious about how I would be accepted by the church and also the clergies.

The reality of the missionary works awaiting us at Kainan Catholic Church was severe to say the least. Contrary to Father Youngkamp's two letters, literally nothing had been set up.

We had arrived in Kainan with complete faith in Father Youngcamp's explanation regarding our living quarters, our stipend, and our health insurance. We thought we had a clear picture of the Kainan Catholic Church community, our supporters, our teachers from the Columban Fathers, and our duties as missioners, as explained in the two letters.

However, according to the Columban Fathers in Wakayama, they were not told of our arrival date—or anything about us for that matter—until a few days before we arrived. We were told that Father Healy (the District Superior) was present at the December Council, where the decision was finalized to assign me to the Wakayama District. However, when we arrived, there was absolutely no understanding or acknowledgement of our proposed role as Columban Lay Missionaries by the Fathers in Wakayama. In retrospect, I cannot believe our boundless naiveté.

Furthermore, as a result of the same lack of communication, the training session by the Columban Fathers of Wakayama, which we were told to expect, never materialized. We were asked to get ready to move to our residence on the following morning. That was shocking news to us. We were worn out from the long flight from Chicago to Osaka, and it was a long drive to the Yakatamachi residence. It was late at night when we arrived at the priests' residence.

Father Tony Cox and Father Sean Corr drove us to our residence right after breakfast. They helped us carry in our five pieces of luggage, introduced us to the women who were waiting for us with lunch already being prepared, and then they left.

I don't remember the contents of our conversations with those women, nor do I remember what was said in the car between Father Cox, Father Corr and us. Carl and I were in shock! After they left us there, we did not hear from any of the Columban Fathers until I made an appointment to see Father Corr at the Yakatamachi Church. One of the Columban Fathers of the Church came every Sunday to celebrate the Mass. However, neither he nor any of the Fathers showed any interest in talking to us after the Mass. We could not understand why were they acting so indifferent to us.

A vacant and badly neglected, two-story priests' residence became our home for the next three years. When we opened the front door and stepped into the vestibule, we took off our shoes and put them in the shoebox. To the left was a living room, a small eating area, and a small kitchen. Straight ahead was the toilet. Just to the right were the stairs, and a little further to the right was the shower and laundry room. The stairs were very steep and made a sharp U-turn half way up. At the top of the stairs was a very small guest bedroom with a single bed in it. To the right was a sitting room with a window air conditioning unit, and an adjoining small bedroom. We used the small bedroom.

We found a couple of chairs but no bed, so we slept on a *Tatami* (straw matting on the floor) with a Futon and a thick bed quilt. The chairs in the bedroom looked as though they were found in the trash. The living room contained a small table with four chairs and a small TV. When we opened the refrigerator, dead cockroaches fell out.

We sat on the floor, as we had no money to buy chairs or a sofa. The only furniture in the bedroom was a low table. We sat on a Japanese floor cushion trying to live like the Japanese used to live in the old days. Today, not too many Japanese live as they did in the old days, but we did. Today, most Japanese have one room furnished as westerners with sofas and chairs, and a bed to sleep on.

The area behind the house was used for dumping trash, wood ashes, coal ashes, and pop cans. It was overgrown with weeds.

I broke down and cried. Carl comforted me and said now that we were here; we would do all we could to live out our commitment of one year.

The week following our arrival, while we were carrying out the bedroom chairs to throw them out with other trash, a couple of nuns came to visit us, apologizing for how the place looked, and said they were only following orders from Father Healy. To this day, I am still not quite sure what they meant.

Over the following few months we rolled up our sleeves, changed our clothes to jeans and shirts, and with buckets of soapy water and cleanser, scrubbed and cleaned our living quarters.

Carl tackled the yard. He collected all the cans and bottles and put them out on trash day. He turned the wood ashes into the ground as he weeded the growth of about six-feet-high weeds, which were probably nurtured from the wood ashes.

A couple of months after our arrival, the money we brought with us was rapidly depleting. Since our understanding from the letter was much different from what we were actually experiencing, I decided to call Father Corr. He was the one in charge of the Columban Fathers' financial matters as well as the pastor of the main church of the Wakayama region, the Yakatamachi Church.

We assumed, from the letter by the Regional Director, that our stipend was to come from the Columban fund, not from the Kainan Church. We later found out that was simply not going to be the case. We were not actually counted as official Columban Lay Missionaries.

Without knowing this, we made an appointment with Father Corr, but we had no car to get there. Fortunately I was able to read and speak Japanese. I looked for a bus schedule in the newspaper to see how we could get from Kainan City to Yakatamachi Catholic Church, Wakayama City, about seven or eight kilometers away.

Once we arrived it didn't take long for the veil of our assumptions to be lifted from our eyes. As far as the Columban Fathers were concerned, we were neither priests nor religious. We were only laity, extraordinary ministers. The way the parishioners understood the word *extraordinary* was the dictionary's definition: very unusual or remarkable, unusually great. Nobody had explained to the parishioners the meaning of the term as used by the Church. A priest is an ordinary, and a laity serving as an Eucharistic minister is extraordinary. These terms the Catholic Church use only feel manipulative and confusing.

We needed to explain the terms of ordinary and *extraordinary* to Mr. Kasai, one of the pillars of the Kainan Church. He was one of the original members of the Kainan Church and the biggest contributor. The right occasion came when the community appointed him to be one of the Extraordinary Eucharistic Ministers. Unfortunately, he started to act, and expected to be treated differently from other laity. He dressed himself in fine white robes. He thought he became a priest. He expected people to treat him as an extraordinary person, as the literal interpretation shown in a dictionary. I explained to him the difference between ordinary and extraordinary as defined by the Church. Graciously, he then realized that even though he was made a Eucharistic Minister, he was, more than ever an ordinary person. One of us.

Once I explained the proper meaning of his position, we were respected and treated warmly. The parishioners decided to help us financially so that we could have a car. The church paid for the annual automobile insurance. We paid for our own health insurance.

When we met Father Corr, I showed him the two letters from Father Youngkamp, which explained what we were to expect financially. At the end of our meeting, Father Corr agreed to pay for the utilities of our residence and gasoline for the car; however, the stipend was to be paid by Kainan. He never mentioned anything about who was paying for the automobile insurance or our health insurance. It seemed as though he actually avoided the subject entirely. Our monthly stipend *as well as* automobile insurance and health insurance should have, according to Father Youngcamp's letter, been paid from the Columban fund, but I did not pursue it any further. We had too many obstacles to overcome. The most immediate obstacle — make our living space somewhat habitable.

Like any other missionaries, we lived within our budget. We never ate at restaurants. We never went to the movies. We did not take a tour of Japan, much less tour the Wakayama Prefecture. We simply could not afford the time or money. The only outside indulgence we enjoyed was an occasional visit to a coffee shop for a good cup of coffee and a pastry. The price of coffee was for just one cup, not limitless refills like in the United States, as we were used to.

Fairly early on, one of the Columban Fathers came to visit us. He told us he had come to welcome us and to offer us his old car. He said he was buying a new car, though there was nothing wrong with the old one, but he was not willing to spend any more money on it. It was the time of Shaken. According to law, every car more than ten years old had to go through an inspection to pass the test of drivability every two years. All we needed was the money to take it to a repair shop to make sure it passed the test. When we presented the case to the community, they offered to pay for that and the annual automobile insurance.

The only thing we asked of the Columban Fathers was to give us two weeks of sabbatical leave annually so we could fly to Los Angeles where my brother lived. While there, we could purchase groceries including: oatmeal, cold cereals, 12 boxes of cake mix, and 12 pounds of Roasted Brothers coffee. We took these staples back with us to Kainan to supplement our cost-of-living expenses for an entire year. While in Los Angeles, we enjoyed the good old American cooking that Carl loved so much. He loved his breakfast of bacon and eggs with lots and lots of syrup on pancakes, and home-cooked roast beef served with mashed potatoes with lots and lots of gravy. Our airline tickets from Osaka to Los Angeles and back to Osaka were covered by my Japan Airlines retirement benefit. The Columban Fathers did not spend any money for the expense of two airfares. They never offered.

While Carl was assessing the condition of the church building, I tried to find a way to re-assimilate to the Japanese way of living. At first, I sensed that the reception by community members was mixed. Some showed curiosity, while some did not express any of their thoughts. I know very well when Japanese do not say "yes" to something, it means "no." How could we win the hearts and minds of each member to help rebuild this badly neglected church? All Carl and I had was our willingness to be accepted. We wanted to help them build up the church, from a physical building to a spiritual gathering place — a place of worship. I needed to know their thoughts.

Following my instincts, I decided to investigate how they felt about our arrival. Were they forced to accept us or not? How much were they told about the need of lay leadership and why? We found out what one of the pillars of the church thought when we visited her. At the time, she was struck down with a severe cold. When we visited her, she asked us bluntly, "What are you doing with your money in America?" We told her that we had left our money in a bank because we would need our money in America when we completed our work in Japan. Hopefully, we would have some money left so we could return to our normal life in America. At that time, I did not mention to her that we were using our own money until we could find out what exactly was happening with the Columbans. From Mrs. Kodama, we discovered that money was one of the concerns connected with our presence. They needed to find one thousand dollars ($1,000.00) in their income to pay our stipend. There were only thirty-six (36) members attending Sunday Mass regularly. Mathematically speaking, they could not afford us.

Since the cost of living in Japan was about twice as much as the cost of living in America, we had to withdraw some of our money from the United States to supplement our cost of living in Japan. It was the only way we could continue. In Japan everything was so inflated. For example, at that time a piece of steak cost fifteen dollars ($15.00) per kilo; one apple cost one dollar ($1.00); a box of cold cereal cost ten dollars ($10.00). Our stipend of one thousand dollars ($1,000) a month did not cover our cost of living.

One day our neighbor told me that every evening at 7:00 PM one of the neighborhood grocery stores had a sale with 50% off on meat, fish, vegetables, and fruits. It was how she saved money. That evening I went there at exactly 7:00 p.m. There was a long line when the store opened. I saw women push themselves wherever they were aiming to go. By the time I got there, everything was sold out. Eventually, I learned the art of pushing and shoving like everyone else in order to get what I needed.

We often wondered when the Columban Fathers of America learned about our reception in Japan; furthermore, why didn't they decide to include us in their decision-making process? We also wondered about the so-called consensus, supposedly reached at the December Council meeting of the Columban Fathers of Japan, which Father Youngkamp wrote to us about. We based many of our decisions from the instructions Father Youngkamp gave us in those initial letters.

In short, the Columban Fathers of America and Japan did not see eye to eye on our viability as official Columban Lay Missionaries. As a result, we were viewed as a special case, which left us very much in limbo. Part of the problem was that the details of this disagreement were only revealed to us later on, after we had sold our house in Chicago and returned for a second and third year of service.

The reason we sold our house was because serving the mission became our top priority. It was our second year when we received a letter from Father Brian Vale, the Regional Director of the Columban Fathers in Japan. In this letter, he reiterated that we were in Japan as a special case. He pointed out that we had not gone through the Lay Missionary Program. The program was originally presented to us as optional, because of my background; and, the fact that I had a Master of Pastoral Studies Degree from Loyola University. We had not signed a formal contract of any kind, as people going through the program would have done. We did not conform to the usual process for being nominated as lay missionaries. These criteria were never mentioned to us at all as conditions for becoming a lay missionary. While the Kainan church gave us a basic living stipend of about one-thousand dollars ($1000.00) a month, it fell far short of the money we needed to survive. The Columban priests only paid for our utilities and gas for our car. Today, as I reflect, I realize that perhaps we were naïve, but additionally, the Columban Fathers were not acting honorably.

With that understanding, I decided at the very least to write a proposal to present as our Lay Missionary Agreement with the Columbans. I followed the official Columban Lay Missionary Program with some amendments, since we were considered a special case. But Father Brian Vale, the Regional Director of the Columban Fathers did not acknowledge my proposed agreement.

Though we put in three years of service, ultimately we were never recognized as official Columban Lay Missionaries, which still remains a painful, bitter disappointment. We were never fully compensated financially either. We ended our time there with the title of "catechists". A catechist is the person who teaches the laity about the Catholic religion, "the main elements of the Christian faith." This was as close as we could get to an official title. But, the Kainan church had its own catechist. So, I decided to work with her. Her name was Imatsu Kazue. She was a lovely woman. I wanted to ensure that she helped educate the children as well as the adults.

WHAT WAS THE ROOT CAUSE OF OUR ADVERSITY?

I was recruited by the Society of Columban Fathers of America to go to Japan and be the administrator of one of their priestless churches on the basis of Canon Law—specifically Can. 517:2, which describes Team Ministry:

Can. 517 [1] When circumstances require it, the pastoral care of a parish or of several parishes together can be entrusted to a team of several priests in *solidum* (jointly) with the requirement, however, that one of them should be the moderator in exercising pastoral care, that is, he should direct their combined activity and answer for it to the bishop. [2] If, the diocesan bishop should decide that due to a dearth of priests a participation in the exercise of the pastoral care of a parish is to be entrusted to a deacon or to some other person who is not a priest or to a community of persons, he is to appoint some priest endowed with the powers and faculties of a pastor to supervise the pastoral care.

On the basis of Canon Law 517:2, the Columban Fathers of Chicago found that I actually qualified as a lay associate. The Columbans in Chicago then contacted Father Youngkamp. Unfortunately Carl and I arrived in Japan before the Columban Fathers in both America and Japan received a response from the Bishop's office in Japan approving Carl and me as lay missionaries. Eighteen months had passed from the inception of this plan until our arrival in Kainan. We thought they had plenty of time to get our approval as lay missionaries sorted out.

Of course, Carl and I did not know anything about the pending negotiations between America, Japan, and the Bishop's office of the Osaka Diocese. We were not stopped when it came time to leave for the mission, nor were we offered anything when we notified the Columbans that we needed to sell our house to stay on for another two years. As a matter of fact, Fr. Cox's response when I notified him was "Great! I need your help!"

Again, maybe we were being too naïve. But, we wanted to be able to concentrate on serving the community for the second and third years. We wanted to finish what we started. After our first year we felt very committed to the cause, the Church, and most importantly, the community.

For these three years, we worked without a title or without proper identity. The local population called us Masako-san and Carl-san. I did the work of a catechist and pastoral associate (or pastoral administrator), as I understood my role to be.

You might ask why is a title important? In Japan, a title is everything. It gives the people a point of reference to embrace you. It is needed to work with people you don't know, and to lead people. Japanese society is very title conscious. Exchanging a business card is the norm. As I said, a title provides the most important point of reference for those who don't know you. We were foreigners, entering a new community with the hope to help them rebuild the old Church into the new Church according to the Second Vatican Council's vision for the Kainan Catholic Church.

At the beginning of the first year I asked my superior, "What is my title, because people want to know?"

"Your role is to be a *catechist*," I was told, "until you are assigned later as a *lay associate*. It will be up to the bishop's office. Our role is simply one of nominating."

I told people to just call me Masako and my husband Carl, because it was very difficult for Japanese to pronounce Streling. They were, of course, uncomfortable calling us by our first names. As I mentioned, the Japanese are very title conscious. When one first meets another person in Japan, exchanging a business card is the norm.

According to the Regional Director of Japan, my superior asked the Archbishop of Osaka several times about appointing me as a lay associate, so I could *"be entrusted with a share in the exercise of the pastoral care of a parish"*. There was no response from the Bishop's office. Eventually, I stopped asking them for my title, because it just seemed like a futile exercise. The bureau-cracy of the Church felt impenetrable.

My situation was the first time the Osaka Archdiocese had a "lay associate". It seemed the Bishop's office was not clear on how to make the first steps into this new area. I understood that fact. Being careful before making a decision is part of the Japanese national characteristic, especially when there is no precedence. But the lack of effective communication and the unwillingness of different parts of the Church to work together to help people who want to help the Church were disappointing. It felt like our good will to serve the church was being manipulated.

Even though Archbishop Yasuda of Osaka had not appointed me as a titled pastoral associate, he addressed both Carl and me as lay missionaries. Archbishop Yasuda treated us with respect as one of his priests.

The Columban Fathers, however, had a big problem both calling and accepting us as lay missionaries.

The Columban Fathers of Japan were not ready to share the church with a lay apostolate in Japan. There were no lay Eucharistic ministers or readers/lectors in their churches rep-resented by the Columban Fathers. To think about the church as a participatory church means that it must accept and share authority and responsibility, with not only the ordained and religious, but also with the laity. This concept was articulated at the Second Vatican Council. The Columban Fathers of America sent us to the Kainan Catholic Church without an official document appointing me as an administrator. February 1995 was the first time we heard any concerns about this voiced by the Church. To be fair, the Japan Region had every reason for denying us from their circle, but they had no cause to treat us as though we were second-class citizens. While they were living like royalty, we were expected to live like paupers. They ate the best food available. We ate the worst. They drank the best liquor stores could offer. Once a month, we treated ourselves to a cup of coffee at a coffee shop. They traveled first class on the fast train. We traveled in second class on the slow train.

It is fair for me to say that Fr. Corr, the pastor and the man with the purse of the Yakatamachi Church had changed his attitude toward us. He became friendlier in the second year. We were invited to his residence at Yakatamachi every Sunday for dinner.

I wondered, if they were so particular about their adherence to the law, why did they not send us back to Chicago? Or stop us before we had departed or before we were commissioned? In the end, the Columban Fathers of the Japan Region did not even offer to commission us back to America at the end of our three years of service. Not only in Japan, but The Columban Fathers of America didn't offer to receive us back as their Columban Lay Missionaries either. It seemed that no one wanted to be responsible for us.

In wondering who would be the one to send us back to the United States when we completed our commitment as lay missionaries, I decided to call Archbishop Yasuda and ask to see him. When I explained the situation, he told me that he would commission us back to America. Perhaps as a sign of seeking our forgiveness and reconciliation, Archbishop Yasuda said to me:

"Even though your record stands on its own, would you like to defend it and your credentials in front of the Osaka Diocesan priests and foreign missionary priests? There will be about two hundred-fifty priests attending one of our monthly diocesan meetings."

I agreed to do it at the July meeting the last month of my ministry. I said that I might try to indict the Osaka Diocese and the Columban Fathers for not living up to Gospel value. To that, the Archbishop nodded his head. I prepared a ton of papers but did not need any of it because I was defending myself in my own language, Japanese. The words flowed from my lips easily and, again, I experienced the power of the Holy Spirit. With His lead, I said what I needed to say. At the end of my own defense, almost all of the Osaka Diocesan priests lined up and asked for my forgiveness, or expressed their sorrow, but none of the foreign missionary priests were among them.

However, one of the three Columban Fathers who was there asked me if he could have my manuscript. It was Father Donal Griffin, who later had my manuscript translated into English.

At Archbishop Yasuda's invitation I was allowed to address the injustice done by him and his priests publicly. When we left, the Kainan Catholic Church was moving toward the model of a participatory church, under the leadership of the Archdiocese of Osaka, Archbishop Yasuda. The Kainan Catholic church was living. The Kainan Catholic church was priestless no more.

Among four priests who had bid to be a pastor of Kainan Church, Father Akeishi of the Archdiocese of Osaka was chosen. Thus, the Kainan Catholic Church came directly under the control of the Osaka Diocese and no longer under the Columban Fathers.

Chapter Eight:
Mission Field

I do not want one to think that I consider my time at Kainan Church as little more than a three-year injustice done to Carl and myself. I do not feel that way. These were three years of memories I cherish. Three years that I will not forget because, disappointment aside, I indeed feel blessed to have found the opportunity to put my education and my love of God to good use in my native Japan. It was there where I found "God in all things" as St. Ignatius of Loyola once said.

Let me describe how we spent each of those three yeas as Columban lay missionaries. I do so in my hope that I can prepare for those who are prospective future missionaries to let them see how the mission field looks like through my experience.

MARIA KINDERGARTEN

Whether a member of the Kainan church or the neighboring Maria Kindergarten, we all used the same gate to enter the property. The Maria Kindergarten was a two-story building directly ahead as you passed through the gate. It was attached to the old priest's residence.

Not too many children who attended Maria Kindergarten were raised Catholic. In fact, most of them were not. The main reason parents chose to send their children to the Montessori Kindergarten was because of their appreciation of the teaching and the hope that their children could benefit from it.

Every Sunday, mothers brought their children to attend Sunday School, catechized by Kazue Imatsu. In Japan, Montessori Kindergarten is usually connected with a Roman Catholic Church. It is always associated with a Christian church. Japanese mothers value most the opportunity to give their children the highest education they can afford. With a resume listing Maria Kindergarten on graduation papers, they could send their children to one of the highly accredited elementary schools, middle schools, and high schools, which then enabled them to choose one of the highest accredited universities rather than a lesser college or university.

One morning, four or five mothers from Maria Kindergarten came to visit me. I invited them into my office and asked if there was something I could do to help them.

"In fact, there is," one of them said, "and that is why we are here to see you. Since you speak both Japanese and English, and read and write both as well, could you teach our children English?"

Another woman added, "We would like your husband to teach us conversational English because he speaks American English. There are many foreign English teachers available, but not with the perfect combinations like you and your husband have. Besides, some of the teachers' accents are so strong we can hardly understand what they are saying."

Some of the foreign teachers were Australians or New Zealanders, and even I had to listen to them closely, because I also had difficulty understanding their accent. There were two Columban Fathers who were from those areas in the Wakayama region.

I thanked the women but declined. Already, I had such a full schedule. My time was limited. I also felt I was not there to teach English, but to help build the Church. Shortly after that meeting, they came with more than a just few mothers, but with nearly all of the kindergartener's mothers. Again, some of them wanted us to teach them English. Again I declined, but they were persistent. I finally said, "The only way I can find it in my heart to teach your children English is if you agree that I will teach them about Jesus and his mother Mary, the Mother of God. *Maria*, this kindergarten your children are attending, is named after her. It is honoring Mary as the mother of God. Additionally, we will not be teaching English to adults."

They agreed, and I met with Mrs. Imatsu, the catechist, informing her that seven more students would be joining her Sunday School class immediately after every Sunday Mass. I taught them English after Mrs. Kazue Imatsu finished her Sunday School session. Every Sunday after lunch at 1:00 PM, Carl and I taught children English. Along with simple ABC English lessons, I used the English words for "pray, praying, prayers, Mary, mother of God, God, Jesus, His father Joseph, and Jesus' family" in their weekly lesson. Carl read the Christmas story and the Easter story in English to train their hearing. Because they were familiar with the names of Jesus and Joseph in the Christmas story, which was taught by the catechist, I only reinforced this story by telling it to them in English words. My purpose in teaching children English was two-fold: one for the children and the other for their parents. I made sure that the children could see the prayerful posture of Mary, Mother of God, who was praying always. I hoped that their mothers would learn from their children about Mary, mother of God. In retrospect, I probably should have taught the parents English as well, but at the time, I was overworked with barely enough time to eat.

The other image I wanted to instill in the children was of the Holy Family. A family should always consist of a supportive father like Joseph, and mothers with love and trust in each other, no matter how tough their life could be. The family is the place where human life begins, is nurtured, and hopefully cherished. In the work-driven society of Japan, the father figure often gets marginalized.

It was difficult for me to teach these children, who were from well-to-do families, about being hungry for food and thirsty for water. They told me they never felt hungry because they said their mothers gave them something to eat when they came home from school at three o'clock in the afternoon. They didn't know how the small children in the Philippines were suffering from hunger because they had not seen anybody who was hungry.

"Besides," one of them told me, "this is not the Philippines, it is Japan."

These children were pretty smart!

Another thing I discussed with the catechist was the idea of having birthday celebrations every month with a homemade cake decorated with candles on it for the children. I wanted these kindergarten students to get to know the children of Catholic families on such an occasion. Carl baked the birthday cake from the 12 boxes of Betty Crocker cake mix every time we went to America for a sabbatical leave. The cakes were so good that everyone thought they were made from scratch. Mrs. Imatsu's daughter, Aki, who was about twelve years old, did the decorating. She was a very artistic girl. Today she works in the field of Art. My heart is filled with the warmth of God's love as I recall those days. When I think of how the child's face brightened as a birthday cake was ushered in, all aglow with candles. It was so wonderful to experience how God makes everything right when one tries to do His Will.

Every Christmas, we invited the students and their parents to celebrate the Mass, including the kindergarten students and their parents. Carl was dressed in a Santa Clause outfit and carried a bag full of presents on his back. He walked among the children, shouting "HO HO HO, Merry Christmas!" in English. He distributed a gift to each one of the children. How marvelous it was to know God worked in the world in spite of the adverse situation in which we were placed.

While Mrs. Imatsu catechized children, I invited interested mothers, including non-Catholics, to study the Bible as literature. I thought as literature, not as religion, the Bible might be more enticing to the non-Catholic audience. I also thought, that in this environment the mothers of kindergarteners might apply for attendance. I had a total of nine applicants. Among them were non-Catholic mothers of Maria Kindergarten. They studied the Bible with the Kainan Catholic women, side-by-side.

Initially, Mrs. Nishimura, the Principal of Maria Kindergarten tried to ignore me. We worked in the same building. She was in her office in the Kindergarten. I was in the old priest's office. Mrs. Nishimura and I would meet often. Every time I saw her I greeted her, but received no response. One day I called and said that I would like to talk. I learned that she feared my coming to the church as an administrator because it would result in me taking over the school and she would lose her job.

"I have no intention of being a principal of a kindergarten," I told her. "In fact, I wouldn't know how. Besides, I am not a priest. My responsibility is to help build the Church. You know more than I how the Church was dying in a literal sense."

It was good that we talked. We laughed a lot and parted. After that she became the best advocate of our cause and sent her son to help Carl in every way possible. Her son understood English more than he would admit. Carl and he often worked together side-by-side. It was wonderful to witness such comraderie between the generations!

THE FIRST YEAR

In spite of the many adversities we faced and disappointments we suffered, we did not lose heart. There were choices. We could have packed up, turned back, and gone home. Instead, we decided to stay for at least a year.

Each morning Carl and I began our work with prayer, asking God to help us as the Columban Fathers had left us there with no further directives. We prayed earnestly, trusting God's guidance and providence, for I had no experience as an administrator of a priestless church, though I had administrative experience in my past work. Carl had been self-employed and had limited administrative experience.

I called the first meeting of the Parish Council Members of the Kainan Catholic Church to introduce ourselves and to explain why we were there to serve them. I knew in my heart that they were the ones we could trust and rely on. This was their church. We were going to rebuild it together. With conviction, the meeting was called. After everyone introduced himself or herself, I left them with one question, "What is Church to you?" I needed to know how much they knew about the meaning of the Church.

The following monthly meeting I asked again, "What is Church to you?" The majority of them said that the church was a building and belonged to priests.

I explained that while it is true that the church is a gathering place where we assemble together to worship, give our thanks to His goodness, and praise His Name, it is not merely a building and does not belong to priests alone. It belongs to all of us — the priests, the religious, and the laity. We call it our faith community where we share our faith in breaking the bread and breaking the word open. During our discussions about the Church, I promised silently to myself that I would help them build a Church based on a new vision, where we would gather to celebrate Eucharistic liturgies; where people could come to talk, laugh, and also share in the different challenges life presents to all of us. In this environment, people might come to church, not only to celebrate the Eucharistic liturgies, but also just for the fun of being there to socialize. Maybe more people might come to church knowing this freedom existed?

One day I inquired as to why the church was so neglected. I asked when it was last painted and decorated. When were the curtains and draperies last laundered? I wanted to know when the priest's residence, office, and property had last been tended to?

I was told that everything belonged to the Columban Fathers because they built the Kainan Catholic Church almost fifty years ago; therefore, the community had never interfered. Obviously, the church had been painted with U.S. Army paint. During the occupational period, to help rebuild the war-torn country, paint was given to anyone who needed it. If I remember correctly, the church was an olive color and had not been painted since its founding in 1957.

I also asked them to make a list of questions for which they wanted answers. Anything they wanted to know, whether it was about Carl and me, their faith, God, Jesus—anything at all. I compiled a master list from the questions collected and answered every single one in due course. Included were such age-old questions as: *Why, do good people suffer and bad people prosper?* When I did not know the answer, I asked my friends and professors in Chicago. Eventually, I made a master list based on their inquiries, which served as a guide to either catechize or educate us all.

It felt overwhelming to grow in faith with these people when I first discovered that many of these veteran Catholics could not answer the one question: *Who is Jesus Christ to you?* Their faith was based purely on *piety*, a way of living to best please God.

One Sunday after Mass, I shared my thoughts with a Columban Father who came to celebrate with us. I asked him how it was that a person might not be able to answer the question: *Who is Jesus Christ to you?* I hoped for some insight or explanation. Instead, he scolded me for "asking such a private question." One woman told me, "I attend Mass every Sunday and confess my sins twice a year. I will be considered a good Catholic and go to heaven." Then she revealed, "I was told not to read the Bible because I might misinterpret it."

With these answers, I knew I had to start from the very beginning, from the meaning of Baptism.

Using my own experience of becoming a Catholic through the RCIA and a couple of key texts (*THE RCIA—Transforming the Church* by Thomas H. Morris, and the Columban Fathers' own text, *Kirisutokyo Koza*, an adaptation of the RCIA), I talked with the family of a Catholic man. His mother was around age 90. We were with his son and son's wife and daughter. The elderly woman told me she decided to become a Catholic because she was impressed by the Catholic Funeral Mass. In Japan the Catholic clergy allow Japanese ancient rites at the end of the Mass. In a touching ceremony, people come forward offering a lighted stick of incense in solemn respect to their ancestors. These people taught me that to build the church, we must understand the wisdom of the Japanese culture.

It was challenging to explain the proclamation of the *kerygma* (the saving death and resurrection of Jesus Christ) to a ninety-year old woman who spent her entire life observing the ancient rites of ancestor worship. I did the best I could by watching, helping, and walking with the Nakanishi family during their journey of faith in ancestor worship to faith in Jesus.

There were no infant Baptisms or marriages celebrated during our three years of missionary works in Kainan, but we celebrated many Funeral Masses together.

More questions arose. How could anyone grow in faith without knowing the spirit of the law? How can one know the love of Christ, or the meaning of the Apostle's Creed, unless someone has been on a quest for Christ? Is it any different theologically if I were to ask myself, *"How could I share my entire life with my husband if I did not have a quest for his person?"*

As I write, St. Paul's words ring loudly in my ears. I marveled at how God worked through the imperfect, the foolish, the weak, and us.

"Rather, God chose the foolish of the world to shame the wise, and God chose the weak of the world to shame the strong"
(1 Corinthians 1:27).

In the next meeting, I called the entire community together. I proposed a new bathroom with a ramp so people with disabilities could have access to it. They would be able to celebrate the Eucharist with us. There were no objections raised. The community members were silent as they listened to my presentation that day.

The first objection came from Mr. Maruta, the president of the Parish Council. I was having a wonderful conversation with Mrs. Kazue Imatsu in the front yard of our church one Saturday afternoon. She was finishing up cleaning the worshipping place and making flower arrangements. Making beautiful flower arrangements to decorate the church for Mass was an important duty of women parishioners. Every woman took turns cleaning and making flower arrangements for every Sunday Mass. She asked me if I would like to join the group, but I declined because I had no talent for making flower arrangements. Instead, I suggested that I could clean the church as well as anyone. She laughed and said they could clean the church without my help. Beside she said you are too busy.

It was then that Mr. Maruta drove in on his scooter. "We don't need to build a new handicapped bathroom," he said, "because we already have one."

Puzzled, I looked at Mrs. Imatsu and asked Mr. Maruta, "Where is the bathroom?"

"It is in the city park," he said.

The city park was two *long* blocks away from our church. How could a handicapped person who walks with a walker reach a bathroom in time? This was my first encounter with Mr. Maruta, the president of the Parish Council. I was a little confused as I listened to his reasoning.

"Carl and I will visit the facility there in the park soon," I replied, "We will give you our evaluation on it at the next meeting."

Not too long after that encounter with Mr. Maruta, Carl and I went to the city park to see the facility. We thought it was too far from the church. It was too difficult for someone with a walker to walk on the unpaved walkway. I was ready to report to Mr. Maruta and the council members about our evaluation of the proposed handicap bathroom at the city park, but Mr. Maruta announced that the council members had agreed to build the new bathroom. Again, I was speechless. He simply said, "We need one so that a handicapped person can also celebrate a weekly Mass together."

This change of heart surprised us. It seemed to change his understanding of charity for the sick, handicapped, and also for the poor. I was told later that he was one of the Kasai clan. Without his dedication to building the Kainan Church and working behind the scenes in various ways to support our efforts, we could not have accomplished much for the Church.

The entire congregation had a strong desire to rebuild the church. The women worked to replace all the curtains and furniture, and Carl decided to renovate the entire church. He began with remodeling my office and the reception room, which were connected to the Maria Kindergarten building. Next, he submitted a written proposal of the approximate cost of paint for the inside of the church. The Council members approved and set up an account with one of the paint shops near us. One day during a Mass, we made the announcement. I asked everyone to save old newspapers and bring them to the church because Carl was collecting them. One of the church members asked me why Carl needed old newspapers, so I explained to her as best I could.

On the following Sundays, they came. Our worship space was covered with newspapers. I explained that the newspapers would prevent the paint from getting on places that Carl did not want it to touch. He tackled the first step in the renovation of the church, which was to paint the worship space. No man volunteered to help him because they said inhaling paint was dangerous to one's health. However, one young man, the son of Mrs. Nishimura, the principal of Maria Kindergarten, came to help Carl hang the old newspapers. With his help, Carl was able to finish preparations for painting, and he single-handedly finished the task. It took every hour available for the next three months for him to complete the painting.

While Carl was renovating the church, I spent most of my time helping the women either sew new curtains, call on the homebound, or visit the sick in Kainan hospital, which was located right next door.

Usually, special projects like sewing curtains would be done on Sunday right after Mass so that we did not interrupt Carl's project during the weekdays. After the women served the workers lunch with tea, sweets, or rice crackers, we gathered in a circle to make the curtains. I joined them. I took that opportunity to get to know them. Sometimes I spoke of biblical stories about Jesus and women, or asked them if they had any questions about the Scripture readings we had just heard that particular Sunday.

On one occasion, a woman asked me, "Why do you not wear a mantilla head-covering?"

A mantilla is a lace veil or shawl often worn by Catholic women. Since I did not know the real reason I simply said, "Women in America do not wear the mantilla. Occasionally, in America you will see a woman with a mantilla on, but they are usually from some other country, such as the Philippines or Spain."

The following Sunday, all the women came to celebrate Eucharistic liturgies without their mantillas.

Then the same woman asked why St. Paul looked down on women, addressing St. Paul's seemingly chauvinistic attitudes about sex and the status of women. I smiled to myself recognizing, in her, much of the frustration I myself once felt. This woman was living in one of the most patriarchal societies that still existed. I promised her that we would meet soon to study about it.

"I praise you because you remember me in everything and hold fast to the traditions, just as I handed them on to you. But I want you to know that Christ is the head of every man, and a husband the head of his wife, and God the head of Christ. Any man who prays or prophesies with his head covered brings shame upon his head. But any woman who prays or prophesies with her head unveiled brings shame upon her head, for it is one and the same thing as if she had had her head shaved. For if a woman does not have her head veiled, she may as well have her hair cut off. But if it is shameful for a woman to have her hair cut off or her head shaved, then she should wear a veil.

A man, on the other hand, should not cover his head, because he is the image and glory of God, but woman is the glory of man. For man did not come from woman, but woman from man; nor

*was man created for woman, but woman for man; for this reason
a woman should have a sign of authority on her head, because of
the angels. Woman is not independent of man or man of woman
in the Lord. For just as woman came from man, so man is born of
woman; but all things are from God.*

*Judge for yourselves: is it proper for a woman to pray to God
with her head unveiled? Does not nature itself teach you that if
a man wears his hair long it is a disgrace to him, whereas if a
woman has long hair it is her glory, because long hair has been
given [her] for a covering? But anyone is inclined to be argumen-
tative, we do not have such a custom, nor do the churches of God"*
(1 Corinthians 11:2-16).

At the following monthly meeting of the Parish Council,
I submitted a proposal to hold a Bible study session in the
morning and evening if they so desired. I knew I would not
have any men in the class. In the work-driven society of Japan,
people just didn't have any time off during the week. Most men
worked from nine in the morning to nine in the evening. Even
today, that seems to be the norm for the younger generation.

I was able to recruit about eight women attendees for a
weekly morning session. A couple of women showed up for the
evening session. As promised, I addressed Paul's attitude toward
women, particularly, the issue of head coverings mentioned
in the first Corinthians. Although Paul's most "chauvinistic"
passage insists that women should wear a head covering when
they pray and prophesy in church, he did not really believe
women to be inferior. He seemed to say that men and women
have equal status and are interdependent: *"For just as woman
came from man, so man is born of woman; but all things are from
God"* (1 Corinthians 11:12). It is true Paul insisted that women
should wear a head covering in church. He appealed to the
hierarchy of subordination wherein God is the head of Christ,
Christ is the head of man/husband, and man/husband is the

head of woman/wife. This thought is in accord with the hierarchy of socio-sexual relations in the ancient world. Since I was born and raised in that culture, I understand that was one way to keep society operating, but not necessarily what I believed and promoted. At the end of the session, I reminded them how Japanese society operates as an ancient world even in this century. Man dominates, woman subordinates i.e. danson jyohi. I also reminded them that they are the ones who give birth to male and female children. Reflect! How do you raise them—differently or equally?

If you don't like the patriarchal society, you must begin the change. You have the power to change. I believe Paul treated men and women equally. Many of his Letters prove it. We had a chance to study Scripture together and tried to see the world as Paul saw it.

"There is neither Jew nor Greek, there is neither slave nor free person, there is not male and female; for you are all one in Christ Jesus" (Gal 3:28).

In the first year of our ministry, I concentrated on helping to build the old church into a participatory church in the physical and spiritual sense, through Carl's humble actions and mine. We showed the community how privileged we were to share our lives with them through the Church. True, we were getting involved in church business, not just on the ritual side of it. We also wanted to build a relationship with everyone who allowed us to come into their lives. "Come join Carl and me every morning in the prayers of the Rosary. Come to Sunday Mass twenty or thirty minutes before it begins and let's talk," I encouraged them. People began talking and sharing how the past week began and ended. We began seeing them smiling more as they entered the church. Toward the end of our three years, I had to ask them, "When the Mass begins can you please stop your socializing?" They were enjoying themselves with others.

SELLING OUR HOUSE

Just as Carl realized that his next renovation project was to re-varnish the pews and renovate the badly neglected church, I knew there were many things I must also do. Gradually, by the end of our first year of missionary work, especially on Holy Thursday at the evening dinner, Carl and I knew we needed more time. As we gathered together to receive the simple meal Carl and I had made for Holy Thursday (spaghetti and meatballs, green salad, and French bread), I knew what I must do. As I broke the bread after the prayer and passed it to the next, I knew what my missionary work entailed: to help the community rebuild the church; help them be fed with the Body and Word of Jesus Christ. As there is no definition for "priestless" in the Oxford Dictionary, I would help them become a church with their own priest, and they would be priestless no more. They would feed one another as they came to the font to be baptized. I would train them to serve the church as a Eucharistic Minister and a Lector. To do that, we decided to sign up for an additional two-year commitment with the Society of Columban Fathers. We met with Father Tony Cox, Director of the Columban Fathers of the Wakayama prefecture. At our meeting, we announced our plan to serve for two more years so we could complete the work we had begun.

At that time, Fr. Cox said nothing of our non-status as missionaries, nor did he mention any reservations on the part of the Columban Fathers or the archdiocese. Rather, he expressed his excitement and welcomed our requested extension of stay at Kainan, because he said he needed my help to implement his ideas.

I must admit I thought his comment was strange. Although, he was the one who had met us at Kansai airport with Father Corr when we arrived in August of 1993. I wondered, after he and Father Corr brought us to this place upon our arrival in

Japan, why did we not see him for many months thereafter? He never mentioned any "grand ideas" originally, why now? What exactly were his ideas? If he had so many "ideas", why did he not articulate them to us? I could not read his mind.

After Father Cox voiced his approval of our commitment to stay an additional two years, we announced our intentions to the council members at the monthly meeting. To stay, we had to return to Park Ridge to sell our house in order to be free to work with the community toward rebuilding the physical and spiritual church. The work we had begun at Kainan Church was just a beginning. There was still so much work to be done. At this announcement, everyone from the community present at the meeting expressed their approval and excitement!

We returned to Park Ridge to sell our house where we had lived for almost thirty years. Our house was sold before it hit the market, thanks to our pastor, Ron Kalas, and the help of a realtor who was a member of Mary Seat of Wisdom Church. We felt that worrying about a house back in Park Ridge might be a hindrance to the commitment we made as lay missionaries. We knew that our first year was but a preview of what missionary work involved, and so we gave heed to the teachings of Jesus' found in the Gospels.

"And another said, "I will follow you, Lord, but first let me say farewell to my family at home." [To him] Jesus said, "No one who sets a hand to the plow and looks to what was left behind is fit for the kingdom of God" (Luke 9:61-62).

Again, perhaps we were being naïve. We loved our little house. We bought the Cape Cods style home in 1964 and were so happy for our accomplishment of buying a home, especially me. It was one of the American dreams that I held for so long. We said to each other, "We did it." Without anyone's financial help and within ten years of our marriage, we did it! What a thrill that was! Without Carl's guidance on how to save money for something important, like a house, it would never have happened. Up until then, I thought money was used to spend on clothes, jewelry, fur coats, collections of crystal, travel, and fancy cars. Simply, to enjoy life's finest offerings. The first car we bought was a Ford. Imagine! I was driving in America! Next we bought a Lincoln Continental and then a Cadillac. I was feeling my sense of accomplishment. In America one can achieve one's highest aims. Whatever one dreams in America, with hard work and determination, dreams will come true.

We shopped at one of the fanciest stores in Chicago, John M. Smyth Furniture Store on Michigan Avenue. We furnished the entire house. I sewed drapes for all the windows except the kitchen. I loved every moment of it. Our house became alive. But there was no one except my husband to share our joy. Without our parents and siblings to share with, I felt our joy was not complete.

In our backyard were a large elm tree, three stories high, an apple tree, a pear tree, and a big magnolia tree. Every spring the magnolia tree produced beautiful pink flowers to the delight of the Park Ridge Garden Club members. They came to admire and take pictures of it. The pictures appeared in the local newspaper every year. I understand from the Garden Club members that our magnolia tree was the largest and most beautiful one in Park Ridge. We buried two of our beloved pets under that tree.

I have so many cherished memories, especially of the two pets that alleviated my loneliness and some of the touch of sadness I felt in my life. The first dog was a poodle we named Hics.

One weekend in 1958, Carl came home early in the morning. He normally came home once a week from his job of driving a truck. The job took him away from me five days a week. Although I missed him very much, I felt grateful for having him home every weekend. One morning, I was still in bed sleeping when he woke me up and put a tiny pup on my chest. The pup could literally fit in my hand. He was a pure black beautiful miniature poodle. Hics became my companion. His love and loyalty eased my loneliness for Carl and for my family back in Okinawa. Carl trained him to walk without a leash. He went everywhere with me. Together, we went to the park, to the beach, even to the weekly visit to the bank. Hics traveled with me on my first trip back home since leaving Okinawa. That was the summer of 1961, seven years after I left Okinawa for America. After a two-week quarantine period was over at Naha Airport, Okinawa, I took Hics to my parents' house in Ishigaki Island and introduced him to everyone in my family. When my parents' dog, named Red, saw Hics living inside of his house, he was quite upset, yet curious. Red circled around his house, not yet quite sure what he should do about Hics. Soon, Red became our protector. Wherever I took Hics for a walk, Red was there with us so the stray dogs would not attack us. Hics had a hard time understanding people in Japan because they spoke a different language than he understood. When my maternal grandmother, Unme, visited us and saw me with Hics instead of a child, she lamented. She even suggested that she should kill him and let me eat it so I might become pregnant. Imagine that!

Hics was very happy to return home after a month-long visit in Okinawa. When we arrived at Midway Airport in Chicago, I claimed him at the international arrival and immigration office at the airport as part of my luggage. When I saw Carl was there waiting, I opened Hics's cage. When he heard Carl's whistle he ran forward, searching for Carl. Hics ran one way, then another. He was so excited that he passed by Carl, still running. Carl whistled again. Hics went by him again, so Carl said, "Come on Hics!" When Hics finally found Carl, he leaped up on his chest and Carl caught him. He was so happy, whining and licking Carl's face to tell him how much he had missed him. When other passengers and their families saw what was happening and that Hics had finally found Carl, everyone started clapping their hands. Seeing how much Hics missed Carl touched me too and brought tears to my eyes. Hics lived until he was 12 years old. He suffered for a couple of years from an injury after a neighbor's large dog got out of their yard and attacked him. Hics died of a heart attack in the summer of 1971 while my parents were visiting us.

For a couple of months I tried to live without Hics, but I could not. I then decided to get a Yorkshire terrier, which was recommended by Hics's veterinarian. I named her Cleopatra — Cleo for short. Cleo had a completely different nature from Hics. She was as smart as he, but her memories of what she learned were short. I had to walk her with a leash, but not for too long a distance. She was happy in our backyard chasing and killing a bird or two. I finally got her out of that murderous spirit and only let her chase the birds. After all, that was her backyard I reasoned. She lived a short seven years and died of kidney failure. Like all dogs, she chewed grass and ran and played in the back yard. I let the veterinarian treat her with kidney dialyses every few weeks for a couple of months, but then decided to put her down. It was a difficult decision. I did not want Carl to go through this heart-breaking experience, so I chose a beautiful fall Saturday morning. The yard was decorated with the colorful leaves on the trees she loved to play under where she chased the birds and squirrels. Soon, it was where she would become one with the earth. That day, Carl would be coming home after driving many miles for his job as a truck driver. When he came home from work, I told him everything about Cleo and how sad she looked. I told Carl that I decided it was time for her to go home and play with Hics in heaven. We hugged each other and cried our hearts out for the second time over the loss of a pet. Carl went to the veterinarian to claim her body. We buried her next to Hics under the magnolia tree. It is fascinating to me, that human beings become so attached to their pets. I believe it only speaks to the energy of the universe that flows thru all of us; from the sun to the trees to the animals, and finally to our hearts.

THE SECOND YEAR

After we sold our house, we returned to Kainan to resume our work. Carl asked Mr. Maruta to help him move the heavy wooden pews, one at a time, from the inside of the church to the carport. There, he could scrape off the old varnish, and re-varnish them in the open air. There were forty pews. By the time he refinished a few, the parishioners were able to actually see the difference with their own eyes. The pews showed their beautiful light natural colors. Four parishioners came to help Carl. Together they finished re-varnishing forty pews. It took them five months.

At the beginning of the third year, the men worked side-by-side with Carl building the church. The last thing Carl built was an altar from a big round wooden spool that was used to hold underground wire. This was at the request of an Osaka Diocesan Priest, Father Akeishi, who would be considered to take over the Kainan Catholic Church when we left. That wooden spool was just a piece of junk when it was given to us.

Carl said that he could use it to make a round alter as Fr. Akeishi wished. He and Mr. Maruta Yoshihiko decided to add more slats to its sides and bought a piece of wood to make a tabletop. They stained and varnished it. It turned out to be a uniquely round altar that they still use today. It was rumored that after we finished our tour of duty on July 28, 1996, the church would be priestless no more. Thank you, my Lord for granting our prayers.

There is one more very amazing story to tell you about Carl. He had very little command of Japanese, yet he was able to communicate with the children of the Maria Kindergarten next door. They loved him and loved to come see what he was doing. He was either working inside the church or outside of it, or hanging laundry on the clotheslines! This scene you would not see in Japan. Men do not wish to be seen in public doing a so-called "woman's job".

When he was working outside, the children came to watch. Carl drew a line on the ground with a long bamboo stick and told them with his limited Japanese vocabulary not to cross the line. He did not want the children to get dirty with varnish or inhale the paint. On the other side of the line, the children watched as Carl continued to talk to them with broken Japanese. They were able to communicate and enjoy each other.

I spent the second and third years working with Father Cox to develop lay leaders, especially in the area of the Eucharistic Ministry and the Ministry of the Word. The purpose was clear. Whenever and wherever Mass cannot be celebrated on Sunday because of the shortage of priests, like Kainan where there was no resident priest, the faithful should not be deprived of the Liturgy of the Word or Liturgy of the Eucharist. I found an answer in developing lay leaders by training and educating them so they could fill the gap and be the agents who would nourish the faithful by both the Word and the Body of Christ.

How presumptuous I was to think that, as a lay mission-ary, I could initiate more education for the Columban Fathers of Wakayama and educate Christian Communities. But I did. I decided to meet the Archbishop of Osaka, Yasuda on this account. With his full support, I approached the young Regional Director of the Columban Fathers of the Wakayama Prefecture, (Father Cox), about the need to train the laity. He decided to take a one-week study and training seminar at the Japan Catholic Study Center at Nagoya. I was to accompany him.

All the while Father Cox and I were on the train ride to Nagoya, I was thinking of how I might convince him that we—missionary priests and laity like myself—had no power to make the Japanese become Christians, or Roman Catholic Christians for that matter. It is, after all, the business of God and the person who is seeking the truth. I noticed that the only thing the Columban Fathers seemed to be focusing on was the baptism of Japanese in increasing numbers. We evangelists can only introduce, articulate, and demonstrate who our God in Jesus is to us, not only through catechism but also through our deeds and actions. There were so many ways to evangelize. The rest is up to the individual. It was up to us to think outside the box.

The five-day seminar offered at the Nagoya Catechetical Research Center (from January 12 to January 16, 1995) taught us how to be a Eucharistic Minister and a Reader/Lector. Upon our return, the education would enable us to instruct the men and women who would be appointed by Father Cox—at the recommendation of their parish priests.

The distance from Osaka to Nagoya is about one hundred thirty-nine (139) miles, or approximately two hundred twenty-four (224) kilometers. We took the train from Osaka to Nagoya, a ride of about two hours, followed by a bus ride to the Center. Everything was located far away from the home parish. Driving the expressway to get to any place was costly. The alternative was to use public transportation, which was quite efficiently run. Train schedules were amazingly accurate and fast.

Father Cox was quite impressed by the seminar. Since he was responsible for directing seven churches of the Wakayama Prefecture—Shingu, Tanabe, Ryujin, Gobo, Koya, Yakatamachi, and Kainan—he decided to invite people of the Nagoya Catechetical Research Center to come to the Yakatamachi Church. They could hold a seminar for all who were recommended by their parish priests. In the case of Kainan, I made the recommendations.

I recommended three men and four women from the Kainan Church. The Seminar was held for three days, from May 5 to May 7, 1995. This was the beginning of the Lay Leadership Training at the Wakayama Prefecture. I reminded them that: "The laypersons appointed should regard the office entrusted to them not so much as an honor, but as a responsibility; and above all, as a service to their brothers and sisters under the authority of the pastor. Thereby they could carry out this responsibility by virtue of their Baptism and Confirmation."[24]

THE THIRD YEAR: OUR LAST YEAR

In April of 1995, after the seminar at Nagoya, I asked Father Cox for permission to go to Chicago to attend a one-week course to learn about the art of leading prayer. It was called Lay Presiding. The course was offered at the Catholic Theological Union in Chicago. The course Father Cox and I attended previously did not have this particular course on the subject we needed, nor did the Institute of Pastoral Studies (IPS) of Loyola University Chicago offer such a course.

While at the Theological Union, I saw one of the Osaka diocesan priests attending the same course. We had never met. I knew enough not to approach a Japanese priest. I was a woman and a laity. He must first approach me if he was interested in meeting me. That is part of the misunderstood humility I was taught and raised in. Nevertheless, he must have thought the way I did. He came all the way from Osaka instead of attending the Diocesan-approved institute in Nagoya. Seeing an Osaka Diocesan Priest studying here told me something very important. They are well versed in theology in English and Japanese. He had mastered the English language well enough to study at

---

24   Congregation For Divine Worship Directory for "Sunday Celebration in Absence of Priest," Vatican City, p.10

the Theological Union in Chicago. It was time that the work of evangelization of the Japanese should be transferred to the Japanese Catholic Dioceses. The job of foreign missionaries had been completed.

I hoped he was reminded that the word and communion service provided by a layman or woman leader was the heart of an assembly. We celebrated on the Lord's Day. There was no priest to preside at Sunday mass. The ordained priests needed to study the reality of the Japanese church in order to understand that their fear might be minimized, and they might move closer to shepherding. Hopefully, their shepherding would include training lay leadership. I felt the urgent need to train the laity so the Kainan Church could receive Holy Communion every Sunday, even after we left.

How else could the sacramental Church exist where there are few priests? I understood that once achieved, this would conclude our lay missionary work.

The course began with the question:

By whose authority do Christian men and women exercise "*presidency* of the *assembly*?"

Fundamentally it is always and ultimately Christ who leads our assemblies and invites us to praise and thanksgiving. It is Christ who speaks the word and makes possible our prayer. It must be the ceaseless effort of every leader of prayer to ponder what God with us means. Thus will we be faithful heralds of Christ's presence, power and love in our assemblies.[25]

Although the ultimate authority that comes from Baptism and Confirmation alone does not give one enough confidence to be a leader of prayer, neither does one's skill nor theology and rubric suffice. Can one memorize the rituals, movements, and liturgical gesture perfectly and recite a well-written reflection on the Word of God? Can one then feel fulfilled to be called a

25   Kathleen Hughes, "Lay Presiding: The Art of Leading Prayer," p.45

leader of prayer? Obviously, a leader of prayer ought to possess all of those qualities I listed above. But still there is something missing that is very central to prayer: spirituality.

Whose spirituality is missing? Our faith tells us that we are made by the free will of God in His own image after His own likeness. And, that He breathed into our nostrils the breath of His life. If this is true, then we have, indeed, inherited His Spirit. His Spirit draws us to His priesthood. We are fashioned as an icon of His. Yet, I have a strong urge to say that I am not qualified to be called an icon of His ministry.

It was difficult for me to lead an assembly for prayer service on Sunday without a priest. I felt that I was weak on theology, rubric and ministry. Simply put, I was scared to death and nervous of not being worthy enough. But with the help of the Spirit I was able to lead Sunday Communion Services without a priest. I taught others how to lead and do the same.

Through His total dependency on God, the Father, Jesus perfected His Mission. He always prayed and never made decisions on His own. He was my master image of presiding. I prayed to God, the Father to send St. Paul to help us every day for our work.

The task of training potential lay leaders in prayer was not easy, to say the least. It took several months, three evenings a week, side-by-side with Sunday reading and reflection. Eventually, we were able to produce the first of Kainan Church's very own seven lay leaders. I called them the "five loaves and two fish" who would lead us to a new Church where laity could lead.

I reminded them that the "Empty Chair" speaks of the One True Shepherd and Teacher of His People, whose advent we await. There is only one True Priest who presides over the Word and Communion Service. In the meantime, we are as His icon. I also reminded them, "You are the model of the future of the Church. We came as your leader to model the future of your church. You must carry on what Carl and I came to show you." That was our last message to them.

PENTECOST SEMINAR IN TOTSUKA, YOKOHAMA, MAY OF 1996

On February 1, 1996, I wrote an official letter to Father Brian Vale, the Regional Director of Japan. I notified him that the last day of our Columban Lay missionary work at the Kainan Catholic Church would be July 28, 1996. I later received a letter from Father Thomas Tehan, the Regional Vice-Director. In his letter, he acknowledged receipt of my letter and assured us that he was looking forward to meeting us at Totsuka for the Pentecost Workshop. He notified us that the Regional Director, Brian Vale, was away from Japan for the month of February.

Father Cox, Father Corr, Carl, and I took a train to attend the Pentecost Workshop held at the Franciscan Retreat House in Totsuka, Yokohama for the week leading up to Pentecost Sunday. The workshop focused on "A Paradigm Shift in the Concept of the Columban Mission in the Third Millennium." Father T. P. Reynolds was the speaker. I was surprised to see Father Tom Tehan instead of Father Vale because we thought we might meet Father Vale in person.

One morning, in Totsuka, I was taking a stroll around the grounds of the Retreat House before the morning session, breathing the fresh air, and feasting my eyes on the beauty and simplicity of the gardens. I always took a walk. This particular morning was no different. A Columban Father approached me and asked my name and capacity. I introduced myself to him, saying that I was a Columban Lay Missionary working with my husband Carl at the priestless Church in Kainan for almost three years. He took a pocket-sized green book and flipped through it, saying he could not find my name or my husband Carl's name in his green book.

I didn't remember the rest of the day clearly. I felt defeated and crushed after finding out there existed a green book known as the Columban Fathers Directory, and, that our names were not listed within it. I went to Father Tehan, who was the Master of Ceremonies that day. While I don't remember exactly what he said, I remember him brushing me off. I don't remember where Father Cox and Father Corr were. In fact the rest of the retreat is somewhat hazy. My memory of the dinner that evening is partially drawn from the recollection of Father Reynolds who, upon request, generously shared his memory of the evening. After the dinner that night, Father Tehan stood up and announced that he would like to recognize certain individuals who were attending:

The first recognition went to Father Joe Finnerty for his 50th anniversary of priesthood. He received a little gift.

Then Carl and I were recognized. "Carl and Masako," he said, "have worked in the Kainan Catholic Church for the last three years and are returning home in July of this year." I received a small gift.

It was as I was opening the gift I heard him say, "Now, I would like to introduce to you the two Columban Lay Missionaries: Alan Tayassali; and Agnes Virata."

I was aghast! Carl and I were sent to Japan a year ahead of Alan and Agnes—who were also from the Chicago Archdiocese.

The Chicago Archdiocese recognized us as Columban Lay Missionaries in their record. We actually worked as lay missionaries for almost three years before them. They on the other hand, were still going through the orientation period in Japan learning the Japanese language and culture.

When I distinctly heard that our names were not in the ranks of the Columban Lay Missionaries, I cried. I cried for me and for Carl. Carl put his arms around me and held me tight and comforted me. We still had two months to finish up our work at Kainan. I did so with a broken heart.

RITE OF COMMISSIONING HOME TO AMERICA

On July 28, 1996 at two o'clock in the afternoon, Archbishop Yasuda and the newly appointed parish priest of the Kainan Church, Father Kenji Akeishi, led the Mass and concelebrated the Rite of Commissioning us back to America with the Columban Fathers of the Wakayama prefecture, Father Corr, Father McNally, Father Eaton, and Father Cox. There was no official representation by the Columban Fathers, or Father Brian Vale, the Regional Director of Japan. We were then sent back to America. At the end of the celebration, we received a certificate of appreciation in which Archbishop Yasuda addressed us as (信徒宣教者) lay apostolate or lay missionaries. God has mysterious ways of showing His justice.

The Kainan Church was full that day with the mothers of Maria Kindergarten and the many friends we met in neighboring churches.

There were cameras and recording machines all over the church. Our work was recognized and appreciated by Archbishop Yasuda, The following is his homily, which was translated into English for Carl by the Osaka Diocese:

Streling Masako-san, you were commissioned from Chicago, Illinois diocese of America to Kainan Catholic Church under the Osaka Archdiocese of Japan in 1993 to assume your place of assignment. You were involved in the work of pastoral ministry at Kainan Church for three years exerting efforts in training your congregation. Having faced the reality of religious organizations where priests do not stay permanently, you must have faced many challenges but at the same time must have felt joy of working as a missionary. You were instrumental in marking an important page in the history of Kainan Church encouraging those residing in the community who worship Jesus Christ. Thank you very much.

Streling Carl-san You came to Japan with your wife, Masako, and supported the work of pastoral ministry at Kainan Church.

I thank you from the bottom of my heart. I understand that this round altar is your masterpiece. You also worked together with the congregation repairing the church inside and out by applying varnishes and painting the long benches, walls, windowsills, etc., renovating the church as a place of worship. You reinforced the feeling of pride our congregation had for the church. Thank you.

I am certain you two must have endured some tough times seeing how tedious the process of making the Japanese church grow compared to your American experience. While witnessing the strengths and weakness of Japanese churches, you trod a path together as we tackled our religious organization to open up and renovate. I thank you for that. I appreciate the fact that you were instrumental in marking a new page in the churches of Japan, Osaka Archdiocese and Kainan Church.

I am truly grateful for your hard work as lay missionaries for the past three years and am thankful that our American counterpart was able to commission the two of you to us.

I offer a heartfelt prayer to our Lord who led and supported the work of these lay missionaries and that they continue to lead their path after they return to America and to further enrich their services as Christians.

(Archbishop Hisao Yasuda, Osaka Archdiocese, Japan)

THE LAST DAYS IN KAINAN CHURCH

Our three years of missionary work would be completed on July 28, 1996. I announced this news to the children and the community. I got a call from the mother of one of my English pupils.

She said, "I am very grateful for all you have done for my daughter. She was a very difficult child to raise. She is an only child. Today she is a beautiful girl, smiling, happy to go to school."

I set up a date to meet with her in my office. She came in with a bag of fruits. Fruit was a very expensive commodity in Japan. I was very appreciative.

I wish I had known before that day, that her daughter's difficult nature sprang partially from the fact that she was the tallest of the children, including the boy students in the class. Carl could have helped her. He felt a tall girl was very beautiful if she stood tall and proud. But being a tall girl in Japan could be a problem for a girl, since the country was still a patriarchal country. Men should be taller and stronger and women should be daintier and fragile. This is true even in this 21st century.

On July 29, 1996, the day of departure, we were getting ready to leave for Kainsai/Osaka airport when the doorbell rang. I thought it might be one of the Columban Fathers. I opened the door. There stood one of the kindergarten students. It was the dentist's son. He just stood there, so we invited him in. After a while, he said he did not want us to leave and cried. He wanted Carl Sensei (teacher) to stay and teach him more. After a while his mother came to take him home. We wonder about him quite often.

The doorbell rang for the second time. I expected to see someone at the door to see us off. It was a mailman this time delivering a special delivery package. It was a letter from Father Kambayashi. I opened it to see what was enclosed. When I started to read, my eyes caught *Father Healy* and the *Columban Fathers*. I closed the letter and put it away in my purse because my heart could not take reading the rest of the letter that day.

As I closed the door behind me for the last time, I made the sign of the cross over the Kainan Church and over our residence, where we lived and worked for the last three years. We left Osaka/Kansai Airport without anyone from the Society of Columban Fathers seeing us off. There was only one person, Kazue Imatsu, one of the Five Loaves and Two Fish, Eucharistic

Ministers representing the Kainan Church. It was very difficult to say farewell to someone like Kazue who had become so much like me. She was a part of me during those three years. We held our tears back, bowed deeply, and stoically parted.

The Gift from Kainan

I sent the following article as a final report of our work in Kainan to the Columban Fathers of America where they are located in St. Columban, Nebraska, shortly after Carl and I arrived in Los Angeles, California. The final report contains the gift we had received of *Five Loaves and Two Fish* from our beloved parishioners of the Kainan Catholic Church. *Five Loaves and Two Fish* are actually seven people. They were such a beautiful group of people, a real miracle of my work at the Kainan Church. So, I called these people *"Five Loaves and Two Fish"*. The Columban Fathers of America published it in their monthly magazine, the September 1996 issue. My writing was heavily edited for their own purpose. It was followed by Father Donal Griffin's: A Farewell To Masako & Carl (see Chapter 10). He was the only one of the Columban Fathers of Japan who publicly defended us and shared our suffering. We are forever grateful to Father Donal Griffin.

FIVE LOAVES AND TWO FISH

By Masako Streling

Carl and I were married for over 40 years when we were commissioned to serve the priestless Kainan Catholic Church in Japan as Columban Lay Missionaries on July 24, 1993 from Mary, Seat of Wisdom Church, Park Ridge, Illinois.

The missionary work that awaited us at Kainan Church was challenging. What made the situation harder was that in title-conscious Japanese society, no one seemed to know what to call me. I said that I was neither a teacher nor a catechist. Then, "Who are you?" the Japanese asked. "Just call me Masako," I said.

Before long I was encouraged to attend the monthly meeting of the clergy. I was the only woman there. Local priests also began asking me, "What is your name, Sister?" or, "Who are you?" I told them that I was not a nun, not a teacher, not a catechist. Then, "Who are you?" they asked. "I am a Columban Lay Missionary who works at the priestless church in Kainan."

After working at Kainan Church for about two years, this title- less missionary worker was referred to simply as a "missionary" in the Catholic newspaper.

Title-less or not, I was not immune from making decisions as long as I was working in a priestless parish. After many prayers and much discernment with my husband Carl, we decided to lead the Kainan community toward the Church envisioned by Vatican II when it used the phrase, "People of God."

How were we to accomplish this? Carl and I decided not to take the route of lecturing, but rather to simply live out our faith. Carl took on the task of renovating the church building and the rectory that had been badly neglected for many years. It took him every waking hour for three months. His effort had its effect and men began to show up one-by-one to help him.

I decided to hold classes focusing on a participatory Church using two texts: *The RCIA, Transforming the Church*, by Thomas H. Morris, and the doctoral thesis of Dr. Ignatius Madya Utama, S.J.

According to Father Utama, a participatory Church can be described from three perspectives: its membership, its leadership, and its involvement in the world.

Addressing the perspective of membership, Father Utama says that we become the People of God because we are called, elected, and united by God through and in Christ. As the People of God, we have equality with respect to the dignity of being Christians, and, as members of the Church with respect to the activity common to all the faithful for the welfare of the Church.

As members of the Church, we are not merely receivers of the Church's ministry, but also active members of the life and ministries of the Church.

What Father Utama says is not new. It is based on a Vatican II document. Nevertheless, to rephrase the idea, we are, regardless of our function in the Church, the right hand of God that is used to help build the Kingdom of God in this world. The Spirit of God Whom we received in Baptism is the same Spirit that descended on Jesus when He was baptized by John the Baptist in the Jordan River. We are baptized, not for the maintenance of the church building, nor to be the right hand of the priest, but to help realize the Kingdom of God in the world.

If we are equal in dignity and co-workers of God, we must continue to learn from the Spirit, who is present in all of us. We cannot say that the responsibility for building the Kingdom of God rests only among the Church hierarchy. It also rests among the baptized as well.

To become co-responsible, we must learn from the Spirit. We also need to admit that change is necessary for growth. We must therefore change our attitude toward change. We must learn from each other, from priests and theologians, as well as from the laity, because the Church is a living and revelatory Church.

Since the arrival of this title-less missionary couple much has happened at the Kainan Church over the last two and a half years.

Under the leadership of Father Cox, fifty-two (52) laity from nine (9) Wakayama churches attended a three-day seminar in 1995 to prepare lay people to be leaders of prayer services in the absence of a priest. These laity can also serve as Ministers of the Eucharist.

With the blessing of the Archbishop, these laity can now be called on to minister to the Church whenever they are needed. The parish of Kainan produced seven such persons, whom I call *Five Loaves and Two Fish*.

There were numerous ministries that needed to be carried on by the people of the parish. These laity needed to be trained. Carl and I decided to send them for further training.

The nearest place where they could study was Osaka, and then only in the evenings. It was not feasible economically or physically to undertake long-term study in Osaka. So I decided to take on teaching them, although teaching is not my cup of tea. I was able to arouse their interest and challenge their minds.

As a result, one person has been studying for over a year at Eichi University, the Catholic University near Osaka, working toward certification as a catechist, in spite of the distance and the economic burden. She is the sole woman among the leaders of this parish.

Unqualified and imperfect as we are, I marveled at how God worked through us. How excited I was to have a hand in training these people!

These loaves and fish are different today. They lead the Liturgy of the Word and share themselves in the most heart-warming manner. Men have learned to work side-by-side, building both the physical and the ideal Church we were working toward.

We left the Kainan Church with mixed feelings because there were still many tasks untouched — youth ministry and lay spirituality, to name only two.

We hope the action of these loaves and fish will multiply and feed the hungry, the neglected, and the lonely in the parish and beyond it.[26]

26   Columban Mission Magazine, September October, 1996, p.26-27

Masako (center) and Carl (top) with mothers, and
their children who attend the parish center. None of
the mothers are Christians; only one boy, because of
a severe heart condition, has been baptized.

JAPANESE REGIONAL NEWSPAPER:
MY FAREWELL ADDRESS

The following article appeared in the Columban monthly newspaper of September 1996. The article was sent to me from Father Griffin. I did not know Fr. Griffin very well. I knew he was one of the Columban Fathers in Japan who taught at the Eichi University, Osaka. He was one of two Columban Fathers I knew of, who mastered the Japanese language and culture. He was, as I said, one of the three participants who attended my farewell speech when I was asked to address the Osaka Diocese on July 24. His translation of my farewell speech from Japanese into English is as follows.

"On Wednesday, July 24, Masako addressed the assembled archbishops (Yasuda and Ikenaga) and priests of the Osaka Archdiocese. It was the monthly priests' meeting and so the hall was crowded. Masako gave an eloquent speech in her native language to the assembly. Her audience hung on her every word—the proverbial pin could be heard dropping. She got a rousing round of applause from all as she ended, and in conclusion Archbishop Yasuda gave both her and Carl some very compassionate and kind words of appreciation.

On Sunday, July 28, Archbishop Yasuda traveled to Kainan with Father Akeishi where they hosted a farewell Eucharistic celebration with the Catholics of Kainan and other parishes in the district to honor Masako and Carl, who left from Kansai Airport for Los Angeles on the evening of July 29."

Masako Streling's farewell address to the assembled bishops and priests of Osaka archdiocese July 24, 1996
Japanese Regional Newsletter September 1996
(*Abridged translation by D.Griffin*)

On July 21, my husband and I completed three years as cooperators of pastoral care in the priestless church of Kainan. Kainan was priestless for two years before we came. For that reason, the attempt at making a community-style pastoral set-up went smoothly. But it cannot be denied that there were three other important factors that also contributed. The first of these was that the Kainan Church was abandoned by the Osaka archdiocese. To echo an expression commonly used in the diocese, it is hardly an overstatement to refer to the Kainan Church as being one that is stuck away in a valley of the Wakayama prefecture. Further, apart from saying Mass for them, the Columbans probably were busy and hardly had any time for contact with the Kainan community. Thirdly, there was no leader in Kainan.

Carl and I were chosen as leaders and sent to the Kainan Church by the Missionary Society of St. Columban in America, but as there had never been such a case before, both the Osaka archdiocese and the Missionary Society of St. Columban in Japan never formally accepted me as a pastoral cooperator [shiboku kyoryokusha]. Yet my qualification as a pastoral coordinator was from Loyola University where, after graduating as a Bachelor of Theology, I went on to earn the degree of Master of Pastoral Theology.

I knew we could expect no moral backup from the Church in Japan, there was only one thing left for us — prayer.

Exactly three years ago, on July 24, 1993, at a solemn Mass in Mary Seat of Wisdom Church, we celebrated the Mass with the pastor and Columban priests. We were then sent as pastoral cooperators to priestless Kainan Church, trusting that the Church would support us as lay missionaries. However, in Kainan, a bitter reality awaited us. Obviously, dialogue between Columban Society in America and the Columban Society in Japan had come to a halt, and there was no structural set-up to welcome us. And not only that, but also that condition has lasted until this very day.

For four days, from May 20 to the 24th, at a Columban gathering in Totsuka, we were told clearly: "You are not Columban lay missionaries. The Columban Society in Japan only supports you as individual missionary workers." This came as a terrible shock to me. My body was already weakened from childhood illness. As a result of this shock I became ill for a while. Based on our achievements for these three years, I naïvely thought these ordained ministers would formally accept us as companions in the Japanese Columban Society. But not one priest supported us publicly. They all ran away.

I do not know the exact meaning of the statement of the Columbans in Japan. But what is clear is that in those same words, there are theological, logical and sacramental problems involved. Because of the way we were treated by the Columban Society in Japan, our three years there felt like nothing more than a fictional story. Why is this? We later discovered that no matter where you search in the Columban Society in Japan, there is absolutely no record of our names. I found it difficult to understand why a religious group would do such an absurd thing in such a casual manner to us — their brother and sister in Christ. Being treated in this manner by our brothers and leaders in the Holy Order was humiliating and hurtful. Nevertheless, no matter how much they may wish to deny our existence and obliterate our names from the Columban Directory, I am certain that as a result of our achievements, the memory of our existence will remain with people — the community of the Kainan church.

For three years, we joined the community at Kainan around the table of the Lord and broke bread together. In our Bible-study meetings, as we sat around the stove on cold nights, we searched together for the meaning of who Christ was for us. We searched for truth. Together, we were consoled by the Rosary as we murmured it around the table of Christ. We took part in the baptism of a family of five people who made their journey modestly to the faith as each came to a realization of self in their search for the Tree of Life. With Carl, we encouraged the men of the parish as they spent long hours learning how to conduct the Sunday Liturgy of the Word, until eventually they got it right. We supported the bravery of people as they made a profession of their faith in their homilies. We look back on so many beautiful things that we shared with the community. These memories will never be erased from our memory.

I would like to go back for a moment to 1992. A few Columban priests back then were worried about the future of the Kainan Church, which was then at the point of death. They discovered an answer to the problem of the pastoral care of the Kainan Church in canon 517 of Canon law. And by that same canon a suitable solution was found in me in America. It was decided, seemingly, between the Columbans in America and Japan. However, when this idea was presented to the Osaka Archdiocese, I heard that a problem arose. Namely there was disagreement between the Columban Society and Osaka Archdiocese over the interpretation of Canon 517. Even as the problem continued unsolved, we arrived in Kainan. But there were eighteen months since then. Why couldn't the Columban Society and the Osaka Archdiocese forestall our dispatch beforehand? Not only that, after we arrived, why were we not terminated after the first year, or the second, or the third? Is it because of a power greater than all of us overcame them? Perhaps this is true. I call that mysterious power the Holy Spirit. Both the Columban Society and the Osaka Archdiocese were afraid of that mysterious power. Sometimes I like to think this is true.

But, why on earth would we want to give up not just one, but three years of our precious lives? Why should we want to sell our house and property that we had spent 40 years of married life building up to stay at the Kainan Church? It was not for admiration or wealth. Nor was it for the joy of bearing those sufferings that as Christians we cannot escape from. Even though I was rejected by the religious leaders of a group, I saw myself reflected in the image of the community that was wandering about leaderless.

The past three years had been years of many painful experiences for us. Yet without the 20th century vision or inspiration of the Columbans in Japan, we would never have had the opportunity of working in the vineyard of Kainan. This was the mystery of God's plan that I try to focus on. My heart is full of gratitude. The opportunity to meet so many Japanese priests also fills me with gratitude. I will treasure their memory. When I returned to America I hoped to continue to serve the Lord with faithfulness based on that apostolic spirit within me, which was tempered even more in the vineyard that is Kainan. Thank you.

Chapter Nine:
New Beginning

RETURN TO AMERICA

*"Masako, the experience of your journey to my people and
back to your people delights me.I hope this book,* Christianity
Rediscovered *by Vincent J. Donovan, Holy Ghost Father, fortifies
your experience of speaking the Good News."*
(Fr. Eugene Geinzer, S.J.)

I met Fr. Eugene Geinzer, S.J. in 1991 at Loyola University
Chicago while pursuing my graduate studies in my "search for
Jesus". At that time, he was teaching. His title was the Director
of Fine Arts. I was on a quest to internalize and believe that the
reality of my beginning was with Jesus. It took many years to
claim that Jesus was my personal God. To come to that end, I
owe Fr. Geinzer a debt of gratitude for helping me. One day he
gave me a drawing of his creation. The drawing depicted the
child Masako praying to the sun. She thought the sun was God.
She shall learn later in her life that the Son is God.

Father Geinzer, S.J. gave me a book called *Christianity
Rediscovered,* before I was sent to Japan. To this day, I still go
back to it and think about my experience of being a lay leader
and a woman in the patriarchal country of Japan. My experi-
ence of serving the Lord, the Kainan Catholic Church, and the
meaning of the lay apostolate are almost indescribable. How

did I ever manage being a lay leader? I often think that Father Eugene Geinzer must have a hidden message for me to discover. He was such a big influence on my journey with Christ.

Broken-hearted, we boarded a Japan Airline flight to Los Angeles with Donovan's book on my lap during the fourteen-hour flight from Kansai Airport to Los Angeles. The scenes and events of the last three years invaded my heart and my mind with many flashbacks of incredibly painful and joyful events. Like a revolving lantern, illusive dreamlike pictures came and went within my mind. The joy the Bishop talked about the day before in his official statement comforted me, but the betrayal and abandonment I felt from the Columban Fathers wounded me.

I will say that we received a small sum of money from Father Vale. It was a personal cheque to put towards our moving expenses. He also offered words of thanks written on a personal card. This unofficial gesture was kind, but it made the lack of responsibility from the Columban Fathers, as an organization, sorely conspicuous.

Apart from the personal cheque from Father Vale, Carl and I were forced to pay for our own moving expenses (both ways). Our moving expenses would have been compensated had we been properly recognized as Lay Missionaries. Thankfully my retirement benefits from Japan Airlines covered our travel costs. Moving was an expensive prospect.

We returned to the United States with no home or church to call our own. My brother and his wife were kind enough to receive us into their home in Los Angeles. In their home, I was able to recuperate. Every day, Carl drove us to Redondo Beach where we walked and listened to the ocean waters, letting the water wash my wounded spirit. My brother lent us his old car until we could buy our own.

Several months later, Carl and I decided to look for a house to rebuild our life in sunny California. The truth is that our missionary experiences had changed us. We could no longer return to our former way of life. As I listened to God's call after we returned to America in the summer of 1996, we searched for a place where we could afford to build a home. We could not afford a new house in Los Angeles.

One day, when we were searching for a retreat house, we found a Benedictine Monastery, on a hill in Oceanside, California. It was called the Prince of Peace Abbey. We attended a one-week retreat there. While Carl was praying and meditating under the cross, he heard and felt in his heart the urge to look around below. So we did. We eventually built a house on three quarters of an acre of land, with a large garden. The following spring, we joined the Mission San Luis Rey Parish.

We became very good friends with Father Ben Innes, the Director of the Old Mission San Luis Rey.

We stayed in San Luis Rey Parish for four years trying to live the life of Christians, as St. Paul so passionately teaches us in his Letters. He urges us to respond to God's gifts by serving others, not in order to be saved but because we have been saved already.

Eventually I volunteered as a case manager at Brother Benno's, serving homeless men and women and the working poor. But my need to find a community where Carl and I could belong and serve together once again was not satisfied. After four years of trying to find our niche at Mission San Luis Rey Parish, I told Father Ben that we should leave the Mission and go elsewhere.

"Do not waste time looking elsewhere," he said. "Go to St. Thomas More Parish. You will find what you are looking for."

He was absolutely right. I met the most welcoming community and Father Peter McGuine, a young pastor. Kathleen Bell, Director of Faith Formation, advised him to let me lead the

Bible Study group of men and women in the morning session using the program of Little Rock Scripture Study. How did they know that the study of scripture is my passion? I accepted, and under Father McGuine's leadership and trust, my ministry began to take its own form, not too clearly, but assuredly.

It has been eight years since I started to lead the Bible Study. Perhaps it is time now for someone else to lead it. The study of the Bible is my only passion. I will always be a student.

TRANSFORMATION

As I said, the mission experience changed my life. I did not return to America the same woman who left for Japan. For one thing, I no longer desired name brand clothes. I am no longer the clotheshorse I once was, always trying to please people. I don't need to dress in different clothes every day. I no longer worry about what people say about me, how I talk, or the way I look. I am no longer a woman running from the term Japanese War Bride. I consider myself American and am no longer concerned with the judgment of others in that regard. I no longer feel as though I need to prove or qualify.

I became an American citizen on February 24, 1959. I was very proud. I remember a few days later mentioning it to a man with whom I worked at the time. He was a supervisor at William Greiner Company, a leather tanning company where I was a bookkeeper.

"You could never become an American," he said.

That shook me, and I resolved at that time to prove myself a worthy American citizen. For years we bought only American automobiles despite the flood of Japanese cars coming into the market.

I also remember a co-worker, years later. She was a Chinese girl who took my position as a bilingual secretary at Japan Airlines in the 1980s.

She said, "Even though you support American ideals, and act like an American, and are married to an American man, you will never be accepted as an American or be called an American. To them, you will always be an *oriental*—always. Would an American call an Italian immigrant an Italian, or a German immigrant a German? No, they are considered American. This is why I will never be considered an American citizen. So, think of me always," said she, "as a Chinese girl who gave this valuable advice to you."

What she said is true, in some respect. I do think of her, I must admit, as a Chinese girl. Nevertheless, I don't mind if people refer to me as an oriental, Japanese, a half-Japanese, a Japanese War Bride, or as an Okinawan, for that matter. Today, that is merely who I am on the outside. My exterior identity is, indeed, Japanese, and my ancestors' blood of the Satsuma samurai and Okinawan flows in my veins. But my true identity, and the most important identity of myself, is that I am a woman created in the image and likeness of God. Furthermore, I am a citizen of America, and I am grateful to be one. There is no other country like the United States of America. My personal American experience testifies to that. I will never forget my responsibilities to be a worthy citizen. It is my privilege.

Where else could I have achieved my dream of obtaining academic degrees at age sixty-three? I chose my personal God, Jesus Christ, as my savior, and he has promised me citizenship in His Kingdom of Heaven. I know I could have never achieved my American Dream without the help of the Spirit. God's hand has led me thus far.

Perhaps in order for Him to introduce me to the mystery of God himself—Trinitarian love—he had to take me away from my native land. He took me away from everything I had and knew and left me in the desert like Abraham, where I suffered from loneliness, thirsted for the water of comfort, and hungered for Japanese food. I hungered for food of comfort—His word. He let me choose, and even then, He was patient. There was no coerciveness in my choosing. I wanted freedom. Freedom was what I wanted from the very beginning of my life. Freedom to be a woman. Freedom to be a child. Freedom to enjoy every stage of my life. Freedom to choose Jesus as my savior, my God, My Lord, the most precious gift of faith.

Thus far, God helped me to achieve everything I wanted in my life, including an academic degree, for which I worked very hard.

Yet, Jesus warns me: *"Do not store up for yourselves treasures on earth" (Matt. 6:19)*. I was like a rich fool in the parable of St. Luke's story in Chapter 12: "Engaged in putting up new and bigger barns to house my accumulated treasures."[27]

"We may have thought that these earthly treasures, from which we have been warned off, were only money and real estate and fine clothes and art objects and jewelry. But they include, more importantly, whatever we are especially proud of—or, for that matter ashamed of, or whatever we think sets us apart and identifies us. Our earthly treasure is our self-image and our self-esteem. Hard words. Absolutely."[28]

However, I am grateful to God for all of my life experiences in order to accumulate worldly treasure in spite of the "hard words" of Jesus. I lived every bit of life, the joys and the struggles. I struggled to achieve and struggled to overcome adversities. Indeed, the worldly treasures I have accumulated did not make my life complete. I felt something was missing. I was enduring life, instead of experiencing the joy of living fully. I have cried my heart out and even cursed my God for my birth. Yet I would not want to change one iota of the life I have lived so far.

---

27   Beatrice Bruteau, "The Easter Mysteries," p.12

28   Ibid, p.12

Now that I have freedom and time to live the life I always wanted to live, what do I need to do? Must I die to my own sense of myself, of who I am and why I am important, before rising to the newness of selfhood with God's help? To meet my self, I must remove my pride, remove what I have craved, remove what I sought for my own glory.

It is my story. All my life I have worked very hard to become a person that other people might like, all the while disliking myself for being that way. Also, all my life I accumulated material things and collected many things to show off to the world, all the while knowing we needed very little to live on. To prove my point, we lived simply while we were doing our three years of missionary commitment, and we were very happy. We had done so once. It seems like it is time for another displacement. Another removal. Paradoxically, a rethinking of one's life that brings displacement and removal, also brings with it, freedom and finding true selfhood.

Chapter Ten:
Reflection

KNOWING MY PLACE

I have written many pages about my birth as a first daughter and how my father lamented my birth because the society of Japan did not value the life of a female child. Yet, he knows as well as I do that without the help of my mother and me, he could not have raised his nine children.

When I was growing up, I was told that my place as a woman was always to be subservient to the male gender and always be smart, tactful, and considerate in assisting them. *Considerate* meant that when I was asked by my grandfather or father—or even my elder brother—for an ashtray, I would be smart enough to also bring a pack of cigarettes and a box of matches.

I was taught never to butt in when my grandfather or other men were talking. I learned not to listen, see, or talk when I was not asked to do so in the presence of men. I was not always successful in knowing my place. It was difficult for me. I was not easily taught my proper place. In our household, nothing was standard or ordinary. My father was a stay-at-home dad, and my mother was a "rice-winner". ("Rice-winner" is the Japanese equivalence of breadwinner — I made that word up!)

My first Christian insight into the place of women came from the Gospel of John and the story of the Woman at the Well.

"He had to pass through Samaria. So he came to a town of Samaria called Sychar, near the plot of land that Jacob had given to his son Joseph. Jacob's well was there. Jesus, tired from his journey, sat down there at the well. It was about noon.

A woman of Samaria came to draw water. Jesus said to her, "Give me a drink." His disciples had gone into the town to buy food. The Samaritan woman said to him, "How can you a Jew, ask me, a Samaritan woman, for a drink?" (For Jews use nothing in common with Samaritan.) Jesus answered and said to her, "If you knew the gift of God and who is saying to you, 'Give me a drink,' you would have asked him and he would have given you a living water."

The woman said to him, "Sir, you do not even have a bucket and the cistern is deep; where then can you get this living water? Are you greater than our father Jacob, who gave us this cistern and drank from it himself with his children and his flocks?" Jesus answered and said to her, "Everyone who drinks this water will be thirsty again; but whoever drinks the water I shall give will never thirst; the water I shall give will become in him a spring of water welling up to eternal life" (John 4:4-14).

The Samaritan woman's boldness brought a smile to my face when I first heard the reading of this wonderful story one Lenten Season. She reminded me—and reminds me still—of myself in every way. Jesus uses Jacob's well (v.6) on side where women come to draw waters and gossip. There He provides her a situation and offers her an equal opportunity for the study of theology. She understands that her real place is to serve Him. By serving Him, she serves the community. At the end of the story, she becomes the first evangelist at Samaria, abandoning the water jar, a woman's job. At that time, only men did evangelization. Yet, Jesus offers her the opportunity to serve Him along with men. This opportunity was also given to me, when I said yes to go to Kainan to serve Him.

When I learned my real place, I abandoned my job of serving my husband and waiting on him hand and foot. I realized that I was raising him like a child. He tells everyone who has an ear to hear, "Masako used to make a plate for me at every meal— even at potluck dinner gatherings—now I have to make my own plate."

The second woman I met through the Gospel was Martha. Martha is essentially every woman who loves to entertain and serve a wonderful meal. The Scripture introduces us to Martha thus:

"As they continued their journey he entered a village where a woman whose name was Martha welcomed him. She had a sister named Mary [who] sat beside the Lord at his feet listening to him speak. Martha, burdened with much serving, came to him and said, "Lord, do you not care that my sister has left me by myself to do the serving? Tell her to help me." The Lord said to her in reply, "Martha, Martha, you are anxious and worried about many things. There is need of only one thing. Mary has chosen the better part and it will not be taken from her" (Luke 10:38-42).

I love Martha because she reminds me of all women, and of myself, of course. I notice that she even tells Jesus what He should do—tell Mary to come out and help her.

Jesus lovingly appeases her. On the surface, Jesus' answer to Martha is quite insensitive.

Is Jesus telling Martha that her proper place is in the kitchen? Or is he suggesting that she need not worry so much about hospitality? I think Martha worried about a great many things, as we all do when we are expecting guests for a dinner party. Martha probably heard what was going on out there in the living room while she was trying to bring everything together. She probably finished chopping the vegetables, kneading the dough, grilling the fish, baking the lamb, and the last preparations of a sweet mixing together. She was able to do all these things by herself. But, after everything was cooked and ready to come out of the oven, she needed one more hand. Any woman in her position can understand why Martha asked Jesus to help her out. The Scripture is silent, but Jesus did help her out at the end of that day. The Scripture is silent, but He, his disciples, and Mary came out to help her bring everything on the table so that everyone could feast that day. At the table, Martha offers a loaf of bread she had just taken from the oven to Jesus, who is the Bread of Life. At the table, as she watches Him breaking the bread, she understands what Jesus is saying to her and that He is welcoming her to be one of His disciples. Discipleship included listening to His teachings of the Kingdom of God carefully so she could pass on the good news to others.

He was talking about her real place, free from all anxiety and free to choose what's important — the "need of only one thing."

Jesus tells me the real place of women is to be with men, sitting at the Lord's feet and listening to what He is saying. Like Mary, who was in a man's place among men, women are to be listening and learning about the Kingdom of God. He is offering an equal opportunity to serve Him. He has shown that women, too, are His friends to serve Him.

That day, Jesus was teaching us everything about the kingdom of God from what was going on in the village as well as in Jerusalem and regions around it. It was not about a meal. Mary understood this message. She chose her real place, to be with Jesus as one of his disciples. Jesus was their guest and also their friend, not only to Mary, but also to Martha. Martha knew He was not an ordinary man. He was more than just a teacher.

When we were commissioned to serve the Kainan Catholic Church in Japan, I was the leader and Carl was my assistant. I was in a man's place. Mary and Martha were with me all along, encouraging me to "be proactive. Pass the message on to others."

Today I want to write about how happy I am that I was born a female child of my father and God! God had a different purpose when He created me and sent me to my parents. I identify with Martha. I always tried to be perfect — a model for my siblings. But we all know we miss a mark. "It is because someone has set the mark and you can measure whether it has been missed and by how much."[29] Most times I missed the mark, but a few times I was right on target. Yet, on a conscious level, I wished I could be free from all those duties and just be me—to be like Mary. I always wanted to be a student. I never wanted to be a teacher. I wanted to be the best student I could be. For that, I was always elected to be in a leadership role. To be a leader, Jesus said, you must serve others.

SERVING

I ponder the word *serving* and its meaning a great deal lately.

According to Scripture, I was made in the image and likeness of God. I was born to serve. I was placed in a training ground, first as the daughter of my parents, then as an employee of various organizations, then as a wife, and then as an administrator of a priestless church in Kainan City, Japan. I still serve my faith community in various capacities today.

I discovered the true meaning of serving one Holy Thursday night just before the celebration of the Last Supper. When a priest enacted Jesus and bent down to wash the feet of the apostles, he showed me what serving truly looks like.

I felt something indescribable in my heart, and I wept and began to understand the true meaning of serving. We are all made to serve each other by feeding each other. We all come to supper at Jesus' table, where "no social class distinction

---

29   Beatrice Bruteau, "The Holy Thursday Revolution," p.39

is allowed. Everyone is equal, all are welcome."[30] One must remember that at that time in world history, everyone eating at the same table was unheard of—scandalous!

Yet Jesus said, "Do it, this is right and this is our salvation."[31] But before we approach the table, we must be washed clean by washing each other's feet.

On the Easter Triduum in 2010, when our pastor bent down to wash our feet on that Holy Thursday evening, I was deeply touched. Why could I not stop weeping? This time — I heard every word of the story, and saw the enactment of it vividly in my mind's eye. No wonder Peter pulls his feet away and reminds Jesus of His proper role when "He (Jesus) leaves His place at the table, takes off His coat, rolls up His sleeves, gets a long towel that He ties around His waist, takes a jug of water and a basin, and begins to wash the feet of His disciples. This is unbelievably shocking. The master is acting like a servant."[32] The message? We are to wash each other's feet by assuming a servant's role in order to serve others. That includes not only priests and laity, but also the very hierarchy of the Church. We have a responsibility not let this beautiful Church erode by the ills of the few.

He was saying to his disciples *follow me*. To serve is our proper role because others receive the same Christ in Him and in us. The two of us are no longer separate individuals. In Him, our neighbor is truly near. No longer are we two separate individuals, but united in the same Christ.

Slow of wit, dull of heart, He seemed to remind me. The Father moves me forward and draws me further into His world slowly but surely. *Forgive yourself*, I heard Him say deep within my heart, *and forgive your parents*. I have cursed my birth many

---

30   Beatrice Bruteau, "The Holy Thursday Revolution," p.52

31   Ibid, p.52-53

32   Ibid, p.59

times, saying to my parents that it was not my choice to be born. I was devastated because I needed to give up my talents and myself. Talents I believed were God given—to help my parents feed their nine children. The responsibility became too much for me to bare. I was helping my father, while my classmates were busily and happily pursuing their own life dreams.

I was only about twenty. I was in so much pain even felt hopeless that I was contemplating taking my own life. Thank God Carl happened to be there to save me. To this day, I can't talk about those dark moments. They are too painful to relive, and I have moved past them thanks to Carl and God's love. I was young and foolish. It was too much of a coincidence that Carl happened to be there that day. I heard His voice within my heart ask me to forgive myself for thinking that I alone helped my parents raise their nine children. True, I sacrificed many parts of myself to serve my parents, but I loved them so. Most importantly, I needed to know that God—the One who carried me when times were tough, or when I was at my limit, He was with me as I strove to complete my service. Through all these triumphant moments, tribulations, and trials of my life, I finally saw Him and understood what serving meant. Without selfless love, I cannot wash other's feet.

Shifting my thinking about who God really was to me was a long journey, until, little by little, I believed that Jesus was my personal God. He was with me every moment of my life, but I did not know His presence until the days of Kainan, where I felt His presence in my suffering of humiliation, rejection, and betrayal. I felt His love very close, helping us complete our work. How can I not acclaim him as my personal God with the thrill of hope? God Who is with us always.

ON RE-EXAMINATION OF MYSELF,
A WOMAN LAYLEADER

ON THE KAINAN EXPERIENCE

My Kainan experience was certainly a mixed blessing. I reflected on the life of Jesus in those days to find meaning more than any other time in my life.

Who were Jesus' friends? Who gave Him a place to rest, or food to eat? Did the men of religious authority provide Him a place to rest or food to eat? According to the Biblical stories Jesus was not a friend of religious authority. Jesus didn't choose the learned Pharisees or Sadducees as His circle of friends. The many writings of the Bible imply that Jesus might have been a Pharisee himself. How else could He win the confrontation with the Pharisees? None of His first twelve disciples were learned men. They were ordinary men like my husband, Carl, and women like me. His circle of friends included lepers, tax collectors, prostitutes, women, children, gentiles, and ordinary people like you and me.

Just like the ones in Jesus' time (the religious authority of a pure Jewish male), the Society of Columban Fathers of Japan could not consider us in their circle of missionaries because they said we did not come from that circle. The people of Kainan, however, thought of us as Columban Lay Missionaries and accepted us as such, just as we thought and believed we were sent as their missionaries. If they had their eyes and hearts in the proper place, as Jesus did, the Columban Fathers would have seen us doing the work of missionaries regardless what their guidelines say about it. Here is what one Kainan parishioner who worked with us closely wrote about us:

The Greatest an Encounter

By Imatsu Kazue written for the 50th Anniversary of the founding of the Kainan Catholic Church

(English Translation by Masako Streling)

About eleven years ago Masako-san was sent as a Columban missionary to us, the priestless Kainan Catholic Church, from America with her husband Carl-san. They worked three years becoming one of us.

Her husband, Carl-san, was an American, though he could not carry a lengthy conversation in Japanese. He was quite humorous, kind, and always considerate of others' feelings. Moreover, he was very skillful with his hands, and he renovated the entire church. He painted the inside and outside of the church, re-varnished the old pews, and made a new round altarpiece. When he finished our old neglected church, it became a beautiful church once again. He worked very closely with the Parish Council President, the late Maruta Yoshihiko. In this new environment, I decided to volunteer my time for Maria Kindergarteners as well as the local elementary students to catechize them. Masako-san and Carl-san agreed to teach them basic English.

One day, Masako-san, without warning put a question to us, "Who is Jesus Christ to you?" Even to this date, I remember very clearly how confused I was at such a sudden inquiry. She taught us the Scripture in depth, shared her thoughts, taught us how to share and pray with Scripture. All the while she was guiding us, I felt her love for Christ. Up until I met her, the Word I heard during the Mass was just passing through my mind. With her guidance, the Word of God remained within me. It might be an exaggeration to say, but to use biblical quotation, "The Word became flesh," and I met the Man Jesus for the first time.

She taught us the necessity of lay leadership in order to maintain a sacramental church because the Church is experiencing a decrease in ordained celibate priests. She initiated a training session provided by the Nagoya Catechetical Research Center for the lay Eucharistic Minister, Reader/Lector, so that we can celebrate communion provided by a lay man or woman leader where there is no priest to preside at Sunday Mass. The seminar was held at the Yakatamachi Church.

She was planning to attend the 50th Anniversary of the founding of the Kainan Catholic Church on November 11, 2007. We received a letter expressing her regret that she could not attend the celebration with us because she was recuperating from a major surgery. If she had, she would have challenged us with questions like, "What was your fifty years of spiritual journey like as a community, and what will it be like for the future?"

For me, I will always remember her query, "Who is Jesus Christ to you?" — and treasure it. I feel the nearness of Jesus, who is always with us while simultaneously feeling the closeness of these two people I met.

I would like to express my renewed gratitude to God for the opportunity of the greatest encounter with these two people, eleven years ago. I dream that we will meet again someday.

Thanks be to God.

Imatsu Kazue

The hearts of the Columban Fathers were, for reasons known only to them, hardened. In truth, for three years we worked in the vineyard of Kainan and lived up to our commitments. Though I have many times, in my mind, played through the months that led up to our departure, and the three years we spent in Kainan, I cannot understand why Carl and I were treated so poorly. I have examined and reexamined all our correspondence with the Columban Fathers. I have read and reread canon law, in hopes of finding some sort of context for those three years. No context, no reason, no compassionate explanation exists. How a society that strives for justice and peace in this world can allow such injustice to befall its own members defies explanation. I ask the question, why, throughout history, does the Church display such dysfunction?

In recent years the Catholic Church has faced many scandals. These scandals have shaken the Church to its very foundation. The most damning elements of these scandals include the cover-up and protection of priests, compounded by failures of hierarchical leadership. The costs—emotional, psychological, physical, and spiritual damage to its people. Why does the Church cover its transgressions in secrets and lies? Why does the Church disassociate from the truth? Why is the leadership of the Church historically mired in dysfunctional behavior?

While what Carl and I suffered pales in comparison to the suffering of victims of sexual and physical abuse, the three years we spend at Kainan cost us a great deal nonetheless. We did not only lose our physical home to the Church, but we lost our faith in the leadership of the Church. We lost a little bit of our spirit to the Church. Our treatment by the Columban Fathers took something out of us. It cost us some of our self-respect, or dignity, and our spirit of our selfhood. What is worse is that these costs, all of them, were needless. Ultimately, we left Japan no longer feeling whole. Nothing made us happy. In this struggle, I found God's mercy, compassion, and love. I then vowed not to give up on the Church.

Telling the truth takes courage. Jesus' freedom encouraged me to speak out about our experience with the Missionary Society of St. Columban. I felt I could no longer hide behind the stoic stance that I was expected to take. Instead, I felt God was offering me some of that same confidence and freedom I used to have as a child. I felt the confidence to stand up for myself.

I remained silent for many years about our time in Kainan to my own detriment. The main reason I remained silent was because I did not want to hurt the many wonderful priests and professors I have met in over the years, a few even among the Columban Fathers. Without their guidance, I could not have become who I am today. I was emotionally torn between Christ-like priests and priests who did not live up to that measure. For over fifteen years, this wrestling in my heart was the reason why I could not face many things about the Church, and myself.

I was spiritually dead, functioning mechanically. I even lost the desire to pray. I am certain now that the reason I had to endure eight surgeries over a five-year period was a result of how I lived. I abused my body because I was not happy. Outwardly I acted normal, but inside I was tormented. I read somewhere about how we can abuse our body by letting stress affect us, resulting in muscular tensions, vulnerability to infection, and even suppression of the immune system.

I regained my health when I decided to speak the truth about my experience working for the Church. I ultimately needed to protect our dignities as children of God. Since I have spoken out and confronted these demons, I have not required any more surgery. I reached the five-year marker for remission of colon cancer in August of 2010!

According to Father Vincent Donavan, in his book *Christianity Rediscovered*, eighty-two percent of the world has not heard the gospel.[33]

"He said to them, "Go into the whole world and
proclaim the gospel to every creature" (Mark 16:15).

Preaching the gospel involves missionary work. What is missionary work? I believe the work of a missionary is to be a faithful witness to the fullness of the Gospel. The Gospel is the door to true, human development. However, Vincent J. Donovan points out what the Gospel is not:

"The gospel is not progress or development. It is not a national building. It is not adult education. It is not a school system. It is not a health campaign. It is not a five-year plan. It is not an economic program. It is not the liberation movement. It is not the black power movement. It is not the civil rights movement. It is not violent revolution.

Our business, as Christians, is the establishment of the kingdom. It is a kingdom that takes its beginning here in this real world and aims at the fulfilling of this world, of bringing this world to its destiny."[34]

Christians are called to participate in realizing that extra dimension. Show what you learned in the Gospel to the world. Live your life according to what the Teacher taught us to the world. Let the world see Jesus in us.

Beatrice Bruteau writes in the preface to *The Holy Thursday Revolution*: "The ills of the world continue in abundance, but efforts to counter them are also vigorous."[35] The ills of the world

---

33   Vincent J. Donovan, "Christianity Rediscovered," p.195

34   Ibid, p.165

35   Beatrice Bruteau, "The Holy Thursday Revolution," p. preface

exhibited by clergies are bad enough, but to protect their ills by the hierarchy is irresponsible. "We still need to go to the root of the trouble in the way we perceive one another and at the same time work out economic and political arrangements that will give relief to oppressed and commoditized people."[36]

The word *politics*, according to Bruteau, means simply "the art of living together in human society [that]… has a human consciousness shaped by memories, emotions, and concepts born of interactions with other people." Taken in this very general sense, she says, "Politics is practically inescapable for even the hermit."[37]

In this general sense, we all learn how to live side-by-side in a family, school or work place, each in his/her position. Even in my pagan upbringing, when I did something wrong, I was either corrected by my parents, teachers, or society because I could not be harmonized in human society. That authority is called, *Okite* (a law or statute). Why should this statute not be applied to every human in the world, whether we are Christian or pagan? Particularly for Christians, we *know* we are sinful.

Clergies choose this awesome opportunity and responsibility so that they can lead people to God. Even a pagan child like me was given the responsibility to be a model for my siblings, and I knew it. But I did not know who was a better teacher than my grandfather, my parents, and teachers. I was looking for a model to follow. I found the Sun, and I decided the Sun was my God. I can affirm that was the beginning of my search for the deepest truth about myself.

I thought the Sun was God, even though we are told that Emperor Showa was our god and our ancestors become gods when they died. They were the ones who would protect us from

36   Ibid, p. preface

37   Ibid, p.3

any harm. But these gods did not protect us. Japan lost World War II. At the end of the war, Emperor Showa announced that he was not a god. Neither were we a superior race as we had been taught. There were also many other gods, according to the tales of old Japan. There was an earth god, rain god, fire god, wind god. However, these gods were not taught as a religion. Rather, the stories associated with these gods were a way of telling the joy, sorrow, suffering, fear, and passion of human lives through these gods' treatment of human situations in naturism. Their livelihood depended on these gods' favor. The Japanese national religion of Shintoism is an offspring of this.

These simple old Japanese tales remind me of the Big Story, the Scripture story of the Creator, who made the sun, fire, earth, heaven, rain and everything else in the heavens and on earth. In Japan, the people of old were aware of an existence of somebody other than themselves who was bigger, stronger, mightier, and more merciful than them. To him, they bowed their heads and asked for their daily bread through a good harvest of rice. This tradition continues even today. It is called Shinto. Shinto, or worshipping fertility, is still an integral part of Japanese rice-cultivation.

"In Japan, growing rice is not just an economic operation. It is also a religious rite that has to be practiced for its own sake, whether or not rice happens to be the most remunerative crop in any locality. So long as rice continues to be cultivated by Japanese peasantry, the agricultural form of Shinto will continue to be practiced in the village shrine and on the farm house holy shelf."[38]

I remember when I was in the first or second grade. A teacher took us to Buddha's temple on a field trip. I remember clearly, even today, how two judges guarded the entrance of the temple. Their bodies looked human, but their faces were like

---

38   Arnold J. Torynbee, "East to West," p.27

beasts with two horns on their heads. Their eyes were like a lion's eyes. Their mouths had fangs like a wolf. Their raised arms held whips. After passing the gate, one beheld a panoramic view of heaven and hell. In between these guards, one saw the transience of human life and how it appeared. They scared me so much that I dared not do anything wrong. I did not want to be judged to go to hell. That day, a monk taught us many things. He insisted that we would not kill any living thing. He included the following story:

One day a bad man was looking for something bad to do. He found a spider coming toward his feet and decided to stop and not step on it. He let the spider go. Later, he died and was sent to hell. In hell, he suffered intense heat and thirst. Surrounding him were fire and other people sentenced to suffer hell. One day, in front of his eyes, he saw a spider web and decided to take hold of it. As the spider pulled him up, the bad man noticed many others were holding his legs to come up with him too. He decided to kick them off because he worried that the web might break and he may not reach to heaven. By doing so, he did not pass the test for heaven. The only good thing he did in his entire life was to save the spider's life that day, which afforded him a chance for heaven. But he failed the final test because he was still so selfish and did not have enough faith that the web would hold everyone. Thus, he condemned himself.

This childhood story reminds me of the parable of the bankrupt creditor:

"That is why the kingdom of heaven may be likened to a king who decided to settle accounts with his servants. When the king began his accounting, a debtor who owed the king a huge amount was brought before him. Since the debtor had no way of paying it back, his master ordered him to be sold, along with his wife, his children, and all his property, in payment of the debt.

*At that, the servant fell down, did him homage, and said, 'Be
patient with me, and I will pay you back in full.' Moved with com-
passion, the master of that servant let him go and forgave him
the loan.*

*When that servant had left, he found one of his fellow servants
who owed him a much smaller amount. He seized him and started
to choke him, demanding, 'Pay back what you owe.'*

*Falling to his knees, his fellow servant begged him, 'Be patient
with me, and I will pay you back.' But he refused. Instead, he
had him put in prison until he paid back the debt. Now when his
fellow servants saw what had happened, they were deeply dis-
turbed, and went to their master and reported the whole affair.
His master summoned him and said to him, 'You wicked servant!
I forgave you your entire debt because you begged me to. Should
you not have had pity on your fellow servant, as I had pity on
you?"* (Matthew 18:23-26).

This is the story of a master who takes the initiative to
forgive one of his debtors a rather heavy debt. But the debtor
does not offer the same mercy to a poor man who owes him
a small amount of money. We know the rest of the story. "The
master, on learning of the harshness and strictness of the bank-
rupt debtor, had him thrown into prison until he could repay
his entire debt. He did not absorb his master's forgiveness at
any deep level and was incapable of performing a similar act of
mercy to his poor [worker]. Thus he condemns himself.[39]

The monk's story struck me. It has stayed with me into adult-
hood. From that day forth I have tried not to harm another
living thing. Carl laughs at me when I try to blow mosquitoes
or insects off my arms instead of swatting at them. It is amazing
even as an adult, as old as I am. I still remember this story, which
still insists that I shall not kill, instead "brush it off"—let it live.

---

39   John Monbourquette, OMI., "How To Forgive A Step-by-step Guide,"
      p.172

The god the monk taught us about that day reminds me of our God, Jesus, who calls us to be forgiving and merciful. This merciful God and Man, Jesus, is merciful even with Judas Iscariot who made the horrendous mistake of betrayal. Jesus also called Judas Iscariot to grasp a string of hope to repent. In His silence, Jesus was with Judas Iscariot's suffering. There is a connection of Jesus with the tales of old Japan, which I reflect on today.

I would like to share the focal point of the stories. In their old Japanese tales, the ancient Japanese expressed the same joy, sorrow, fear, reverence, wonder, suffering, rage, and passion — the absurdities of life. Even though they were not aware of the good news of the Gospel, they met the God of the Gospel in their sub-consciousness. They met the God of the Gospel in a way that was true to them and their cultural traditions.

It is with a sense of humility that I admit failing to recognize this point when I had the chance. I could have used this Japanese sensitivity to evangelize or to help the Japanese when we spoke about God to those veteran Catholics. Instead, I was too distracted with many thoughts of bringing what I had learned in America as the only way to speak about God or to share our reflections with them without thinking about the cultural differences between the two countries. I looked at the Japanese as another American when evangelizing in the land of Japan.

"An evangelist or a missionary must respect the culture of a people, not destroy it. The incarnation of the Gospel, the flesh and blood which must grow on the Gospel, is up to the people of a culture."[40] Had we walked with them instead of acting as though we were their savior?

I should have realized then that Japan is the only country where Catholics can marry in the Shinto Rite, celebrate Sunday liturgy in a Catholic Church, or be buried in a Buddhist funeral rite, and still be called a Catholic. A Shinto, a Catholic, and a

---

40   Vincent J. Donovan, "Christianity Rediscovered," p.30

Buddhist can co-exist in Japan. It might be the task of future missionaries to learn the traditional spiritual life of Japan first. Their spirituality is fused together with their Confucian ethics and their Shinto ritual. Confucianism, Buddhism and Shintoism live happily together side by side.

Yet, I learned that their spiritual hunger was not satisfied with these three religions. What about the prospects for Christianity itself? We must find the language and music to feed spiritual hunger and to soothe the searching soul with the good news of Jesus.

As I understand it, Good News is Jesus' Word to show us how we treat each other. Jesus uses the words, "Love one another as I have loved you." The ability to realize our own potential and our own Kingdom on Earth is based on love.

ON A WOMAN LAYLEADER

"Whoever wishes to be first among you shall be your slave. Just so, the Son of Man did not come to be served but to serve…" (Matthew 20:27-28).

Were my experiences of being the first lay and woman missionary of St. Columban in Japan positive? Absolutely.

I was given an opportunity not only to really reflect on what Jesus taught to his disciples over two thousand years ago, but I was also given the opportunity to be a servant in His example.

I was keenly aware of my responsibility as a leader of the Kainan Catholic Church, both as a Christian and as a descendant of the samurai. I served my beloved community of Kainan with a sense of humility, privilege and honor.

It would be naïve to think I would not experience suffering, betrayal, contempt, humiliation, and rejection. I am very well aware of the words Jesus spoke to His disciples.

Much like the missionaries before me, I was not immune from persecution of some kind. Indeed, I suffered my portion of it. It hurts because persecution came from within the Church. The entity I became a missionary to serve. But always, through these experiences of pain and suffering, I experienced an extraordinary presence of the Spirit. As a result, I became a courageous witness of Jesus' presence in my life to complete our works as missionaries. So why do I need to address the Kainan experiences further?

Simply put, blessing comes with responsibility. What is my responsibility as His least of vineyard workers in this situation? Was His gift to keep only for myself? Was the reason I accepted the offer of Columban Fathers John Burger and Jim Hastings to serve in Kainan because I understood the gift I was given must be shared with others? Or was the reason to let the world know how deep and wide was His justice in His compassion and mercy during the time of our trials and confusion?

Is it not my responsibility to let the world know that, "Out of our littleness, our emptiness, our nothingness God's greatness will flower in an astonishing way"?

Richard Rohr reminds us that: "The genius of the biblical revelation is that it gives us permission and even direction to take conscious ownership of our own story at every level and every part of our life and experience. God will use all of this material, even the negative parts, to bring us to life and love."[41] Rohr also reminds us that: "The biblical tradition takes all three levels seriously: My Story, Our story and The Story." [42]

I often think about the Missionary Society of the Columban Fathers and the Osaka Diocese, particularly of Father Akeishi and Archbishop Yasuda.

---

41   Richard Rohr, "Things Hidden Scripture As Spirituality," p.24

42   Ibid, p.24

Father Akeishi and Archbishop Yasuda are the fruits of one of the seeds sown on the good soil by the first Jesuit Missionary of St. Francis Xavier, one of the original seven members of St. Ignatius, who was sent by St. Ignatius de Loyola, a military officer, to Kagoshima, Japan where my ancestors, Satsuma samurais, lived and died. He had arrived on the 15th of August 1549 to introduce Christianity.

Japan at this same time was going through an era of great unrest. Shogunate, a military leader, became an absolute power demanding the warriors' class (samurai) to serve them by oppressing the farmers to pay taxes to maintain the power of Shogunate. They sometimes paid with their lives. Military men (samurais) were expected to live and die for serving the Shogunate.

I remember my education with the Jesuits at Loyola University Chicago. This was where I heard the tradition of St. Ignatius of Loyola said, "Go Forth and Set the World on Fire!"

Is it just an irony or coincidence that I found St. Ignatius of Loyola is known as the soldier saint? Perhaps, as a descendant of the Satsuma Samurai warriors — this is why St. Ignatius became my favorite saint. I chose to study at Loyola University Chicago. I was then sent to Japan, where the great missionary St. Francis Xavier, who was one of the original "companions," of St. Ignatius of Loyola, evangelized. I was sent to the Kainan Catholic Church named after St. Francis de Sales, whose education was formed by the Jesuits. I did not know all these historical facts before I said yes to my duties. Was my parallel experience in Japan with the earliest Jesuits' experience just coincidence? All I know is everything in the world and everything that exists throughout the space-time continuum is connected. I don't believe in coincidence.

CHRISTIANITY HAS FAILED IN JAPAN

Japanese Christians occupy only one percent of the population of Japan. The Catholic Church represents about 0.5 percent of the population according to Father McCartin. Indeed, they are no more than a tiny minority. He offers his assessment as to why "Christianity has failed in Japan" in an article he wrote for the September 1996 issue of the "Japanese Regional Newsletter of the Columban Fathers of Japan." In it, he discusses a number of topics.

As one of the missionaries and a native Japanese woman who worked in the same country, I found Fr. McCartin's article interesting because while his words speak to an all inclusive Church, the actions of the Columban Fathers, his own order, were anything but.

"We have been here 400 years," McCartin begins, "and even with generous helpings of martyr's blood, Christianity has not taken root." He then goes on to question the motivation of those early martyrs, suggesting that they did not die for Christ but out of "misplaced stubbornness." To suggest this is not only disrespectful to all martyrs throughout history, but it is also inaccurate and irresponsible. In fact, when the edict banning Christianity was issued by the Shogunate in 1587-1716, many Christians accepted martyrdom to hold on to their faith in Jesus. Some went underground. They are known as the "Hidden Christians" according to Ann. M. Barrington's book, "Japan's Hidden Christians". She continues to inform us that, "it is generally accepted that in 1614 there were approximately three hundred thousand (300,000) Christians hiding in Japan. By the time of the final *sakoku* (closed country) edict in 1639, it is estimated that there remained about 150,000 Christians."[43] To place any of the failure—as Fr. McCartin sees it—of Christianity

---

43   Ann M. Barrington, "Japan's Hidden Christians," p.27

at the feet of those who gave up their lives is simply, closed minded and sophomoric. Christianity exists exactly because of the ultimate sacrifices human beings have made throughout history, for the greater glory of God.

History tells us about the first martyrs, St. Paul Miki and his companions. The Roman Catholic Church canonized them on June 8, 1862 under Pope Pius IX. There were twenty-six (26) martyrs of Japan executed by crucifixion on February 5, 1597 at Nagasaki. My own ancestry, the Shogunate and Samurai were part of this tirade. Many early Christian missionaries were martyred from the swords of the Samurai and Shogunate. It is ironic that as a descendent of the samurai who took part in torturing and murdering Christians over 400 years ago, I now endure the mental and emotional torture from dysfunctional priests within the Catholic Church. I wish to recommend the book, *Silence* written by Shusaku Endo, which describes the unthinkable, inhumane methods inflicted upon the early martyrs. The book provides detailed accounts of the persecution of Christian communities and the suppression of the Church in this period. It is a moving account based on true gut-wrenching stories, describing how Japanese Christians held onto their faith and passed it on to generations after them. Christianity is not dead in Japan. Perhaps the true spirit of Christ is dead within the priests and hierarchy who make up the Catholic Church. Priests who put their heads in the sand while they know of other priests who commit dirty deeds, like pedophilia. Priests who use the wealth and generosity of the laity to serve their own lifestyle rather than the needs of the community. Priests who put themselves before the people they serve. Priests who act like hypocrites, as the old Pharisees in the stories of the Bible.

Fr. McCartin is right, Christianity is all but dead within the walls of the Church. But Christianity thrives outside the

Church, within the hearts of communities around the world. Communities like the one I served in the vineyard of Kainan.

I worked with people in the mission field of the Kainan Catholic Church for three years. I can assure you that Christianity has not failed in Japan. I believe that the Columban Missionary works of the last fifty some years in Japan might have failed. It is clear that the message of Christianity expressed in the actions of the Columban Fathers did not impact the community in Kainian. If it had, I would have not come into a situation where a priestless church literally didn't have priests to lead them to a deeper faith. The hypocrisy of Fr. McCartin's words is evident in the actions of the priests in his own order.

Father McCartin claims:

"Our God does not have the power to attract the Japanese", he claims, as though God is a magician. He continues, "We should abandon Christianity. We need a new religion. This new religion would teach that each person, and indeed the whole of creation, is a manifestation of the divine, and that as such each person is equal before God. There is no difference between women and men, between Japanese and gaijin, between blue collars, white collars, and dirty collars. It would spell this out: that Koreans, burakumin, foreign laborers, homeless people, the handicapped, and people in Third World countries, etc. are all equal. This means no more oppressing, and exploiting the Philippines. No more dumping nuclear waste in the ocean. Living at a much lower level than we are now. Eating little or no meat and less seafood. No one could come to 'church' in a Mercedes. No one could come in a car unless it had at least four people in it.

In this new religion, women and men would be equal. There would be women priests, bishops, and popes. People would be respected in this new religion. Celibacy would be optional. A priest could marry after ordination. People would have a say in the choice of priests and bishops."

Fr. McCartin's new religion is the "old" message of Jesus Christ. It was founded by St. Paul and St. Barnabas, the first Christians in Antioch (ACTS 11:26). This was the message that the Columban Fathers should have carried with them when they were sent to Japan fifty years ago. McCartin's words are beautiful, but the actions of his own order contradict everything he espouses. Before he preaches about a "new religion", maybe he should clean up his own house of hypocrisy.

What the public has seen thru the millennia is the reality of the Church. Priests, Bishops, Cardinals — I call them company men. The Catholic Church has become big business. It's another corporation, the oldest corporation on the planet. How many hierarchies have we now seen teach and practice differently from Jesus' teachings and what He died for?

The true message of love, compassion and understanding is the message that the Columban Fathers *should* have carried with them when they were sent to Japan fifty years ago. I make such an audacious statement after many years of reflection on our experience as their Columban Lay Missionaries working in Japan.

I wonder, how many other missionaries throughout history had their good will manipulated by the "needs" of the Church?

God has given to every member of the Church the office of priest, prophet, and king. Every member of the Church includes laity. One of the Columban Fathers adamantly objected to me thinking about training the laity to be lectors and communion ministers. "Only priests can read and give communion," he said. "Otherwise, the Eucharist is simply a piece of bread and a glass of wine." He had forgotten that at the consecration of bread and wine, it truly becomes the Body and Blood of Christ. This metamorphosis, the Catholic Church calls transubstantiation.

(Catechism of the Catholic Church 1377). Transubstantiation occurs regardless of whose hand gives communion, albeit ordained priest or baptized Catholic laity.

Because of their mindset, we were treated as outsiders, not as equals as they are in our humanity. We were only lay, not holy and as clean as they. What is clear is that in so many priests' words there are theological, logical and sacramental problems involved.

This kind of thinking of domination inherited from the past must die. Bruteau lists "domination as the Ills of the World."[44] "Only through reverent attention to and acceptance of the gifts of all the Spirit remain unquenched for the Church to flourish anew."[45]

To bring together a culture and the gospel, Donovan, in *Christianity Rediscovered* reminds us: "Christ Himself said, 'I did not come to do away with the law (the Jewish culture and religion), but to fulfill it' (Matthew 5:17). The Church, an evangelist, or a missionary, must respect the culture of the people they are trying to help, not destroy it. The incarnation of the gospel, the flesh and blood, which must grow on the gospel, is up to the people of a culture."[46] The Columban Fathers failed to understand the Japanese culture and the Gospel messages completely before they tried to evangelize the Japanese. They thought the Gospel message and culture were two different things. The only thing they were concentrating on was to baptize Japanese in more numbers. Some Japanese even told me that the reason they became a Christian was because it was fashionable to be one, just like speaking English is fashionable for some. The hypocrisy is frightening.

44   Beatrice Bruteau, "The Holy Thursday Revolution," p.3

45   Drew Christiansen, S.J. "America The National Catholic Weekly-May 31, 2010" p.5

46   Vincent J. Donovan, "Christianity Rediscovered," p.30

It took me twenty years to begin to understand Catholicism, yet even today I am still searching and learning the truth Jesus taught us.

How could the Columbans evangelize the Japanese with limited knowledge to master the Japanese language? If the Columbans' actions modeled what Christ was like, maybe they could have attracted more Japanese into becoming Christians without mastering the Japanese language.

I know there were many factors involved in my becoming a Catholic. The main reason was that my neighbors treated me like I was one of them. This was a very Christ-like action.

Perhaps, the heads of the Columban Fathers did not understand the meaning of justice, even though Jesus taught the meaning of justice as I quote Pope Benedict XVI's message of the Lenten Season: "The common understanding of 'justice,' he said "is to give each person his or her due."

We are all God's children no matter what stratum we are placed in this world. How could the Japanese see the person of Jesus in the Columban Fathers in the everyday lives they led? We could not find the person of Jesus in most of them, particularly in their Directors and their Superior General. None of them ever asked us whether or not they could be of any help. I felt their attitude toward the community was quite condescending. The fruit of personal experience must always be found in our love and service toward others. We did not find these qualities in most of the priests affiliated with the Columbans. And I suspect, that many communities around the world have also had similar experiences. The Catholic Church seems to have become a group of institutionalized men, with no real regard or understanding of the outside world. Their only concern seems to be maintaining their own institution, not serving or really loving the world community.

To people searching for meaning in life, the ritual the priests performed in Sunday mass did not provide an answer either. Rituals are merely a means toward an end. If that end is not kept, the ritualistic religious rites become an empty form of hypocrisy.

LETTER FROM FATHER KAMBAYASHI

Thirteen years after leaving Kainan, on one December day in 2009, while I was gathering materials to write, I noticed the unread letter from Father Kambayashi (Archdiocese of Osaka, Japan) dated July 27, 1996. I received this letter the day I left Kainan but I could not finish reading it because I was so broken hearted that day. After I finished reading it, thirteen years later, I decided to have it translated in English by Fumiko Uno:

When I apologize to others, I first recognize what I might have done (confirm facts), and what mistakes I may have made and what steps I ought to take so as not to repeat the same mistakes. And in case of having incurred damage, I must pay in some way because it won't count as an apology unless I do that, and it would only further insult the other party.

At the monthly clergy meeting of July 24, 1996 (Masako's farewell address), she recounted her life as a lay missionary from beginning to the end. And so regarding the circumstances of the couple since their arrival to Japan, I myself decided to check into the situation by asking the parties involved and looking up records at the time of Mr. & Mrs. Streling's arrival in Japan and circumstances leading up to the current.

The following was conveyed by Father Healy, who was the regional head of Wakayama district at the time of the couple's arrival to Japan (currently works at the headquarters of the St. Columban Society in Tokyo). St. Columban Society Fathers in Chicago recommended the couple to the regional head as candidates for lay missionaries. The regional head replied, however, that he could not accept them as "St. Columban Society's pastoral missionaries" on two accounts. One was the age limit. The Society of St. Columban has a policy of appointing young people as lay missionaries. The other was on providing a specified training to candidates of lay missionaries of the St. Columban Society. This was advised but Masako felt that it was unnecessary because of her master's degree in theology from Loyola University. Since Masako had a strong desire to work in pastoral ministry, the St. Columban Society of Japan was approached by the Chicago Region as to whether or not they would accept her though not as a "lay missionary of the St. Columban Society." Upon hearing this, priests at the Wakayama district of the St. Columban Society replied that they would not mind having her work there even if not as an appointed "missionary of the St. Columban Society" and that they would welcome her to serve at the priestless Kainan Church. So there was no formal contract drawn up with the Japan district that the St. Columban Society of Chicago was sending a lay missionary of their own to them. The St. Columban Society of Japan however, decided to supply living expenses with the realization that the cost of living must be assured. (To the question by Kambayashi that Masako mentioned of an extremely solemn Commissioning Sending ceremony at the time of her departure, Father Healy replied that it must have been a sending off ceremony by a small parish and not one sponsored by the St. Columban Society).

Father Healy met with Archbishop Yasuda at the same time asking for permission for the Strelings to work at Kainan Church and to offer them a certain title. Although the Archbishop gladly granted the permission for the couple to serve at Kainan Church, his response was that he could not think of a title because the church congregation could not readily understand what a lay missionary's work entailed. Father Healy then suggested the title of "catechists" for the time being for three months. To this, the archbishop said it sounded good. Before the first three months were up, Father Healy had to return home on a sabbatical leave. So he went back to see the archbishop to seek an approval on the title of "ministry supporter." But he went back home before receiving an answer.

Father Cox, who took the position as the successor, asked the archbishop as follows: The Strelings, who are working at Kainan Church as "catechists" with the commitment of one-year, desire to work at the church longer. In order to make preparations for that, they would like to temporarily return to America. They are currently referred to as catechists so that the Japanese congregation can understand that more readily, but in the future, we need to modify the title to something like "pastoral missionary." Please come up with suitable title.

Father Cox made this plea on January 1994. This meeting was attended by Father Kambayashi for the purpose of taking notes as instructed the archbishop. There is no evidence in any of the parish records that there were any subsequent discussions on the matter.

My conclusions are as follows:

Masako was not accepted as a formal lay missionary of the Missionary Society of St. Columban. In other words, she was not commissioned by the St. Columban Society of America per se. Aside from how Masako perceived this, however, the St. Columban Society of Japan understood that they entered into a contract with Masako on an individual basis.

The St. Columban Society of Japan (Wakayama District) felt, however, that Masako needed some title to be serving at Kainan Church. And they decided the title should be offered by the archbishop, thereby asking him to do so. Seeing that both Father Healy and Father Cox made the same request to the archbishop, one can realize that they were aware of having the St. Columban Society support Masako, part of which was to offer her a title.

Though the archbishop agreed that the title of catechist was good for the time being, this issue must have escaped his memory while contemplating this and establishing a more suitable title. When asked about this, the archbishop said that he didn't remember if he replied to Father Cox or what he said if he did. If the archbishop gave an answer of some sort to Father Cox, the Father would have relayed the message to Masako. The person asking for an answer could rarely forget to pass the word.

I can assume how this "memory lapse" occurred and offer the following explanation: The archbishop delegates responsibilities of pastoral ministry to the St. Columban Society for the Wakayama district, adopting the method of offering his permissions on items that were discussed and concluded by the St. Columban Society. And so he must have felt that the title the St. Columban Society would come up with would be a suitable title. Seeing how these events unfolded, I reflected on my failure and thought of what I could have done differently myself.

Though I [Kambayashi] was present at the meeting between the archbishop and Father Cox, I took notes of the meeting and merely submitted them to the archbishop. To deal with his "forgetfulness" of late, the archbishop was letting a staff member attend these proceedings. He did so not only for the purpose of note-taking but to have a staff member handle some of the administrative tasks. But at that time (January 1994), I had worked as an administrator for merely a year and was not very aware of the archbishop's intentions. I felt that my duty was to take notes, submit them to the archbishop and wait for his instructions. And if I didn't hear from him, I didn't make inquiries. I feel now that I should have been more proactive in this regard by approaching the archbishop that this issue was yet to be solved, to consult the clergy advisory board, or suggest some title myself. However, as I was not aware of the circumstances leading to Masako's arrival in Japan and the situation at the Wakayama district, I didn't realize *the importance of deciding a title for Masako to work at Kainan Church nor have the parish formally appoint her. And I also thought the issue was already taken care of. Therefore, as far as the administrative office was concerned, my intention was to treat her equally as a priest by sending her information, inviting her to the monthly clergy meeting, seminars, etc. But the most crucial point at the beginning was amiss.*

So that similar mistakes are not repeated in the future, I intend to be thorough in assuming my duties as an assistant to the archbishop as mentioned above.

Furthermore, I want to pay attention to creating an environment where the congregation can fully demonstrate their capacity to serve the church. And I want to exert effort in becoming a director whom the congregation can easily consult with when they experience tough times due to lack of a given environment.

Lastly, as for making up for my mistakes, I will report to the priests at the next monthly clergy meeting to seek their forgiveness on my mistakes. It must have taken courage for you to speak at the monthly meeting. I appreciated your suggestions. I am sorry that there was poor support while you were working at the church. Please convey my regret to your husband also.

Please accept my apologies for now. I have a final request. I would be grateful if you could compile a report on the last three years and send it to me. Thank you.

Hirokazu Kambayashi

When I read Father Kambayashi's meticulous report asking for our forgiveness on behalf of the Osaka Archdiocese and promising to report to the priests at the August 1996 next meeting of clergy to seek their forgiveness, I was deeply touched. It did, however, make the lack of formal apology from the Columban Fathers of Japan, America and Ireland all the more conspicuous.

I know from subsequently dated letters that Father Kambayashi was as good as his word. He did follow up with the parties involved, bringing the matter up in August of 1996.

"Therefore, if you bring your gift to the altar, and there recall
that your brother has anything against you, leave your gift there at
the altar, go first and be reconciled with your brother, and then
come and offer your gift" (Matthew 5:23-24).

THREE LETTERS

I decided to include the three letters that I received. They are the responses to Fr. Kambayashi's pursuit of truth.

The First Letter: Father Brendan O'Sullivan, Director of US Region, dated Sept. 6, 1996.

In this letter Father O'Sullivan, was reporting to Father Nicholas Murray, Superior General in Dublin Ireland, states unequivocally:

We, the US Region, consider that Carl and Masako Streling are
Columban Lay Missionaries.† We saw unique qualities in Masako
Streling, who had completed her MA in Pastoral Studies at Loyola
University in Chicago and her fluency in Japanese.

We contacted Father Vincent Youngkamp, the Regional
Director in Japan and offered to facilitate Masako and Carl
going as lay missionaries to Japan if the Columbans in Japan
were interested. Father Youngkamp was very interested. Masako
felt called to mission, specifically mission in Japan. Seeing Father
Youngkamp was very interested in Masako, she offered to meet
him at Haneda Airport.

At the Commissioning Ceremony at Mary Seat of Wisdom
Parish in Park Ridge, Illinois, Carl and Masako were sent as
Columban lay missionaries.

We were aware that we were not following the Society of St.
Columban Lay Missionary program guidelines. He listed three
reasons: We were excited by the notion of having people of this

caliber doing mission work in Japan. Father Youngkamp and the
American Region agreed that we should just go ahead and do it.
We did not bother to write it up and sign a contract. We felt that
we had a good agreement and the support of people in both the
US and Japan and let it go at that.

In retrospect that might not have been wise. It might have been
better to clearly define what it is that we were about.

In fact there were a number of irregularities in our situa-
tion, known to Father O'Sullivan, which were never made clear
to Carl or me at the time. Unfortunately we have never heard
the position of the Columban Fathers of Japan on this issue,
for Father Youngkamp was, at the time of this correspondence,
no longer Regional Director of Japan and Father Brian Vale,
though copied never responded himself. The lack of response
from Japan was highly disappointing.

The Second Letter: Rev. Nicholas Murray, Superior
General of the Missionary Society of St. Columban, Central
Administration, Dublin, Ireland, dated Sept. 18, 1996.

This letter was addressed to us and copied to Frs. Vale and
O'Sullivan. Rev. Murray opens by stating:

I would like to take this opportunity to express my personal
thanks to you for years of dedicated service you have gener-
ously given to the Church in Japan as Lay Missionaries with
the Columban Fathers.† On behalf of our Society I would like
to convey our appreciation and gratitude for your commitment
to the people in Kainan Parish, your valuable participation and
contribution to the Columbans in the Wakayama district and the
Archdiocese of Osaka...

You can be assured that your journeying with us has enriched
us Columbans as we strive to promote partnership with lay people
in our missionary task ... Having been pioneers in the days of
fledgling Lay Mission in Japan you will undoubtedly have accu-
mulated valuable insights and wisdom that comes from practical

personal experience. Consequently your opinions on development in Lay Mission will be of value to us.

As you settle back to life in the US allow me to wish you many years of happiness together as well as fruitful service to your local Church. We will always be delighted to consider you as part of our Columban family. You will have a special place in our Masses and prayers and please keep us in yours.

The Third Letter: Father Donal Griffin, dated October 8, 1996.

We received the third letter from Father Griffin, one of the Columban Fathers of Wakayama and a professor of Eichi University of Osaka. It was sent in response to a letter I sent after receiving Father O'Sullivan's letter but before receiving Father Murray's letter. Sadly Father Griffin passed away shortly after sending this letter.

I just receive your letter dated September 19th. Glad to hear that both of you and Carl are settling back into life in the States.

The Letter to the Superior General from the present Director of the American region of the Society of St. Columban, Father Brendan O'Sullivan who was the Lay Missionary Coordinator that sent you as a Columban Lay Missionary to Japan, is the most authoritative that can be had, I think.

Father Vale sent each one of us a copy of Father O'Sullivan's letter to the Superior General. We here in Wakayama and elsewhere in Japan are all quite satisfied with what Father O'Sullivan wrote to the Superior General concerning your status as a Columban Lay Missionary. Three times in his brief letter he deliberately wrote of you as a Columban Lay Missionary. When I rang Father Youngkamp recently about Father Sullivan's letter, he was in total agreement with it and said that he always regarded you as a Columban Lay Missionary.

Father Healy's explanation to Father Kambayashi is at odds with Father Youngkamp's memory of the events and doesn't fit the facts as they were known back then three years ago. There is a certain amount of fantasy on Father Healy's part in his report to Father Kambayashi, I feel.

With his letter, Father Griffin also enclosed a copy of the Japanese Regional Newsletter of July 1996. The newsletter contained Father Griffin's transcription of my farewell speech (see chapter 7) and the following article:

A Farewell to Masako and Carl by Donal Griffin

Three years have elapsed since they came among us here in Wakayama. Their arrival was unobtrusive and went almost without notice then. But in time both Masako and Carl Streling made a contribution to the Church in Wakayama, which in retrospect can be seen, as extraordinary and quite remarkable. Only with the passage of time will a proper evaluation be able to be made of their presence as Columban Lay Missionaries—not only in the parish of Kainan where they worked, but in the district of Wakayama as a whole.

Masako continues to amaze when one considers that as a female pastor she was very much a pioneer: she invades with aplomb the hitherto male bastion of the priests—their sitting room, their conference room. She not only strove courageously to defend her corner against all-comers, but also quite often vanquished her male colleagues in stimulating debates. No female missionary, even a religious, has ever before been in the position or command in a parish in Wakayama—or as far as I know, in Japan as a whole—until Masako arrived. (This is not to underrate the roles played by ladies as catechists and parish officers—those are different matters.)

Full justice cannot adequately be done here to the contribution that Masako made to the people and the parish of Kainan during her all-to-brief sojourns there. But, judging from the warm, harmonious atmosphere that can be felt there now, she has worked

wonders to develop Kainan Parish into a kinder, friendlier com-
munity than it had been for some time. The obvious affection that
she is regarded with by her own sex, especially in Kainan, points
up the fact that leadership in the Church as a whole has been too
long the prerogative of the male. The advent of Masako and her
experience as a (lay) pastor had made it clear that henceforth in
guiding the Church a greater contribution by females of the species
is called for—not only in Wakayama, but everywhere else as well.

While I praise Masako I cannot forget what Carl, too, has
done for the Church in Kainan. His contribution in fact is more
easily described if for no other reason than that it is more visible.
The tiny church building in Kainan never had much going for it.
Cramped and crammed with ponderous pews, it never did much
to elevate one's spirits to the supernatural. Carl did something,
which no one had thought of doing before; he stripped the pews
of their wretched-looking coatings of paint to reveal the natural
wood. Then he lightly varnished in such a way as to enhance the
beauty of the timber. As a result there is now lightness and indeed
airiness about the church, which has made it quite attractive. He
also spent a lot of time repairing the old presbytery. It was gloomy
and cluttered with wires running all over. Carl did a fine job in
renovating the whole house, hiding electrical wires, sanding down
the floors and painting all the rooms. It is now a bright, clean-
looking place, which the children of the parish love to use for
Sunday school.

We, Columbans of Wakayama, and the Catholic community of
Kainan Parish owe both Masako and Carl a tremendous debt of
gratitude. We shall remember them with kindness for many a long
year to come. Thank you Masako! Thank you Carl!

We shall miss you!

[gratitude]

I cried when we first received the letter and the article by Father Donal Griffin. It made us feel so good, like we were touched by an angel. Father Griffin was the only Columban priest who publicly defended our cause and praised our work.

MY RESIGNATION LETTER

After six years of discernment following our return to America, I decided to write a resignation letter to Father John Burger, Regional Director of the US Region. The date was April 11, 2002.

In it I expressed the reasons for my resignation, but I did not receive any response from Father Burger, so I accepted *no response* as his answer.

Chapter Eleven:
Road to Forgiveness

SECOND TRIALS: EIGHT SURGERIES INCLUDING COLON CANCER

"Yet I am always with you; you take hold of my right hand." (Psalm 73:23).

As a child I held on tightly to my brother's hand when we boarded a train in Taiwan to pay our annual visit to my grandfather in Yaeyama. I must have been seven years old and my brother nine. I held on tightly to my father's hand when I was discharged from a hospital after recovering from acute pneumonia. Finally, I held tightly to my husband's hand for fear of falling down each of the eight times I was discharged from the hospital between 2003 and 2007.

During those years I endured four back surgeries. The surgeries included two lower back and two neck spinal fusions, (front and back). I also endured two rotator cuff repairs, one hysterectomy, and colon cancer.

The figures of my brother, my father, and my husband moved thru my mind like a dream. I will carry them with me to the end of my life. I realize now that, like my father and later my husband, Jesus was also holding on tightly to my hand at every crucial moment of my life so that I wouldn't fall. Holding on tightly to one another is part of Jesus' recurring message in

Scripture. Oh, my Lord, please let the real wisdom of the child not be lost. Let trustfulness, and a willingness to be led, taught, and raised by You to true maturity according to your plan (rather than mine) be fulfilled.

How did I get through those difficult years? I was able to live because of the sacrament I received each time. At the suggestion of our Pastor, Father Michael Ratajczak, I received the sacrament of the *Anointing of the Sick*, when I suffered early stage four colon cancer. The experience of a five-time recipient of the sacrament of the *Anointing of the Sick* is indescribable. Like any other experience with God, it is difficult to find adequate words to describe, except to say God's grace in those moments gave me calmness, peace, and freedom from anxiety every time I was taken into the surgery. When I look back, I realize the sacrament I received was the beginning of my recovery.

The sacrament of the *Anointing of the Sick* is one of the seven sacraments, which Catholics can receive as one of the gifts of the Holy Spirit.

I also want to share my experience meeting Jesus. I met Him personally after they brought me to my room following the first surgery. He showed me His agonized and lifeless face crowned with thorns. When He let me see His face in agony, I understood what His love meant. I finally understood the Crucifixion is ultimate love. I no longer asked, *"What have I done that was so bad that God let Jesus die on the Tree?"* In those moments of my complete suffering, I finally understood.

I now know what His love feels like, and as I write these words, I cannot stop crying for my ignorance of old. He was there with me all the while in my times of need: *"This is my blood of the covenant, which will be shed on behalf of many for the forgiveness of sins"* (Matthew 26:28). Some might say that I was hallucinating or still under anesthesia. Whatever state I may have been in, I saw Him. I was healed of each sickness. I endured seven other surgeries and chemotherapies. I was given an extended life. How can I not proclaim to Him that He is my friend, my healer, and my life?

I don't know why I was healed. I know that I was one of many before me who have been healed. When I surrendered to Him, every one of my eight sicknesses was healed. Perhaps, it was a sign for all of us to see as an act of His divine mercy. Perhaps, it was a sign for us to see that His healings are signs of His love.

Many points were offered for me to ponder. My remission was no guarantee that I would be forever free from cancer. The cancer could come back. Perhaps the healing process the next time could be the process of entering into His kingdom, a kingdom where there would be no sickness, no death. It would be the final healing.

Freedom from anxiety began with the gift of the Holy Spirit in the sacrament of the *Anointing of the Sick*. I remember at that time I lost all of my hair on my head. It was just after the second chemotherapy. I screamed when I scrubbed my hair with all my energy as it all fell out. It was the most eerie feeling to see my entire head of hair in my hands and on the floor of the shower room, leaving me completely bald. That scene reminded me of a ghost story I had seen in a movie as a child. Losing my entire head of hair did not bother me as a woman. I did not even want to wear a wig. Instead, I learned to cover my bald head with a turban until my hair grew back. As it grew back, I decided to go natural. No more permanent, no more color, just a short haircut. I felt free. I was freed from a woman's vanity of being fashionable.

It was a wakeup call for me again to get my act together. I could no longer be a Sunday-only-Catholic, thinking I had done my share of serving since my Baptism. Indeed, I had served the Church, including the three years as a lay missionary in Japan.

However, it was again a call reminding me of the lifetime commitment I made at my Baptism to be His disciple and to get involved with the faith community using my whole heart. It was my payback time again. *"How can I repay the Lord for all the good done for me?" (Psalm 116:12).* It was time to give back all that I had been given, including this new life, my talents, my knowledge lived and learned, and my own enthusiasm and weaknesses. I used my talents to improve not only my own life, but also the lives of others.

Surviving cancer was also a sign for me to make sure I lived this new gift of life fully. I wanted to live this new life with gratitude and humility, not with arrogance. In the scripture passages after the healing stories, Jesus tells us that self-righteousness and human pride can lead one to a bigger sin seven times worse than the first. I took note of this wisdom as I now moved forward with vigor for a new life.

Jesus also said, "Your faith healed you." I hung onto His word of trust in me so very tightly in my heart. Even my little bit of faith was enough for Him to heal me.

Our prayers might not always be granted as we petition, according to St. Paul. His intense prayers were rejected when he begged the Lord for the thorn in Paul's flesh to leave him. Three times the Lord rejected his requests. Instead, the Lord said to him, "My grace I gave is sufficient for you, for power is made perfect in your weakness." When I was sick, I prayed intensely that our Lord would take me home because I had enough. I did not want my husband to suffer any more. Taking care of me for five years was enough for him, too. So again, I learned from St. Paul's teaching to trust God's presence as power in my life when I was powerless. Put simply, what I learned during this period of my life was precisely what cradle Catholics were saying to me, that was to offer my life up to God.

Offer yourself up to God. Offer everything—what you are, pride, self-dignity—and let God help you. I didn't have enough energy left within me to even stand up on my own after the eighth chemotherapy. My husband helped me wash my naked body in the shower. I did not have any strength to cover my nakedness. I lost everything, including all my dignity that had held me up so far. I even lost most of my bodily hair, including my eyebrows and eyelashes. Stripped of everything, I was totally dependent on Carl. Such a situation forced me to realize that what I received from Carl was a pure gift from God, not because I deserved it, but because God is mercy and God is compassion.

The only thing I could do on my own was hold my two hands together in prayer. My soul prayed for me. In my human weakness, the power of Christ came into my life as power many times over. The power of Jesus held Carl and me up during this period of our lives. We never feared or lost hope. We lived each day in His care.

Which brings me again to the days in Kainan and what we accomplished there with our limited knowledge and experiences. Were the accomplishments in Kainan our accomplishments? Absolutely not. It was Jesus who granted us the power to complete our mission by giving us the collaboration of the community of the Kainan Catholic Church.

I also learned of the power of Jesus through our weakness, in our ups and downs of everyday life. He came into our lives to demonstrate the all-encompassing nature of God's love for us.

I am reminded that the fighting spirit of my descendants, the samurai, was His gift. It was a call for a courageous stance during difficult times. I am also reminded that just as the Creator breathed life into the nostrils of the first human creature, making him a living being, so I breathe deep of Jesus' breath of life into me, empowering me to live this gift of a new and extended life.   Until He calls me by name someday, which I hope He will. Until He holds up His wounded hands to me; until He welcomes me back to our final home, the Kingdom of God, where there is no death, pain, loneliness, or tears; until I am reunited with my paternal grandparents, my maternal grandmother, my parents, my brother and my two pets, Hics and Cleo, and all my friends of the past and present; until then, I will live with His peace, the same peace He left with us as He departed from us.

Chapter Twelve:
Repentance, Forgiveness, & Reconciliation

RATIONALE — Truth

In her book, *Forgiveness and Other Acts of Love,* psychotherapist and author Stephanie Dowrick suggests:

"Forgiveness deeply offends the rational mind. When someone has hurt us, wounded us, abused us; when someone has stolen peace of mind or safety from us; when someone has harmed or taken the life of someone we love; or when someone has simply misunderstood or offended us, there is no reason why we should let that offence go. No reason why we should try to understand it. No reason why we should hope for enlightenment for that person. No reason why, from our own pain and darkness, we should summon compassion and insight for that person as well as for ourselves.

To grope our way towards forgiveness, we may need momentarily to circumvent the rational mind, or transcend it. Yet the rational mind is the known ground that we share. There is no easy way to talk of circumventing or transcending it. And there is certainly no easy way to put forgiveness into practice."[47]

---

47   Stephanie Dowrick, "Forgiveness & Other Acts of Love," p.291

Frankly, there is no easy way to talk about forgiveness. All I know is that I feel it in my body, though my rational mind cannot recognize forgiveness. The experience is subtle—like something has left me. I can now talk about it without anger. I may even be feeling sorrow or regret as to why I need to expose the hurtful experience.

The fact is, what passed between (or failed to pass between) myself and the Columban Fathers wounded me on a fundamental level. Whether malicious, intentional or not, it crippled my peace of mind and robbed me of my equilibrium for years after the fact, and there are simply no logical or rational arguments to act as a balm for those kinds of wounds. In the years after my return, those wounds festered and, I believe, made me physically ill.

By sharing the truth of what happened, in as logical and factual way as possible, I am, I hope, letting the pain go. I am facing the past and recognizing it for what it was. I am trying to be as honest with myself as I can be, for the telling of truth is like cleaning a wound. Only once a wound is cleaned can the healing begin. God heals us and liberates us from all ills if we allow Him to. By cleaning my wounds fully I am opening them up to God.

Carl and I withdrew from involvement with the Columban Fathers as of April 12, 2002. I no longer felt energized by their presence. Instead, every time I was among them, I felt like an abused wife who cannot leave her abuser. Likewise we felt as though the Columban Fathers did not welcome us anymore. They were trying their best to avoid us. It was an unhealthy relationship, which Carl and I finally had to step away from.

I was, for a very long time, afraid to come forward with the truth about how we were treated, afraid of the reaction it might provoke, afraid that it might lead to rejection and/or isolation. In short, I was afraid of being belittled again.

How often did I struggle within myself during my lifetime with that kind of thought? *If I tell you how I really feel, you might not like me anymore.* I am supposed to be a Christian who is able to carry my own cross all the way to Calvary and forgive all the people who persecuted and humiliated me. I am ashamed to admit that I could not. I am merely a finite being with flesh and blood. It was easier for me to be quiet about the whole thing and hope it might go away. The self-denial did not go away, even after I reasoned to myself and said publicly that I had gained more than I suffered. People might tell me that, as a Christian, I should not seek revenge, but instead turn my other cheek to be struck.

But what I seek is not revenge. Vengeance we are told is God's prerogative and God's alone. I don't wish the Columbans any harm. I am asking that they simply accept their responsibility to live up to the call of the priesthood.

In his address to the Irish people, Pope Benedict XVI, on behalf of the Church, finally apologized to the victims of sexual abuse by stating, "Only decisive action carried out with complete honesty and transparency will restore the respect and good will of the Irish people toward the Church." That was in his forty-six hundred word letter to Irish Catholics dated on March 20, 2010.

Decisive action, that is both honest and transparent. I would certainly accept that from the Columban Fathers. With that I would be able to forgive and even reconcile with them to some degree. It would go a long way to healing my wounds and restoring my wounded heart. Thus am I compelled by the Spirit to write, no matter what the outcome might be? To face this truth and act on it takes all my being and courage. But I am a descendent of the Satsuma samurai. I will continue to act with honor. I will continue to perform my duty to God.

On June 27, 2010, during Sunday mass, I was reminded when I heard the Gospel reading of Jesus: *"When the days for his being taken up were fulfilled, he resolutely determined to journey to Jerusalem" (Luke 9:51).* His human freedom led Him to His death. But death also led Him to His resurrection.

I have hope in Jesus, in His resurrection. Thus, I am resolutely determined to keep writing.

How do we overcome the suffering caused by another whether through violence, betrayal, or abuse? How do we reconcile and forgive? These are questions I have been struggling with for over fifteen years, Questions for which there are no easy answers. I think of Anne Rice, one of my favorite novelists. As I was writing this memoir, she announced that she had decided to quit being a Christian. In regard to her decision, she explained: "It is simply impossible for me to belong to this quarrelsome, hostile, disputatious, and deservedly infamous group—quitting being a Christian does not mean that I have lost faith in Christ. My faith in Christ is central to my life."

I felt sad to read Rice's statements. Why could she not stay with us and help make changes instead of quitting? Nevertheless, I agree with some of what she said. In fact, I myself have issues with the hierarchy of the church, which I am addressing. Rice reminds me of myself in many ways because of the long spiritual journey she took from a life of atheism to the life of a Roman Catholic Christian.

According to Stephanie Dowrick, a practicing psychotherapist in Sydney, Australia, and currently chair of the Women's Press, in London, "[she] has absolutely no interest in resurrecting the idea of sin. She is actually quite uncomfortable linking it to this discussion about forgiveness. But [she said] it is difficult not to think about sin when what she is doing here is considering the kind of action that put victims of those actions into a terrible dilemma about whether or not they can forgive. This is not a trivial matter. If your life has been mauled and torn apart by another human being, and then you are mauling and tearing apart your own conscience about whether or how you should forgive that human being, this is absolutely not a trivial matter."[48]

I was torn between the Christian ethics that dictated for me to forgive the Columbans while my God given self-dignity was fighting against it. Moreover, whenever I thought about Christian forgiveness that I could not adhere to, I suffered my self-contempt. How could I forgive those in the Society of St. Columban whom I felt betrayed and abandoned me; and, who caused me so much suffering as a result? *I am a victim*, I reasoned, *how can I forgive them? They should ask for my forgiveness*. I was paralyzed.

Instead of affirming my wounded self and my incapacity to rise up to a transforming state of forgiving and forgetting the hurt, I further affirmed my worthlessness for not being holy enough to be able to forgive and forget. Christians should be able to forgive and forget.

Was I naïve to expect that priests and men of the cloth could be free from human failings? Free from the petty jealousies, cruelties, and politics of life—and entirely given over to the words and deeds of Christ? Yes, I was probably being naïve. But as my husband Carl said when we started our relationship with the Church, "if we can't trust a priest, who can we trust?" Trust and doing the right thing by God and for the people is what priests historically, supposedly embody. Should not priests and men of the cloth live up to the platitudes they preach? If the Church and its priests pledge themselves as direct links to God, should they not also be held accountable in their actions as links to the divine? If not, then hypocrisy becomes their measuring stick. Hypocrisy we have seen thru the ages, from acts of financial corruption, governmental influence, sexual abuse, neglect, even murder at the hands of these men, including bishops, cardinals and even various popes throughout history. Sadly, their own

48   Stephanie Dorwick, "Forgiveness & Other Acts of Love," p.311

actions beg to question the entire structure, meaning and legitimacy of the Church.

In his book, *Brokenness & Blessing Towards A Biblical Spirituality*, Frances M. Young writes that Augustine thinks this struggle and the wrestling that I was dealing with, "is [your effort] to hold onto Christ, which means the struggle to love one's enemy. For if you love your enemy, you do, indeed, hold on to Christ."[49]

In my struggle to hold onto Christ, I found a healing book recommended by my friend and mentor, Kathleen Bell, *Things Hidden: Scripture as Spirituality* by Richard Rohr. Rohr says, "Jesus is not too interested in moral purity because he knows that any preoccupation with repressing the shadow does not lead us into personal transformation, empathy, compassion or patience, but invariably into one of two certain paths: denial or disguise, repression or hypocrisy."[50]

Indeed, to put all our brokenness of the human condition under this rigid umbrella and talk about *sin* is missing a mark. Love is Christ's Law. He came to heal this broken world. He broke off from the rigidity of Judaism. A rigidity which prevented them from reaching out to others and from loving. We have reduced ourselves to the Pharisaic narrowness that Jesus warned against.

If Catholicism is about one sort of legalism or another, suggesting that certain actions are wrong because they are forbidden by law and a juridical definition of law that is not about reaching out to the world. If Catholicism is about not reaching out to the issues of pro-choice, homosexuals, contraception, divorce and remarriage; and, if we are not loving one another like Jesus did, how are we going to reconcile all these groups of

---

49   Frances M. Young, "Brokeness & Blessing," p. 45

50   Richard Rohr, "Things Hidden Scripture as Spirituality" p. 77

Christ's people who are excluded from the Eucharist? How can we bring them into the Church to be restored in the Eucharist? How are we going to help people heal?

My spiritual directors, teachers, and the Society of St. Columban Fathers are Roman Catholic priests. I, and many people around the world thought they who bore the name "Roman Catholic priest" could walk on water and were holy men. I did not have room in my heart to believe that they could fail. To say that they are only *human*—like you and I—does not sit quite right with my sense of justice. It rings of hypocrisy.

As a descendant of the samurai, somehow I thought priests and men of the cloth should be held more accountable for what they do. Should they not do more than the average poor, simple folks like Carl and I? Should they not practice the morality they preach? Should they not be held to a higher standard?

Truth is, they do bad things as we do, and they also do good things as we do. Priests are human beings, and they make mistakes. However, a priest's duty is to be an example for the public. A priest is supposed to be our conduit to God, our moral compass, someone we trust. We bare our souls to them, trust them with our children, our families. They need to be held to a higher standard.

I often thought about leaving the Church after the painful experience with the leaders of the Society of Columban Fathers and my inability to forgive them. But I could not leave my beloved community despite these unsettling ideas. Where would I go? There is no perfect society in this world we live in today. Even Jesus recruited imperfect men. These unsettling ideas were not enough for me to leave, but they were enough to make me feel unfulfilled until I found my original quest for the mystery of the cross. "No other world religion has the revelation of the Cross."[51]

---

51   Richard Rohr, "Things Hidden Scripture as Spirituality," p.204

My Jesuit friends said to me again and again, "If you leave, you would be outside of Church and unable, then, to help it to change."

I prayed for the conversion of my heart because I noticed myself no longer feeling passion in everything I did. I became like a robot moving and doing what I was told to do mechanically, especially in my confessions of sin. I thought, *"How can I forgive them?"* I reflected on my shameful behavior in the confession of sins as the minimum requisite for receiving absolution. The sacrament became a formality as a practicing Catholic on my part, leaving me with a large void in my heart.

I deeply felt the need for the sacrament of *Reconciliation*. Yet I could not help myself from wondering how did Jesus help sinners not to sin—to live responsibly. To these huge, complicated mandates, the Church has revised the sacrament of *Confession* to what is now known as the sacrament of *Reconciliation* because it confers on the sinner the love of God who reconciles. With this change, I wonder if the lines of people at the confessionals are any different.

How does one who is spiritually aware, like myself, exercise one's responsibility and duty as taught by the Church, and still manage to be happy in the 21st century?

In essence, sin creates a radical inability in the individual. Sin creates the inability to love God above all things. The all too human condition of sin disables us, distances us from love and laughter and the fullness of who we really are. We must arrive at an understanding of sin, not primarily as an action we do, but as a condition of the self we are. Christians today, need reconciliation no less than those who went before us, and doing so is not any easier. In short, we are broken; therefore, we are called for correction.

For me, and I am sure for many, it is "necessary to discover and embrace a redeeming narrative. [And] not let the memory [of the past] corrode our sense of safety and self but rather be turned into a force that gives us strength to withstand it."[52]

One way to move toward redemption, for me, is remembering without holding a grudge or yearning for revenge, as in the samurai tradition of my grandfather. Rather it is recalling an honest and candid account of the mercy of God who aroused me to hold onto the memory of the hurt I suffered during our missionary works at the vineyard of Kainan. The memory of hurt is an important acknowledgment before forgiveness, repentance, and reconciliation can begin, because the scars we receive from hurt, humiliation, and betrayal become part of us. These scars will not be erased from our body and memory. The scars of our hurts are our witness that we loved God simultaneously as we witnessed God's love.

Why the memory of suffering? Love is Christ's law. For me it is focused on love of God and love of neighbor and my struggles in the vineyard of Kainan to love those who hurt me as commanded by Christ. It was very difficult for me to follow His Law of Love. I betrayed this vision of Christ's law many times, particularly over the last fifteen years. However, Christ came to heal the broken world. He came to heal my life when I was tormented by inner demons like self-pity. When I was broken and lame I found His blessedness.

Those wounds He wore on His body help us remember His mercy, His love and the death he suffered. They are part of His identity even in heaven. My wounds, too, that I receive are part of my identity today, and I will carry them forever into eternity as proof that I loved the Kainan Catholic Church as I loved Jesus.

How do we forgive those who hurt us?

One might consider the Gospel's injunction to forgive one's enemies, *who have hurt us "not seven times . . . but seventy-seven*

---

52   Robert J. Schreiter, CPPS, "Reconciliation Mission & Ministry in Changing Social Order," p.36

times" (Matthew 18:22), as an example of how repentance and forgiveness, based on a change of heart ultimately frees the victim from the values of the oppressor and makes the victim capable of establishing a new kind of relationship with the oppressor. The victim is asked to show forbearance towards the perpetrator, not because the perpetrator is innocent, but to 'make something new' through forgiveness as a sign of the kingdom come into the world."[53] But it is not humanly possible. Only with Christ is everything possible.

EVERYTHING IS POSSIBLE WITH CHRIST

> *"They brought the boy to him. And when he saw him, the spirit immediately threw the boy into convulsions. As he fell to the ground, he began to roll around and foam at the mouth. Then Jesus questioned his father, "How long has this been happening to him?" He replied, "Since childhood. It has often thrown him into fire and into water to kill him. But if you can do anything, have compassion on us and help us." Jesus said to him, "If you can! Everything is possible to one who has faith" (Mark 9:20-23).*

Though it is based on my own shallow understanding, I also came to a conclusion reached by the German Jesuit Theologian Karl Rahner, namely that everything is possible with Christ—even for me.

I could not even articulate what was really hurting me then.

Oh, the days and months when I cried out in my silence, and also loudly in the presence of God, to take this pain and help me be a good Christian so I could forgive those priests who hurt Carl and me! Crying out was my appeal to God exclaiming what I felt reached beyond my ability to cope.

---

53   Joseph Favazza, "Reconciliation: On the Border Between Theological and Political Pra," p.9

I thought, *"How can I rebuild my trust again in the Church with this state of mind? Am I in the right group? I don't want to wait to reach another twenty-year marker again to decide whether I am in the right group or not, the Roman Catholic Church. How do I get beyond the present mistrust?"* In my search for truth, I fell into a neurotic state of mind.

Then one day, during my morning walk, from nowhere I felt a soft breeze touching my face, urging me to take out my pen and paper and continue writing. Writing allowed me to reflect on my life as a child, as an adult, as a lay leader of the Kainan Catholic Church, and simultaneously about God's movement in the various stages of my life. I felt energy and movement in my heart. It was *Ki*, the Japanese would say—telling me that I can do it again. Telling me that I am fully human with the capacity to rise up and affirm my own human worth to the world once more.

For Nouwen, this movement is found in his writing. "Not only my own unique way of being in the world, but also my ability to give words to it, I experienced a deep spiritual satisfaction. I come in touch with the Spirit of God within me and experience how I am led to new places."[54] I decided to finish this difficult chapter instead of succumbing to the negative feelings whispering to me to give it up.

Gradually I realized the necessity of reflecting on the Big Story—Scripture—which I have read and studied. It became the only book I wanted to read and rely on. It is full of human histories of hurt, humiliation, and all kinds of human sins of shame and guilt, of feeling and wanting to revenge, and wanting to destroy one's self.

I could not forgive for fifteen years, but in the Old Testament narratives, I found some sense of spiritual survival. I was able

---

54   Edited by Robert Durback "Seeds of Hope — A Henri Nouwen Reader," p.79

to think of forgiveness and reconciliation. During the writing of this section I felt the profound experience of Jesus' love. I decided to meditate on the Crucifixion narrative, especially the following passages:

"When they came to the place called the Skull, they crucified him and the criminals there, one on his right, the other on his left. Then Jesus said, "Father, forgive them, they know not what they do" (Luke 23:33-34).

Who are *they*?

Instinctively I knew that these passages provided a key to lead me out of darkness to light. According to the Scriptural passage, Jesus prayed to his Father to forgive them, the killers, *for they know not what they do*. He prayed for forgiveness of their sins because of their ignorance of Him.

The highest court and supreme council members composed of the elders, the high priests and scribes known as the Sanhedrin in Jerusalem, knew what they were doing according to the law. They were the religious authority and knew the law. They found Jesus guilty for blasphemy and sentenced Him to death. Accordingly, they let the Roman authority crucify Him with two other sinners. They thought of Him as a sinner, a blasphemer, but they did not know He was the Messiah, equal to God.

They know not what they do—What did Jesus mean when he said that? I found the key words to understand Jesus' saying in St. Paul's Letter to Timothy when St. Paul explains who he once was.

"I am grateful to him who has strengthened me, Christ Jesus our Lord, because he considered me trustworthy in appointing me to the ministry. I was once a blasphemer and a persecutor and an arrogant man, but I have been mercifully treated because I acted out of ignorance in my unbelief" (1 Timothy 1:12-13).

Unbelief is ignorance of who Jesus is — the Truth. If they had known who Jesus was, they could not have hung Him on the tree.

Knowledge in all these passages is about belief in Jesus. It is about a belief that He is God's only Son, our Lord our God and the Savior of the world. Therefore, Jesus calls us his friend, and brothers and sisters, and gathers us, especially those who are lost, like me, into his fold. I was struggling against an endless feeling of guilt and shame. Guilt and shame caused by the inaction of priests, and other ministers of the Church. I needed to be freed. I was in a state of unhappiness.

The Church includes not only hierarchy and ordained priests, but also laity. Yet we are all struggling to get Jesus' teachings right, even two thousand years later, we are struggling to treat each other as Jesus' brothers and sisters:

"I give you a new commandment: love one another.
As I have loved you, so you also should love one another"
(John 13:34).

For me, to love your neighbor as yourself is a very difficult mandate to follow. This mandate of love includes my difficult siblings and people who treated us as trash and enemies. The first ingredient needed to love your neighbors requires a certain sacrifice on your part. For example, to love my husband, my nearest neighbor, at times requires giving up a piece of myself. There is no true love without sacrifice, especially in human love. Although we have been married for over fifty-eight years, I did not always agree with what Carl thought and did. I am sure he felt the same way about me. We are two separate beings, man and woman, raised in two different households with two different sets of ideals and values. Yet I am mandated to follow these commandments when I made the decision to believe in Jesus Christ and to follow Him. But I often neglect to love myself. To put myself in equal footing with my neighbor is very difficult. I was raised to put myself last.

For me, truly, it is not easy to be a Christian—especially a Catholic. Even in the recent past, we Catholics, especially priests, have shown the world poor examples in the way we have lived, which is far from the way Jesus lived and died for us. Do we have legitimate reason to be forgiven our faults for being human? No, but we can understand why we do what we hate:

"What I do, I do not understand. For I do not do what I want, but I do what I hate. So now it is no longer I who do it, but sin that dwells in me. For I know that good does not dwell in me, that is, in my flesh. The willing is ready at hand, but doing the good is not. For I do not do the good I want, but I do the evil I do not want. Now if I do what I do not want, it is no longer I who do it, but the sin that dwells in me. So, then, I discover the principle that when I want to do right, evil is at hand. For I take delight in the law of God, in my inner self, but I see in my members another principle at war with the law of my mind, taking me captive to the law of sin that dwells in my members. Miserable one that I am!" (Romans 7:15, 17-24).

Citing all these texts is not enough for me to convince myself. Nor is completing this chapter with as much clarity and exactness as I can muster enough for me to convince myself. For I too, must confess that I do not have true knowledge of Jesus, the Truth.

One day in the year 2010, many years after I wrote the letter to Fr. John Burger, I received a letter from Father Arturo Aguilar, Superior, US Region of the Society of St. Columbans.

The letterhead read: *Columban Fathers Legacy Society.* The contents of the letter states:

"Simply, our recognition of your important contribution to our missionary efforts and an expression, not just in words, of our gratitude to you..."—For a fleeting moment, I thought, *We*

are finally accepted as the First Lay Missionary in Japan!" The letter continued...*"we are pleased to announce the formation of the Columban Fathers Legacy Society."* I was puzzled because we had no connection with the Columbans since I wrote the last letter to Father John Burger. In the letter I asked the Columbans to cease all correspondence and refrain from sending us any information regarding the Columbans.

So I decided to speak with Father Reynolds, a Columban Father and a professor of New Testament Study at Loyola University Chicago, to find out the meaning of the letter. That was in May of 2010. Among the many things we spoke of in our conversation, I mentioned to him that I was writing a memoir that included our Kainan experience with the Columban Fathers. He said to me affirmatively and assuredly to keep writing and not to give up. He then offered to send me two books of Robert J. Schreiter: *Reconciliation, Mission & Ministry in a Changing Social Order* and *The Ministry of Reconciliation: Spirituality & Strategies*. I was surprised that the titles of these two books both dealt with reconciliation. Fr. Reynolds must have guessed that part of my writing was dealing with forgiveness and reconciliation. I am grateful he guessed it right.

Schreiter's books confirmed that my doubts and hopes were real. His writings explained why it took almost fourteen years to even think about forgiving.

In addition, Schreiter points out many things I struggled with especially: "They (perpetrators) want the victims of violence to let bygones be bygones and exercise a Christian forgiveness." Unfortunately, he said that this suggestion sometimes comes from Catholic priests. I thought if I claimed myself a good Catholic, I should be able to forgive and forget, but I could not. The more I failed to forgive them in my heart, the more self-contemptuous I became.

That was my struggle. Schreiter confirmed my struggle and explained why I was experiencing such intense internal conflict.

According to Schreiter, "While reconciliation as a 'hasty peace' bears a superficial resemblance to Christian reconciliation, it is actually quite far from it. By calling on those who have suffered to forget or overlook their suffering, the would-be reconcilers are, in fact, continuing the oppressive situation by saying, in effect, that the experiences of those who suffered are not important."[55] No wonder it took almost fourteen years to get to a point where I might begin to forgive. Even then, a couple of events had to happen for me to put pen to paper and start writing down what hurt me. Favazza calls it *"truth-telling"*.[56] Truth-telling was not by my initiative, but it was by God's initiative. I started to move closer to my own truth and reconciliation. "Reconciliation involves," Schreiter says, "a fundamental repair to human lives of those who have suffered. That repair takes time."[57]

Why so much time? The hurt and damage was so real to me.

How could I reconcile with people who hurt me so much? I could not. Again, it is God who reconciles us to God's self. Reconciliation is not a human work. Schreiter begins by looking at the Bible for defining reconciliation. He looks toward two of St. Paul's authentic writings that appear in Romans and the Second Letters to Corinthians. Then I remembered St. Paul's writings on reconciliation.

"And all this is from God, who has reconciled us to himself through Christ and given us the ministry of reconciliation, namely,

---

55   Robert J. Schreiter, CPPS., "Reconciliation Mision & Ministry in Changing Social Order," p.19

56   Joseph Favazza, "Reconciliation: On the Border Between Theological and Political Pra," p.2

57   Robert J. Schreiter, CPPS., "Reconciliation Mission & Ministry in Changing Social Order," p.21

God was reconciling the world to himself in Christ, not counting their trespasses against them and entrusting to us the message of reconciliation" (2 Corinthians 5:18-19).

Schreiter stresses that, "The reconciliation that Christians have to offer in overcoming the enmity created by suffering is not something they find in themselves, but something they recognize as coming from God. Thus the question is not how can I bring myself, as victim, to forgive those who have insulted me and humiliated me so deeply. It is rather, how can I discover the mercy of God welling up in my own life and where does that lead me?

Reconciliation, then, is not a process that we initiate or achieve. We discover it already active in God, through Christ."[58]

Who or where does a call to genuine reconciliation originate? "Somewhat paradoxically," Schreiter says, "It is more likely to come from those who have suffered most in the situation. The reason for this, quite simply, is that we cannot forgive ourselves for the wrongdoing of our past. Those whom we have injured must do that. Not to realize this is to confuse reconciliation with repentance. Repentance can originate from the side of those who have perpetrated violence, but reconciliation and forgiveness must come from the side of those who have suffered violence." [59] How true that is, I thought. I was drawing strength from experiencing the mercy and love of God who walked with me all of my life. God was who nudged me all those years to call for forgiveness and reconciliation.

With this awareness and knowledge of His love, came the courage once again to reach out in trust, to ask Him for His forgiveness for not recognizing Him; and, to ask for His reconciling grace, so that I could become the agent of reconciliation.

---

58   Ibid, p.43

59   Ibid, p.21

In a few words, psychologist Dowrick also explains that waiting is a crucial stage in forgiveness. "It may also be that this settling allows the issue of forgiveness to move from the head to the heart, which is where it belongs."[60]

Among the many writers, theologians and philosophers I've studied, Linda Barker-Revell also has similar things to say about forgiveness: "Forgiveness is a state of grace. It can't be applied as a concept. Compassion can rise up, but forgiveness is God-given, spirit-given. It is an ineffable feeling."[61] How true that is! Forgiveness is an act of love, God-given, spirit-given. It is indeed an ineffable feeling.

Though we do not always recognize His hand at work, I saw and recognized His hand as clearly as I could see my own. It was outstretched to help me forgive "an unnatural act," slowly but surely. Indeed, everything is possible with Christ.

Philip Yancey writes:

From the Gospels' accounts, it seems forgiveness was not easy for God, either.

"If it is possible, may this cup be taken from me," Jesus prayed, contemplating the cost. The sweat rolled off him like drops of blood. There was no other way. Finally, in one of his last statements before dying, he said, "Forgive them" — all of them, the Roman soldiers, the religious leaders, his disciples who had fled in darkness, you, me — "forgive them, for they do not know what they are doing." Only by becoming a human being could the Son of God truly say, "They do not know what they are doing." Having lived among us, he now understood. [62]

---

60   Stephanie Dowrick, "Forgiveness & Other Acts of Love," p.300

61   Ibid, p.300

62   Philip Yancey, "What so Amazing about Grace?" p.107

Chapter Thirteen:
One Thing We Sought

"Experience of Self, experience of God"

What we thought we sought and wanted originally, and what we actually received at the end of our journey was not the same. It took me almost fifteen years to trek to the mountain where I experienced God. It was re-discovery of self and affirmation of my own strength, giftedness and responsibility. The Kainan experience was not all about restoration of our status. That was only part of it.

I was so obsessed with one thing, that I missed the mark—the focus. The focus should have been on Jesus, not on myself. My experience at Kainan was to help me understand and interpret my life's meaning. Carl and I *were* Columban Lay Missionaries. With this affirmation in my heart, I felt assured that the real reasons I sought to be reinstated in the Columban Directory were wrong, for that status belonged to us regardless.

That being said, why have I been feeling the struggle for so many years inside of me? I have explicitly and implicitly filled many pages in this memoir with *why* I should and could not forgive them. The Columban Fathers never even acknowledged their misdeeds, much less acknowledged our rightful status, I thought.

I found an answer in Barbara E. Reid's article entitled "Out of Sheer Silence" in the August 2011 issue of *America Magazine*. I was reflecting on a Sunday Reading.

"Whoever wishes to come after me must deny himself, take up his cross, and follow me" (Matthew 16:24).

"True to today's Gospel," Reid says, "Jesus Himself increasingly came to understand what lay ahead for Him from His own denial of self in finding His true life." She asks, "How do you find yourself?" I know one way to find myself was to stand up as I did at age seven, pointing at myself—*"Banu!," I exclaimed. (It is I!)* Even at that age I did not let anyone wipe their feet on me any more. Why would I now? I felt I knew myself more at that tender young age, than I did when trying to process what happened to me by the misdeeds of the Columban Fathers as an adult.

God was showing me the way to understand why my journey took so long. How else was I able to fill the pages of this memoir? But my heart was not ready to accept such an awesome gift of grace through what I was writing—both with my own words and with the help of many other worthy authors' words.

Barbara E. Reid tells how "...women in La Paz, Bolivia gradually learned to interpret the Gospel differently so their consciousness of themselves as lovable and precious in God's eyes could be heightened." In their process of learning from a misread and misinterpreted Gospel, they came to discover that silently and heroically submitting to the abuse and injustice they endured from their fathers, uncles, and husbands was not their way of denying themselves to take up their own crosses and follow Jesus. "What these women came to discover was the way in which a misreading of today's Gospel had obliterated their sense of self and kept them cowering in abusive relationships."[63]

---

63   Barbara E. Reid, "The Word, America Magazine, August 15-22, 2011" p.31

What fortified me further was her reminder that Jesus spent his entire life "…resisting and eradicating as fully as possible suffering that comes from abuse and injustice." I wept for my imperfect knowledge of Jesus, the Truth.

What does it mean to deny myself and take up my cross? "The repercussions one is willing to risk for the sake of living and proclaiming the Gospel," says Reid, "is what it means to "deny oneself and take up one's Cross."

One does not have to go to Bolivia to find abuse justified by such an interpretation of the cross.

Like the women of Bolivia, I struggled within myself because I misread and misinterpreted the cross. I did not trust my own worth. I assumed I should have submitted to their abuse and injustice in order to deny myself. I assumed that to suffer from self-denial was the way to identify with the crucified Christ. This negative assessment of my humanity as a woman was the consequence of my life experiences under a patriarchy. With that mind set, I suffered self-inflicted guilt and shame. I somehow neglected to remember that Jesus worked his entire life to resist and eradicate suffering that comes from abuse and injustice. It followed that the image of God had changed since I consciously turned away from demeaning female identity toward new ownership of the female self as God's good gift. It was not an intellectual and rhetorical understanding, it was an "aha!" moment of joy, born of brokenness and misunderstanding.

In discovering the real meaning of taking up the cross, I was given the grace of forgiveness of myself for feeling guilty and shame for not being able to carry my own cross. Simultaneously, I received the grace to forgive the Columban Fathers' errors precisely because we, ordained priests, religious, and laity, share a common humanity, a common faith in God. In their errors, God came in His justice to help us do our work as their missionaries.

It should no longer be my concern whether the Society of St. Columban officially recognized our deeds or not.

In His justice, God let us know our true self. Carl knew he was sent as their missionary to do His (Jesus') work. I knew I was sent as their missionary to do His (Jesus') work. But they tried to deny our true identity by denying our rightful status with them. They almost succeeded.

But God faithfully and patiently waited for us to acknowledge that we were and are Jesus' disciples — His missionaries who were sent to Kainan to spread the Good News of Jesus. That is our true self-identity.

With this rediscovered understanding of my true self, my freedom was born to be able to live life to the fullest. In His justice, perhaps God is allowing me to write His truth. This necessary death from my pride and anger to the resurrection of forgiveness took many years. This purification period also took a series of illnesses. But by the grace of God, I am healed physically and spiritually.

Any missionaries who are sent to do the work of God should never lose sight of who we are. Whether sent by the Columban Missionary Society or by other missionary societies, we are mandated by Jesus to spread the good news of Jesus to the ends of the world. We have St. Paul, the first missionary, to assure us that the Lord loves us. No matter what happens on the way, His Grace gets us through. "*My grace is sufficient for you, for my power is made perfect in weakness*" (*2 Corinthians 12:9).*

Everything happened for a reason. To follow Jesus, one can never escape rejection, betrayal, persecution, and even death. The gospel offers a paradox: We must allow the self to die in order to live for God in Christ. Only then will we grow and bear much fruit for the well-being of the world. For me, that is what it means to carry my own cross.

Chapter Fourteen:
Gratitude

Now Jesus and his disciples set out for the villages of
Caesarea Philippi. Along the way he asked his disciples,
"Who do people say that I am?" (Mark 8:27).

"Who do people say that I am?" Jesus simultaneously asks of us, "Who do you say that you are?" For so long I let the authorities dictate my worth and who I was. As a result, I impulsively cast myself as a victim rather than an individual empowered by Jesus' teachings that the realty of origin begins with Christ. It took an entire lifetime to really internalize and believe that the reality of my beginning is with Him; and, that I am created in His image and the likeness of God. Only then, could I finally own the meaning of my suffering—and the joy I felt—working with the people of Kainan Catholic Church.

Empowered by His Spirit, I finally come to the final pages of my story, the journey of a descendant of the Satsuma Samurai. Almost four years ago I decided to share a "sacred telling of my life... like the Wisdom Books of the Bible, are sacred texts,"[64] For me, my story is sacred. I feel it is a story that needs to be shared.

The blossoms of the coral tree always reminded me of the beginning of school. When I discovered them again in

---

64   Peter Gilmour, "The Wisdom of Memoir-Reading & Writing Life's
      sacred Texts," p.160

California, I was reminded that my entire life is a journey of learning.

How wonderful God is to allow me to live the gift of an extended life, so that I have a chance to write about my experience at Kainan. How fortunate I am to have His gift of love to finally forgive the Society of St. Columban, and myself, for being human. I know the risen Christ will be with us always until the end of time. Ultimately, He will transform us into one family of love and peace.

At the beginning of this book, I explained that I wrote it because I felt Spirit-driven. In her book *She Who Is,* Elizabeth Johnson, a Catholic sister and theologian, writes about what Spirit is. "Divine Spirit is not understood to be independently personal, as its symbolization in wind, fire, light, and water makes clear, but is the creative and freeing power of God let loose in the world. More than most terms for God's dynamism, it evokes a universal perspective and signifies divine activity in its widest reaches."[65]

How wonderful God is! He uses our experiences of being lost or hurt to demonstrate that Christ Jesus came into the world to save sinners. I meditate on Jesus' life in my daily prayers. He was a Jew, an outsider, and a failure, according to religious authorities of those days. He suffered and gave His life to give us life. Because of Jesus' suffering, God raised Him up, according to St. Paul in his Letter to the Romans. That is my faith.

I am grateful for a merciful God who has allowed me to experience the mystery of suffering in the Kainan experience; and, in my life as a child and young adult in a world of persistent violations of sexism. God vindicated all these sufferings, humiliations, and the pain of loneliness. Without these experiences and the creative and freeing power of God, I would not have

---

65   Elizabeth A. Johnson, "She Who Is, The Mystery of God in Feminist Theological Discourse," p.83

become the person I am today. The Spirit affirms the person I am, BANU (it is I). As a child of seven, when my name was called on that first day of school, I stood up, pointed at my chest, and said "Banu". I knew who I was. But, according to Beatrice Bruteau, when the young child said "I" (Banu), "the body was indicated. This description of the self continues into adulthood with our concern for the appearance of the body and its ability to perform."[66] Thus, my description of the self has been changed since that day.

Today, I am a "woman equally created in the image and likeness of God, equally redeemed by Christ, equally sanctified by the Holy Spirit. Women are equally involved in the ongoing tragedy of sin and the mystery of grace. Women are equally called to mission in this world, equally destined for life with God in glory."[67] With that knowledge, I ask every day for His guidance in our "daily bread" and "his forgiveness and mercy" to live each day as His gift. To live as His co-workers, as brothers and sisters whose lives are completely dependent on His providence.

"The world is one interdependent whole, and each one of us is part of that One Whole. Each of us must realize with respect to every 'other' that *'I am in my Father and you are in me, and I am in you' (John 14:20)*. This is why the Zen monk, Shojun Bando, also says, 'Unless everybody else attains Enlightenment, I cannot truly attain Enlightenment, so my destiny and everybody's destiny are one.'"[68]

Here I am in my most sacred and exposed place of my own humanity as a woman, as God's gift. It is here I find traces of our often hidden God speaking eloquently between the duties of my daily life cooking, washing, ironing, and scrubbing the

66 Beatrice Bruteau, "What We Can Learn From the East," p.49

67 Elizabeth A. Johnson, "She Who Is, The Mystery of God in Feminist Theological Discourse," p.8

68 Beatrice Bruteau, "What We Can Learn From East," p.101

toilets, reading, reflecting, and meditating on the Big Story, the Sacred Scripture. I am able to assume the traditional roles of woman with a renewed spirit of joy. Here I also celebrate the traditional role of men working within ministries. In my sacred and exposed space, I embrace both roles of man and woman.

The winds are blowing again this morning, renewing His universe both literally and metaphorically. "God who is utterly committed to the *bumanum*, whose glory is the human being and, specifically, within women fully alive, does the symbol of the suffering God release its empowering power."[69]

---

69   Elizabeth A. Johnson, "She Who Is, The Mystery of God in Feminist Theological Discourse," p.271

Chapter Fifteen:
Special Moments

I dedicated this memoir to my husband, Carl, for our 58th anniversary. I wrote the following prose after the celebration of our 48th wedding anniversary. I still feel the same way about my beloved, even stronger.

"As the body is clothed in cloth
And the muscles in the skin
And the bones in the muscles
And the heart in the chest,
So are we, body and soul
Clothed in the Goodness of God
And enclosed."[70]

MY BELOVED

I Love Carl.
He was my savior for whom I am forever grateful.
He appeared from nowhere, saved me from the
destruction of my life.
That was one summer evening of 1952
a long time ago
in the darkest night of my life when
he appeared from nowhere, and saved me.
I owe him my life.

---

70   Stephanie Dowrick, "Forgiveness & Other Acts of Love," p.111

He is my husband.
We celebrated our 48th wedding anniversary just the
    other day,
on November 5, 2001.
As with everything,
the shape and form of love also changes.
Though our celebration lacked the physical passion of
    young lovers,
our desire to be together is yet stronger than ever.
In San Diego, walking along the beach,
the smell of ocean brought me back to the little village
where I was born and raised.
Ishigaki Island, the most southerly of Ryukyu Islands,
commonly known as Yaeyama.
Feeling the warmth of the sun on my back,
feeling his hand tightly holding mine, I felt the presence of
    the Loving God,
who led him to me.
That was many years ago.
The same God who told me to leave everything I possess,
the country, the family, the friends and the little village I
    love so very much, for this man.
It was the most difficult thing I had ever done.
I had to choose one from these two goods.
He had the greater gift to bestow on me.
We shopped in the Horton Plaza.
I found a pair of boots that they say is the 'in-thing.'
The words of the Bible come to my mind: "there is nothing
    new under the Sun."
He found a beautiful shirt, one of liturgical color, green.
Our needs are always simple and ordinary.
We learned together to be humble,
and to enjoy in the ordinary.

Wonderful to be together just him and me,
to create each day of our life anew.
Some call it history.
I call it our love story.
Between sipping the Starbuck coffee and sweets,
we reminisced the last 48 years of our lives being together.
In the evening we strolled together the streets of the Gas
    Light District.
We found the right restaurant just for him and me, where I
    learned how a humble
tossed salad could be made so romantically,
when the maker arranges colors and the shapes of the greens
the love of serving.
It was the first time I tasted black pastas since I left
    Okinawa, which brought
memory of my mother's cooking, the squid soup with
    its ink.
That was long ago.
Yet the smell of the ocean and the taste of the squid soup
    were so delicious and
unforgettable. (The black pastas are created when the chef
    cooks pastas with the ink of squids.)
It seems we enjoy being together more than ever,
Sharing even the simplest meals together is more than the
    best of jewels money can buy.
We toasted our 48th year of togetherness.
God was the only guest with us celebrating our special day.
I know we did not earn God's love
He simply loved the two of us who are so utterly alone, and
    simple and naïve.
I was never afraid of being alone
even though I was left alone most of my young life.
Carl's truck-driving job took him away from me.

Now I know why I was not afraid.

For letting me realize my lost dream,

the One who helped Carl to bring me to this vast country of
the U.S.A.

sustained me all the while.

Now I know.

It must have been doubly hard for Carl to love the way he
has loved me.

I know.

When I see the deep lines on his forehead,

when I see him polishing his Harley Davidson Motorcycle,

he is with himself and his God.

I sometime weep,

because I had hurt him so.

I cannot know his deep thoughts and his deep pain.

Only I know the lines on his face tell the stories of pain and
joy of loving me.

I love you honey.

I pray that God allows me more time

to be with you and less time with myself.

Thank you honey for letting me be me.

Thank you for letting me realize my lost dream.

I wanted to be a lawyer,

but God had His own plan.

He inspired me and led me to study the highest law on the
earth and in the heavens.

No man would allow his wife to spend six years of his life
separately so she can be a student in search of her God
and His Law.

Thank you honey for being with me for three years
in Wakayama,

those years were most precious and spiritual.

We have grown spiritually together.

You are a very gentle, uncomplicated and honest man
that is a special gift from God.
Is it any wonder why God is so close to you?
Hold on to it and not let anybody mess it up,
Not even I dare mess it up.
In contrast, God made me so complicated,
So he gave you to me as His Gift to complement each other
to walk our life journey together to eternity.

Epilogue:
God's Providence

*"You made the moon to mark the seasons; the sun that knows the
hour for its setting. You bring darkness and night falls, then all
the beasts of the forest roam abroad.
The young lion roar for their prey;
they seek their food from God"*
(Psalm 104:19–21).

I no longer question and argue with God. He has provided me
with many mentors and saints. Through them, I have learned
to take the right path to either succeed in the working world
or to emulate people's ways with hope that would help lead me
toward a deeper relationship with God.

As Mary, mother of God, I learned to ponder and reflect what
the Samaritan woman, the first missionary woman of that day
had done. I did not know why the Samaritan woman attracted
me. I listened to her story on one Lenten Sunday morning when
Father Ron Kales read the Gospel of "The Samaritan Woman"
(John 4:4-42). I did not know she was regarded as an outsider,
the product of a mixed marriage. She was considered a "half
Jew" as I was "half Japanese". I learned to ponder and realize how
marvelous it was that God introduced Ignatius Loyola, a man
who speaks of God as one who plants deep within us our desires
to be with God, continually inviting us to embrace spirituality.

I ponder many things in my daily prayers, particularly the
mysteries of suffering. I marvel at the fact that I experience joy

and peace in my heart in spite of all the difficult things I have lived through and experienced.

What I suffered were in truth, the real consequences of social and cultural sins. I am sure my father had suffered tremendously knowing that, without my sacrificial help, he could not raise his nine children. It was a difficult time. The Japanese nation was rising out of the defeat to America. I was always faithful to my filial duties, especially at that time in history. My religious sensitivities are rooted in my father's teachings. Who I am today, I owe in large part to him. My father was a very educated and spiritual man. Though he did not belong to any religious organization, he showed religious sensitivities in all he did and said. Where does my strength and courage come from? It is from my mother, my grandmother, Unme, and my grandfather, Kimura Naotaro. I believe it is also from my family tradition of the samurai, where loyalty, honor, tenacity, and service are most important. From my family tradition, I learned to honor Kimura and hold them dearly in my heart. My family and its traditions are the core and root of myself.

I write this last paragraph of my memoir with a burst of happiness. How liberating it is to finish such a task! No more worrying about whether or not I can finish. I am so happy I decided to compile my memoir. In doing so I have rediscovered the value of my own Japanese tradition. I have rediscovered the delicate sense of beauty in nature, in art, and in the acceptance of life that is as fleeting and sad in its literature. Although my tradition, art and literature touch my heart more deeply in my native language, there are always lingering unanswered questions, such as, whether or not God exists; if life ends at death, then what is the meaning of suffering? Throughout my life, I had many, many questions. I found the answers in the cross of Jesus Christ, the man and God, who promises eternal life with Him in His Kingdom, (John 3:16). I can see how carefully God has been taking care of me all these years. How can I not proclaim that He is my personal God, my savior, who in dying on the cross performed an extraordinary deed to save humanity? As I examine my journey through life—living in dehumanizing poverty, suffering, humiliation, and discrimination, indeed, I find God in all of my experiences. My favorite saint and hero, Saint Ignatius of Loyola, is continually guiding me his way, "Finding God in All Things". As I feel the love and warmth of the sun on my face today, I now know, the sun is God, the Lord's light. God is in all of us. God is truly in all things. My most beautiful journey continues as I walk closer toward eternity. Thanks be to God.

Acknowledgements

With my deepest gratitude for my mentors:
Father John Powell, SJ., Father Richard Costigan, SJ., PhD,
Father Eugene Michael Geinzer, SJ.,
Father Michael Ratajczak; Father T. P. Reynolds,
Matthew Ferraro, Final Editor, Composer and Friend,
Peter Gilmour, PhD.

For my deepest gratitude for my proofreaders:
Elizabeth Roberts,
Karen Oshinski, the final proofreader, and Friend.

Finally, I would like to thank Betty Klevitter, of Lansing,
Michigan, who helped me retrieve the two published
articles in 2010, allowing me to better understand
who I was as a young immigrant in America.

FOOTNOTES

1. George H. Kerr, Okinawa The History of an Island People, (Tokyo: Tuttle Publishing, Revised Edition, 2000), p. 22

2. Ibid, p.21

3. Ibid, p.22

4. Ibid, p.449

5. Ibid, p.4

6. Ibid, p.4

7. Ibid, p.130

8. Ibid, p.382

9. Ibid, p.448

10. Wikipedia — Bushido

11. Wikipedia –Saigo Takamori & Satsuma Rebellion/ Seinan-no-eki

12. Wikipedia-/The Film, "The Last Samurai"

13. William Least Heat-Moon, Blue Highways — A Journey into America, (Boston: Houghton Mifflin Company, 1991), p.87

14. Ibid, p.87

15. George H. Kerr, Okinawa The History of an Island People, (Tokyo: Tuttle Publishing, Revised Edition, 2000), p. 464

16. Ibid, p.469

17. Ibid, p.468

18. IIbid, p.4-5

19. Ibid, p.5

20. Ibid, p.471

21. http://Conservapedia.com/Empero Hirohito

22. Miki Ward Crawford, Katie Kaori Hayashi, Shizuko Suenaga, Japanese War Brides in America: An Oral History, (Santa Barbara: Prager Publishing, 2009), p.61

23. Ibid, p.67

24. Congregation For Divine Worship Directory for "Sunday Celebration in Absence of a Priest," (June 2, 1988), Vatican City, P. 10

25. Kathleen Hughes, Lay Presiding: The Art of Leading Prayer, (Collegeville: The Liturgical Press), p. 45

26. Columan Mission Magazine September, October 1996, p.26-27

27. Beatrice Bruteau, The Easter Mysteries, (New York: The Crossroad Publishing Company, 1995), p.12

28. Ibid, p.12

29. Beatrice Bruteau, The Holy Thursday Revolution, (New York: Orbis Books, Maryknoll, 2005), p.39

30. Ibid, p.52

31. Ibid, p.52-53

32. Ibid, P.59

33. Vincent J. Donovan, Christianity Rediscovered, (New York: Orbis Books, Maryknoll, Nineth Print, 1991), p.195

34. Ibid, p.165

35. Beatrice Bruteau, The Holy Thursday Revolution, (New York: Orbis Books, Maryknoll), p. preface

36. Ibid, p. preface

37. Ibid, p.3

38. Arnold J. Torynbee, East to West, (Osaka: Oxford University Press), p.27

39. John Monbourquette, OMI., How To Forgive A Step-by-step Guide, (Cincinnati, Ohio: Novalis, St. Anthony Messenger Press, 2000), p.172

40. Vincent J. Donovan, Christianity Rediscovered, (New York: Orbis Books, Maryknoll, Nineth Print, 1991) p.30

41. Richard Rohr, Things Hidden Scripture As Spirituality, (Cincinnati, Ohio: St. Anthony Messenger, Press, 2007), p.24

42. Ibid, p.24

43. Ann M. Barrington, "Japan's Hidden Christians,"p.27

44. Beatrice Bruteau, The Holy Thursday Revolution, (New York: Orbis Books Maryknoll), p.3

45. Drew Christiansen, S.J., The Spirit's Gifts, Editorial, America The National Catholic Weekly Magazine May 31, 2010, (New York: America Published by Jesuit of the United States), p.5

46. Vincent J. Donovan, Christianity Rediscovered, (New York: Orbis Books, Maryknoll, Nineth Print, 1991), p.30

47. Stephanie Dowrick, Forgiveness & Other Acts of Love, (New York, London: W. W. Norton & Company, 1967), p.291

48. Ibid, p. 311

49. Frances M. Young, Brokenness & Blessing, (Grand Rapids: Baker Academic Publishing, 2007),p.45

50. Richard Rohr, Things Hidden Scripture as Spirituality, (Cincinnati, Ohio: St. Anthony Messenger Press, 2007), p.77

51. Ibid, p. 204

52. Robert J. Schreiter, C.P.P.S, Reconciliation Mission & Ministry in Changing Social Order, (Maryknoll, New York: Orbis Books, 1997), p.36

53. Joseph Favazza, Reconciliation: On the Border Between Theological and Political Pra, (Joseph-favazza-article. htm.9/21/2010), p.9

54. Edited by Robert Durback, Seeds of Hope — A Henri Nouwen Reader, (New York London Toronto Sydney Auckland: Image Books Doubleday, 1989), p.79

55. Robert J. Schreiter, C.P.P.S., Reconciliation Mission & Ministry in Changing Social Order, (Maryknoll, New York: Orbis Books, 1997), p.19

56. Joseph Favazza, Reconciliation: On the Border Between Theological and Political Pra, (Josph-favazza-article. htm.9/21/2010), p.2

57. Robert J. Schreiter, C.P.P.S., Reconciliation Mission & Ministry in Changing Social Order, (Maryknoll, New York: Orbis Books,1997), p.21

58. Ibid, p.43

59. Ibid, p.21

60. Stephanie Dowrick, Forgiveness & Other Acts of Love, (New York: W. W. Norton & Company, 1997), P. 300

61. Ibid, p.300

62. Philip Yancey, What's So Amazing about Grace, (Zondervan, Grand Rapids, MI, 1997), p.107

63. Barbara E. Reid, The Word, America The National Catholic Weekly Magazine August 15-22, 2011, (New York: America Published by Jesuit of the United States), p.31

64. Peter Gilmour, The Wisdom of Memoir-Reading & Writing Life's Sacred Texts, (Winona, Minnesota: Saint Mary's Press Christian Brothers Publication, 1997), p.160

65. Elizabeth A. Johnson, She Who Is, The Mystery of God in Feminist Theological Discourse, (Crossroad, New York, 1996), p.83

66. Beatrice Bruteau, What We Can Learn From the East, (The Crossroad, New York, 1995), p.49

67. Elizabeth A. Johnson, She Who Is, The Mystery of God in Feminist Theological Discourse, (Crossroad, New York, 1996), p.8

68. Beatrice Bruteau, What We Can Learn From the East, (The Crossroad, New York, 1995,) p.101

69. Elizabeth A. Johnson, She Who Is, The Mystery of God in Feminist Theological Discourse, (Crossroad, New York, 1996,) p.271

70. Stephanie Dowrick, Forgiveness & Other Acts of Love, (W.W. Norton & Company, New York, London, 1997), p.111

About the Author

Masako was born in June of 1931, on the Yaeyama Islands, in the Okinawa prefecture of Japan, the eldest daughter of a large family who were descendants of the Satsuma Samurai Clan. Growing up during the war, she and her family faced many perils and hardships. She met her husband Carl on a military base in Okinawa in the spring of 1951; they were married in the fall of 1953; and in July of 1954, Masako came to the United States to begin a new life. At the Easter Vigil, of 1985, through the celebration of the Easter Sacraments, she became full member of the Catholic Church. After a sixteen-year career with Japan Airlines, she embarked on a course of study that included a Bachelor of Arts, Cum Laude, major in Theology and a Master in Pastoral Studies from Loyola University Chicago. In 1993 she and Carl were commissioned by the Chicago Archdiocese and sent as Lay Missionaries by the Society of St. Columban to the priestless Kainan church in the Osaka Archdiocese of Japan, where they served for three years. Masako and Carl are today part of the St. Thomas More Parish in Oceanside, California.